Exile from the Kingdom

Albert Camus *(Courtesy of Jean Camus)*

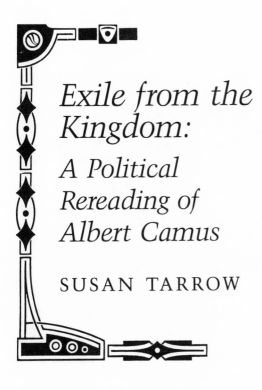

Exile from the Kingdom:

A Political Rereading of Albert Camus

SUSAN TARROW

The University of Alabama Press

Copyright © 1985 by
The University of Alabama Press
University, Alabama 35486
All rights reserved
Manufactured in the United States of America

Publication of this book was aided, in part, by the Hull Memo-
rial Publication Fund of Cornell University.

Library of Congress Cataloging in Publication Data

Tarrow, Susan, 1939–
  Exile from the kingdom.

  Bibliography: p.
  Includes index.
    1. Camus, Albert, 1913–1960—Political and social
views. 2. Politics in literature. 3. Political science
—Philosophy. I. Title.
PQ2605.A3734Z7368   1985   848'.91409   83-18265
ISBN 0-8173-0211-5

For my parents

Contents

Acknowledgments

Several years ago, a well-known French Communist intellectual asked me, "Why on earth are you studying Camus?" This book is my long overdue answer to that challenge, and I want to thank all those who offered help and encouragement along the often tortuous path to publication. Foremost among them is David Grossvogel, who read the manuscript in most of its versions, and succeeded in combining critical appraisal of the text with moral support for the writer. I have also profited from the perceptive comments of Jacques Béreaud, Nelly Furman, Anita Grossvogel, and Alain Seznec. Germaine Brée generously shared her knowledge and expertise in Camusian scholarship, and Jacqueline Lévi-Valensi provided vital information and cordial hospitality during the early stages of my research.

I am indebted to the late Madame Albert Camus for granting me a personal interview despite her failing health; her sister Christiane Faure and Jean Camus also offered new insights into the man himself. Marguerite Dobrenn kindly allowed me to read the correspondence in her possession, and Paul Raffi shared with me his memories of Algiers in the 1930s and of his friend Camus.

A semester in Paris was funded in part by a Berkowitz travel grant awarded by the Department of Romance Studies at Cornell University. I am also grateful to the Center for Advanced Study in the Behavioral Sciences at Stanford for generously providing a room with a view and a typewriter at a crucial juncture in the composition of the manuscript.

Sarah and Chris nobly suffered the rigors of the Parisian school system for my sake, and have retained a gratifying taste for fresh bread and ripe Brie, if not for French verbs *à tous les temps.* Michèle LeDoeuff guided me deftly through Parisian intellectual circles, while Mitzi and George Stein helped to make Paris an unexpectedly friendly city.

My husband has provided constant support of every kind. I thank him for sharing the tribulations of writing and for providing an invaluable nonspecialist's reading of the manuscript, but especially for his patience in enduring the not inconsiderable competition of Camus in his life—he should be forgiven if *he* is not moved to reread Albert Camus!

All quotations from the works of Camus are drawn from the French editions, published in Paris by Gallimard; page references correspond to those editions, which are listed at the beginning of the Bibliography. Permission to quote in English, and to use my own translations, was graciously accorded by Alfred A. Knopf in the United States and by Hamish Hamilton in the United Kingdom. A list of Camus's works in English appears at the end of the Bibliography.

Exile from the Kingdom

LIST OF ABBREVIATED TITLES

Carnets I (1935–1942)	(*CI*)
Carnets II (1942–1951)	(*CII*)
Correspondance (1932–1960)	(*Corr.*)
Ecrits de jeunesse	(*EJ*)
Essais	(*E*)
Fragments d'un combat	(*Fragments*)
Journaux de voyage	(*JV*)
La Mort heureuse	(*MH*)
Théâtre, récits, nouvelles	(*TRN*)

Introduction

> L'oeuvre d'art, par le seul
> fait qu'elle existe, nie les
> conquêtes de l'idéologie. . . .
> L'action politique et la
> création sont les deux faces
> d'une même révolte contre les
> désordres du monde.
> —"The Witness of Freedom"

More than twenty years have passed since Camus's death, and numerous books and articles have been written about both the man and his work. During the period of the cold war, the controversies raging over the validity of Communist ideology in Eastern Europe and of movements of national liberation in the colonies made impartial judgments difficult. Philosophical differences deteriorated into polemics, and Camus was dismissed as a *belle âme*, his political thought considered reactionary and even irrelevant. As recently as 1978, when Herbert Lottman published his biography of Camus in Paris, reviewers noted that only an "outsider" could have achieved such an objective portrait, since Camus remains a highly controversial figure in French intellectual circles.

Though his reputation suffered a partial eclipse, his work continued to be widely read, and sales of his books are still higher than those of most other contemporary writers.[1] In Eastern Europe his work remained popular. Jean Daniel comments (*Le Nouvel Observateur*, 27 Nov. 1979): "Clandestine translations in Eastern Europe, the books requested of Western diplomats in Moscow, the discussions among Communist students in Warsaw, the testimony of Sakharov, Chafarevitch and

1]

Zinoviev: everything points to the fact that Camus found his true public elsewhere." The recently published correspondence between Camus and Pasternak supports this claim (Tall, 1980).

In a period when the defense of individual human rights has become a major topic of concern, it seems appropriate that Camus's work should undergo a revival. In the late seventies, his journalistic work in Algeria was edited, and other articles republished. Articles of reevaluation have appeared in a variety of journals, and two major colloquia have drawn scholars from many countries. This renewed interest reflects a general climate in which history and literature are being subjected to a new optic. The publication in the West of Solzhenitsyn's *The Gulag Archipelago* inspired fresh attempts to look at the course of history and to determine whether such iniquities as the gulag could have been avoided; and the appearance on the Parisian scene of the so-called new philosophers, who brand themselves as anti-Marxist, was symptomatic of a wider disillusionment with the inherited forms of Marxism, a disillusionment that is evident on the left as well as on the right.

This study of the political aspects of Camus's fiction attempts to avoid the dogmatic limitations of ideology and polemic that in the past have restricted many analyses to a repetition of the notorious quarrel in 1952 between Camus and Sartre. These analyses concentrated on the problem of whether, in the political arena, the end can justify any means. It was an issue that sharply divided French intellectuals at the time: Sartre took the view that no revolutionary society is perfect, and that excesses must be viewed in the larger perspective of total achievement, whereas Camus asserted that any end could be irrevocably tarnished by such means as violence and oppression.

The major differences between Camus and Sartre, however, are in their beginnings. Camus's origins and experiences had little in common with those of his fellow writers in Paris, and they had a profound effect on his political and artistic choices.

The basis of Camus's moral commitment was revolt against

the absurd nature of the human condition. "This problem [of revolt] could be clarified by a comparative study of artistic creation and political action, considered as two essential manifestations of human revolt," wrote Camus in 1945, adding in a footnote, "the aim of artistic effort being an *ideal* work in which *creation would be corrected*" ("Note on Revolt," *E*, p. 1696, my emphasis). I shall show how Camus's life in Algeria led him to the formation of his dual commitment, which was the source of perpetual inner conflict: the aim of the rebel is to "correct" the world, but art and political action have different rules. Ultimately it is art that claims Camus's fidelity, because "contradictions are not resolved in a purely logical synthesis or compromise, but in a creative work" (p. 1715). Camus's art, however, reveals the battle scars incurred by his action in the political arena. Journalism, which constituted his major but not sole political activity, was "the story of a failure" (p. 899). My rereading of Camus's fiction is based on this story, and reveals the way in which Camus constantly reassessed and reworked the central problem, that of finding "a new way of living together among men" (Silone, p. 119), a possible kingdom.

Camus's search always led him back to his origins. His background—his development in a poor, illiterate *pied-noir* family in Algiers under a colonial regime, the death of his father before his first birthday, his education in French schools with the aid of scholarships, his experience of class and racial prejudice—contributed to a basically unchanging view of the world.[2] In spite of higher education and literary lionization, Camus retained tastes and attitudes that were unquestionably those of the working class (Abbou, "Deuxième vie," p. 284). Serge Doubrovsky has stressed a fundamental difference between Camus and, for example, Gide: "Whereas Gide experiences everything in the plural, Camus experiences things in the singular. His solar experience is one of destitution and denudation. His is a 'proletarian' relationship to the world, the relationship of someone who has nothing and whose contact with objects is not expressed in terms of having. Camus's domain is *being*. . . . The only possession is a rejoicing which is a participation" (p. 77). Even when his Nobel Prize money allowed him to live "without worrying about tomorrow, to live as a privileged person," Camus did not know "how to possess" (*E*, p. 7). Critics who found evidence of bourgeois values in his work were themselves engaged in a bourgeois reading: "They asked of the text something it refused to offer: for Camus, the text is not capital to consume or invest; it is the experience of a denuding that leads to true knowledge" (Morot-Sir, p. 203).

This "denudation," stripping down to the bare bone, is reflected in Camus's political attitudes as well as in his art. It was poverty that inspired his search for social justice, and his early attempts at writing. *La Douleur* by André de Richaud "was the first book that spoke to me of what I knew: a mother, poverty, beautiful evenings. . . . *La Douleur* gave me a glimpse of the world of creation" (*E*, pp. 1117–18).

For Camus, writing was a physiological necessity, but he needed physical solitude and chastity, removal from the world to a desert, a convent, a diving-bell, in order to combat the natural violence and anarchy in his character.[3] His notebooks reiterate the need for organization and solitude. In his writing, his aim was a purity of expression he termed "classical." But in the political sphere, such purity was impossible: here the process of denudation involved tearing apart the veils of rhetoric and mystification woven by ideologies, in order to deal with the concrete realities of life.

The emphasis that Camus placed on the body has been explained as a feature typical of the "Mediterranean" temperament. This somewhat spurious generalization is unconvincing. It is more likely that the experience of chronic illness deepened his perception of the body as the vital source of all human activity. A healthy man rarely pays attention to his body; for Camus, recurrent bouts of tuberculosis served as constant reminders of his mortality, as well as spurring him to new affirmations of the essential value of life. A sick body is yet another form of oppression. This sense of the role of the body in one's life is reflected in Camus's horror at the infliction of pain on individuals, his intransigent opposition to violence, torture, and the death penalty.

It was the human body that inspired Camus's ideas on limits. The body can never go beyond its inherent capabilities: that is what is essential to every human being, and Camus's theory of the Absurd is based on his awareness of the gap between one's aspirations and one's physical limitations. As Clamence remarks wryly in *The Fall*, "We play at being immortal, and after a few weeks, we can hardly drag ourselves through to the next day" (*TRN*, p. 1529). Individuals may have different aspirations, different values, a different culture, but what they have in common is the body, which is the basis for a code of respect. Just as the body must be accepted as it is, so must the world. The physical basis of Camus's moral vision led him to emphasize the here and now, viable possibilities within the realm of the known world, rather than optimistic visions of a new world, of human progress, or a wager on some transcendental path to perfection. "The world is beautiful, and outside it there is no salvation" (*E*, p. 87).

Camus's essay on the Absurd, *The Myth of Sisyphus*, demonstrates that limits are not necessarily negative. "There is only one useful action, that which would remake man and the earth. I shall never remake man. But one must act 'as if.' For the path of struggle brings me face to face with the flesh. The flesh, even humiliated flesh, is my only certainty. I can live only with that one certainty. The creature is my homeland" (*E*, p. 166). Thus Camus seeks solutions within a fixed framework, a method that involves a constant return to beginnings, a renewed attempt at finding the right way, a permanent state of reassessment.

The theme of *recommencement* runs all through Camus's work on every level. In his early fiction, he links the life of the protagonist to the daily cycle of nature; both Mersault (*A Happy*

Death) and Meursault (*The Stranger*) adapt themselves to the rhythm of the day, starting afresh each morning. The feeling of oneness with the beauty of the world, that Camus first expressed in the lyrical essay, "Nuptials at Tipasa," published in 1939, is repeated almost fifteen years later in "Return to Tipasa" in relation to the theme of renewal. "There the world began every day in a light that was always new. . . . In the middle of winter, I learned at last that there was within me an invincible summer" (*E*, p. 874).

In *The Plague*, where men are separated from the natural world, the struggle is harder. Dr. Rieux's strength lies in his ability to start again each morning, refusing to allow fatigue or inevitable defeat to interfere with his goals. His profession is by its very nature limited by the possibilities of human physiology, so his task is situated in a natural framework. In *The Fall*, Clamence reiterates his monologue every time he finds an appropriately silent bourgeois interlocutor. The short stories of *Exile and the Kingdom* continue the pattern of questioning and starting again.

In the political arena, the theme of finding solutions within fixed limits is an essential component in Camus's thought. His notion of the Absurd is specifically linked with Sisyphus, the ideal proponent of the need for a fresh start, and it leads to the idea of metaphysical revolt. If Sisyphus is condemned to limited action, he must find value in it: if man is limited to his human condition, he must seek solutions within that realm.

In *The Rebel* Camus moves from metaphysical revolt to political or historical revolt, concludes with a condemnation of Marxist revolution and posits in its place a constantly maintained stance of rebellion. Eric Werner, in his invaluable study of the thought of Camus and Sartre, points out that for Camus the revolutionary ideal is unattainable, and masks the real questions, which are not political but metaphysical—that is, the problem of the Absurd. To Camus, the ultimate scandal of human life is death, which paradoxically also gives it meaning.

History, "in claiming to deliver us from the Absurd, . . . robs us of the *hic et nunc*" (Werner, p. 236). Temporary servitude in the interest of an uncertain revolutionary goal is a price that Camus was unwilling to pay, or to exact from others. He never separated abstract thought from concrete examples of its consequences, and thus questioned ideas and ideals in the light of current reality.

It was a stance that excluded repose, and Camus lived the tension he propounded. During the post-Liberation period in France, when a new beginning seemed possible, Camus's political message stressed the dangers of weariness, smugness, passivity, comfort—we must never be tired. That is the privilege of the bourgeoisie. This tension existed less between art and life, "beauty and the humiliated" (*E*, p. 875), than within their combination, "a double memory." "In all I have done or said, . . . I seem to recognize these two forces, even when they contradict one another. I could not deny the light in which I was born, and I was not willing to refuse the tasks of our times" (p. 874).

Camus's refusal to accept the necessity of revolution and his determination to remain within the boundaries of rebellion have been criticized as reactive and ineffectual. Social change demands that people change, but Camus always asserted that the given variables must be the starting-point. In art as in politics, limits must be recognized. The political problems that concerned Camus—justice, freedom, tyranny, oppression—also concern the artist in his work. They are inextricably linked by a common basis of moral values, which in turn stem from human nature as it is, both good and bad.

Recent criticism has brought out the wealth of auto-representation in Camus's fiction, the allegory of the artist at work, the writer writing. This allegory is more obvious in his early texts, where the limits necessary to artistic creation are set artificially. Mersault withdraws physically from the pressures of work and social intercourse, while Meursault escapes them through a persistent indifference. The later texts reveal more subtly the natural boundaries of art. Rieux is both rebel and writer, using the same tools for both occupations. Clamence too reveals his political aims and position through the form as well as the content of his text. Grand and Jonas may be ironic portrayals of Camus himself, but they represent the artist who must constantly return to a blank page and start again.

The blank page is as terrifying to the artist in Camus as the *tabula rasa* is to his political self. For him writing was a violent act of self-torture to which he was driven by physical necessity as much as by the haunting threat of sterility and failure. It was also an act of revolt, the creation of a world untouched by the Absurd. Revolution, on the other hand, involved the destruction of humanistic values and, in too many instances, the torture and suffering of others.

Camus's moral stance in both politics and art was derived from his experience of growing up in a poor polyglot neighborhood. His education in the French school system gave him the tools he needed to act in those two spheres. The primary tool was language, which can communicate abstract thought. But Camus wanted it to express the concrete, and was repeatedly coming up against the ambiguity of language, the impossibility of adequately expressing experience or the ideas it inspired. Thus there was always a tension, a fear of betraying his true intention.

The power of language also created a distance that separated him from his background. In his own family, conversation was not the major means of communication; he and his mother rarely spoke to each other, and his grandmother disciplined him with a whip. But for Camus, the French language was not only the means by which he earned his livelihood, but also the medium that gave expression to his creative gifts. It alienated him from his social environment, to which he felt a deeply ingrained loyalty. So his attitude to language would remain ambivalent: it could be used to mask the truth as easily as to communicate it; it was a source of power and yet inadequate; it labeled him as

French when he had little sympathy for France; it was the medium of propaganda as well as of poetry. Yet it was the only alternative to silence. And the privilege of language entailed the responsibility of bearing witness on behalf of those less privileged than he. Camus's public silence in the late 1950s was in one sense a rejection of the French side of his nature, the intellectual side, in a situation where logic could not resolve the problem of Algeria as he saw it. He found himself between two cultures, and never succeeded in bridging the gap permanently.

Not only in his own experience, but in Algerian society too, Camus found a dualism in language, for he grew up in a bilingual country. Although he never learned more than street Arabic and knew no Kabyl, he felt he understood Algerians and had a sensitivity to their pride and justifiable anger; this was exceptional in a European, even one of left-wing sympathies like Camus. Yet he could never cross the dividing line, and the one ineradicable mark of his Frenchness, and thus his affiliation with colonialism, was the language he used. It was not an ideal medium for Camus, although he fashioned it with evident success. The controlled style and often moralistic tone of some of his writing belies his naturally exuberant nature, a nature that prompted him to rely more on gesture, on physical communication, than on words. His abiding involvement with the theater, as author, actor, and director, underlines his natural affinity to a genre in which the body plays a role equal to that of language.

Camus's beliefs led him into political action, both in Algiers before World War II and in the latter months of the Resistance during the Nazi occupation of France. In both cases his activities were in journalism, which he found a satisfactory way of combining commitment and art. His commitment was unambiguous, and he was able to attain a clarity of expression that had always been his goal. "Danger makes for classicism" (E, p. 1490). His lucid style reflected his political aims: to reject the mystifications of ideology and to denounce falsehood. But political action and its repercussions, exacerbated by the steadily deteriorating situation in Algeria, led Camus into a period of withdrawal, during which he again questioned his moral precepts. The cleavage between art and political action had never been wider. The conclusion that ambiguity reigns in the realm of morals too was a painful discovery. The awareness of moral and political ambiguities is reflected in the purposefully ambiguous texts of *The Fall* and *Exile and the Kingdom*, where language is an appropriate medium, since it expresses that ambiguity.

It is evident that for Camus, politics was not a separate intellectual sphere of activity. It was an integral part of his life and art, and was thus both limited and enriched by it. He spent the first twenty-seven years of his life in Algeria, where a childhood of hardship and sickness was compensated by the beauty of the countryside surrounding Algiers and the Mediterranean landscape, which was available to all who lived there, regardless of their situation. An oppressive colonial society, which was already under pressure and reacting with predictable violence, provided Camus with firsthand experience of racism and social prejudice, and he developed a profound antipathy towards paternalism, particularly in its political forms: colonialism, Fascism, and finally, Marxism. Life as a struggle—against illness, injustice, apathy, ideology, death—is at the core of Camus's work. Commitment to this struggle involves discomfort; the desire for comfort and the clarity of absolutes must be constantly resisted. Revolt is a daily task.

Camus was a prolific writer in many areas of literature, and his work has engendered volumes of critical material. Little attention has been paid, however, to the combination of journalism and fiction. I have limited my study to these two areas because they demonstrate, in different ways, the close correlation between history and art in Camus's experience. Much of his journalism has not been republished and seems dated, and his fiction has been read tendentiously in the light of his refusal to support Algerian independence in the late 1950s. I propose a more balanced view based on Camus's own texts.

A study of the journalistic material, which comprises Camus's responses to the changing political and social events of the period between 1936 and 1959, aims to elucidate its author's immediate reactions to the world of history. The articles written for *Alger-Républicain* and for *Combat* have a certain spontaneity, due to the need to produce material on an almost daily basis, which left little time for revisions; it was through these articles that Camus engaged in direct political action, by attacking specific manifestations of injustice, corruption, and even stupidity in government policies. Although he felt that his writing had no lasting impact, his articles were considered sufficiently subversive by the governor-general in Algeria to be censored and ultimately suppressed, and *Combat* proved to be one of the most respected of postwar newspapers.

Camus's fictional texts, on the other hand, were the result of long months of painstaking revisions, and here the tensions between history and art are revealed. Political attitudes are not overtly expressed; they are implied, but are often distorted or dispersed by their passage through the prism of his creative imagination. "In contrast to newspaper articles or essays in general, the literary message is a doubled message" (Maillard, p. 10).

The essays provide a further source of material and I shall refer to them in relation to some of the constants in his thought. Political aims are most evident in Camus's plays, and Gay-Crosier has discussed this least successful branch of Camus's writing in relation to his philosophy and politics, arriving at the conclusion that it was Camus's rigid refusal to go beyond the limits of his own experience that led him into an impasse in the 1950s (*Théâtre*, pp. 160–62). Camus's interest in the theater was partly due to the nature of the enterprise: it involved gesture as well as language, it was the product of teamwork rather than hierarchy,[4] and its aim was ephemeral and within reach. This allowed the questions to be posed again, differently. The great variety of form and style evident in the fictional texts alone bears witness to this incessant questioning, an attempt to attack problems from different angles, as if the creative act itself could somehow achieve a synthesis.

My reading of Camus's fiction makes no claim to being definitive. Any single method or approach must necessarily impoverish the text, and in some cases my reading may run counter to Camus's own stated intentions. However, an author cannot be aware of all the possibilities of his texts, and my reading explores some of their implications, without diminishing the merits of other points of view or, I hope, betraying Camus's position.

I shall discuss Camus's journalism and fiction in chronological order because his work reveals how closely his thought was linked to historical events. Each work is enriched by his experience and his reappraisal of past texts. Camus himself declared that "a man's work is nothing but this long progression, searching via the detours of art for the two or three simple and great images to which his heart first responded" (*E*, p. 13). It may return to its starting point, but it moves forward. Camus was always questioning his own work; indeed, he was his own severest critic. He changed his mind and was not afraid to say so. "Let's suppose that a thinker, after publishing a few works, declares in a new book: 'I've been following the wrong path up till now. I am going to start everything again. I think now that I was wrong,' no one would take him seriously any more. And yet he would prove he was worthy of being a thinker" (*CII*, p. 58). Camus's sense of responsibility as a writer made him correct past mistakes even at the expense of his own reputation. Thus his writing changes in response to his encounters with political reality as well as to his experimentations with artistic form.

My study has incorporated most of the material published in the 1970s and early 1980s, as well as journalistic articles that have not appeared in any edition of Camus's work. Private conversations and unpublished correspondence have also been drawn on. All the sources provide a remarkably consistent and coherent view of the world, one that has proven relevant to the modern era. Camus's voice, which he feared was merely crying in the wilderness, is echoed today by intellectuals and politicians who have recognized the accuracy of Camus's warning of the threat of abstraction in the nuclear age.

Many political labels have been pinned on Camus, running the gamut from "anarcho-syndicalist" through "liberal humanist" to "bourgeois reactionary." These labels have little meaning, especially in France, where candidates can run for office on such tickets as "extrême centre," and where "modérés" are conservatives. It is Clamence, the ragged hero of *The Fall*, who understands that classifying people is one of the hellish activities of modern life. I shall not try to fit Camus into a new slot in the political spectrum, but rather to demonstrate the difficulty of such a classification. Camus's strength, and ultimately his weakness, lay in the ambivalence of his political positions, his capacity to understand both sides of a question. "I am not cut out for politics because I am incapable of wanting or accepting the death of an adversary" (*CII*, p. 154).

The essential dualism of Camus's vision has its roots in his own history, and although it was the cause of much personal anguish for him, it sparked his creative energy. And the perspicacity of that vision is partly due to his "capacity to stand back from Europe, even when he was deeply immersed in its history, and view it through the eyes of a stranger" (Pierce, p. 35). Camus himself asserted that "it is constantly my lot to remain apart" (*CI*, p. 173). "I have spent my life trying to get in the swim, to be 'normal,' and not on the fringe" (*Corr.*, p. 167).

Camus was destined to remain on the fringe for most of his life. He had no faith in systems, and so refused the inflexible principles of any ideology, preferring a pragmatic approach to political problems. Thus he rarely committed himself to any political group. Sartre summed up his invaluable role and his impact on his time in an obituary: "Anyone who read or thought about [his work] came up against the human values he held in his clenched fist; he questioned the political act" (*France-Observateur,* 7 Jan. 1960).

1

Algiers: The Early Years

Je n'ai jamais rien écrit qui
ne se rattache, de près ou de
loin, à la terre où je suis né.
—Interview for *Franc-Tireur*

Camus's early political activities in Algiers have now
been well documented. In his 1965 study of Camus's political
commitment, Emmett Parker listed the writer's contributions
to *Alger-Républicain* and *Soir-Républicain,* the two Algiers
newspapers for which he worked between 1938 and 1940. But
until 1978, only the articles published in *Algerian Reports* and
reprinted in the Pléiade edition of Camus's *Essais* were available
in print. Some of Roger Quilliot's conjectures in that edition
have been disproven by subsequent research: an exhaustive biography by Herbert Lottman, followed by that of Patrick McCarthy, and a critical edition of Camus's journalism in Algiers by
André Abbou and Jacqueline Lévi-Valensi, have recently thrown
new light on this period.

These years are crucial to an understanding of Camus's life
and work, for they form the basis for the positions taken during
the mature years of his life, which he spent in France. In Algeria
he experienced several major reversals in his personal as well as
in his political life: ill health, a failed marriage, an unsatisfactory novel, a brief and subsequently disillusioning adherence to
the French Communist party. The ambiguities of his political
commitment are evident in the system of values he maintained;
he emphasized concrete realities as opposed to abstract princi-

15]

ples, and voiced an uneasy feeling that Marxist philosophy was lacking a vital component, a sense of the sacred that was more closely akin to the beauty of the world than to any religious transcendence. The conflicting claims of poet and activist are already apparent.

Camus himself was vague, and even reticent, about his motives and activities during these years. In a review of Paul Nizan's *La Conspiration*, published in *Alger-Républicain* (11 Nov. 1938), he asserted that joining a political party was a personal affair, like getting married. He did in fact marry in June 1934; it seems this was a period of personal commitment. This first marriage, to the daughter of a wealthy Algiers doctor, was an unhappy and short-lived experience, however; the couple's Bohemian way of life proclaimed a joyous rebellion against conventional mores, but the wife's addiction to morphine and her infidelity led to a painful separation and divorce two years later.

Camus's commitment to a political party also ended in rejection, although in this context he played a more positive role in his own fate. Jean Grenier, Camus's teacher and mentor, asserts that he encouraged Camus to join the Communist party because he felt that his pupil, concerned as he was with social problems, had the makings of a first-rate politician (Grenier, p. 44). But Grenier himself viewed party membership as an easy commitment, and independence as a positive position, and when Camus discovered the fact later, he felt betrayed. "I did not understand how you could have advised me to become a Communist and then taken a stand against Communism" (*Corr.*, p. 180). A year after his break with the party in 1937, Camus had reassessed the event. He wrote to Grenier, "Courage was not on our side, but on yours. My only excuse, if I have one, is that I cannot detach myself from those among whom I was born and whom I could not abandon. Communism has unfairly annexed their cause. I understand now that if I have a duty, it is to give the best of myself to my people, I mean, to try and defend them against lies. But the time has not yet come because all the issues

are clouded" (*Corr.*, 1938, p. 31). Camus was never a totally convinced party member. In a letter that Grenier dates 24 August
1934, but which in fact dates from 1935,[1] he spelled out his
motives and misgivings.

> Everything attracts me to them. . . . I think about it a good deal
> and it seems to me that the excesses of Communism are based on
> a certain number of misunderstandings that can be rejected with-
> out any harm. And then Communism sometimes differs from
> Communists. What has held me back for a long time, what holds
> back so many minds, I think, is the Communists' lack of a sense
> of religion. It is the Marxists' claim of constructing an ethic that
> may suffice man completely. . . . But perhaps one can also under-
> stand Communism as a preparation, as an askesis which will
> prepare the ground for more spiritual activities. In short a will to
> escape from pseudo-idealisms, from feigned optimisms, to estab-
> lish a state of affairs in which man may find anew the sense of his
> eternity. I do not say that this is orthodox. (Grenier, pp. 45–46)

That indeed is an understatement. Camus's comments show
a desire to dispense with nineteenth-century utopias and to
seek some more immediate action, but it is apparent that he
cannot wholeheartedly endorse all aspects of Communism. His
belief that what he calls the "excesses" (*outrances*) of Communism can be repudiated shows a certain naïveté concerning the
ideology and discipline of mass movements; and it is regrettable
that he was not more specific as to the nature of these excesses
and "misunderstandings" (*malentendus*). The word *malentendu* suggests not only "misunderstanding" but also "mishear-
ing," not merely a difficulty in interpretation but a problem of
communication. Obviously language plays a vital role in facili-
tating communication, and a dual-language society confronts
this barrier constantly. Camus was to exploit an aspect of *outrances* based on a certain number of misunderstandings in his
play *The Misunderstanding* (*Le Malentendu*).

A study of the party in Algeria during those crucial years in
Camus's political development reveals some cause for disillu-

sionment, and throws light on the reasons for his later anti-Communist views, as well as on the developing structure of his thought. The 1930s in Algeria was a time of uncertainty and upheaval for the French Communist party (PCF). Strict Leninist dogma called for an end to colonization, and for the withdrawal of the oppressive rulers. But the Algerian situation presented a dilemma that was never satisfactorily resolved, because the membership of the party was largely made up of Algerians of European origin, who were deeply imbued with the racist prejudices of the *pied-noir* tradition. When the party attempted to recruit among the Moslems, European members accused the leaders of neglecting their interests. European workers shied away from the PCF in favor of other left-wing organizations. Throughout the French education system, textbooks inculcated children of all classes with the myth of the civilizing mission of colonial conquests, and the *pieds-noirs* supported this view because their very existence as a relatively privileged class depended on the strength and stability of French rule in Algeria (Sivan, p. 60).

So an atmosphere of fraternal solidarity in a common struggle for justice and equality was not to be found in the Algerian section of the PCF: European members were divided, and the few Moslem members resentful; Amar Ouzegane declared that Arabs left the party in disillusionment because they were treated as "poor relations" (Sivan, p. 69).[2] As Sivan comments, "In this climate of ostracism, a 'poor white' Algerian would have needed extraordinary emotional and intellectual resources to believe that the struggle for de-colonization was both timely and desirable, and that it had any chance of realization" (p. 63).

Camus's conception of politics already reveals his awareness of ambiguities, of the gap between political rhetoric and political activity. "I shall always object to putting a volume of *Capital* between life and man" (Grenier, p. 46). Abstract ideology can become a barrier, its rhetoric can separate people and their needs from political reality.

Somewhat more surprising, in view of Camus's early rejection of Christianity, is his attitude toward the materialistic aspects of Communism, the absence of any sense of religion.[3] The human soul needs nourishment, he argued, as well as the body, and ideology ignores the need for beauty; the poet in Camus is already outstripping the philosopher. Nevertheless, he hopes that the experience might prove a "preparation," an idea that he later denounces in *The Rebel* as the common fault of both Communism and Christianity. The notion of askesis or self-discipline is one to which he will return; even at twenty-one he recognized the basic anarchy of his personality, and in 1959 he confessed to Jean-Claude Brisville, "My anarchy is deep and unbridled" (*E*, p. 1921). Here he views Communism as an almost mystical venture—askesis leading to more "spiritual activities"—but he also realizes the value of the discipline imposed by the party.

This opposition of askesis and anarchy reveals a fundamental aspect of Camus's personality, which is reflected in his political commitments. Askesis implies a system of *self*-discipline rather than one imposed by a group. His notebooks express some of his misgivings about Communism; in March 1936 he wrote:

> Grenier on Communism: 'The basic question is this; should one, for an ideal of justice, accept stupid ideas?' One can answer yes, this is a fine thing to do. Or no, which is honest.
>
> With a due sense of proportion, the problem of Christianity. Should the believer be concerned with the contradictions in the Gospels and the excesses of the Church? Does belief in Christianity mean accepting Noah's Ark and defending the Inquisition? or the tribunal that condemned Galileo?
>
> But on the other hand, how can one reconcile Communism and disgust? If I try the extreme forms, to the extent of absurdity and uselessness, then I reject Communism. And this concern for religion . . . (*CI*, p. 29)

In this entry lies the germ of another constant in Camus's thought, the idea of rebellion. His response to the arbitrary imposition of contradictory dogmas is to say "no." The notebook entry reveals his hesitation in taking anything on trust, a rejection of party discipline, for he is already questioning the means involved in achieving the end, an ideal of justice. The letter to Grenier shows that Camus aimed at more immediate returns: "I have such a strong desire to *see* a reduction in the amount of unhappiness and bitterness that poisons mankind" (my emphasis). There was also a need to recapture his "roots"; he was attracted by "ideas that lead me back to my origins, to my childhood friends, to everything that makes up my sensibility" (Grenier, p. 46). He must already have felt estranged from the other members of his family and his old neighbors merely by virtue of his education. He mentions being embarrassed at taking a *lycée* friend to his shabby home in a poor neighborhood. "It was a long time before he could unburden himself of certain secrets; for example, by ascribing to Jacques Corméry, the hero of *The First Man*, 'the shame and the shame of being ashamed' that he had experienced himself when, on being admitted to the Lycée Bugeaud, he was on the point of writing on his identity card, opposite the heading 'parents' profession', the word 'servant'" (Viallaneix, p. 23).[4]

It is clear that Camus was not totally convinced that Communism was the answer to the problems of human society. His assertion that "every doctrine can and should evolve" (Grenier, p. 46) proved to be a false hope. Indeed, the failure of the Communist party in Algeria was largely due to its rigidity in the face of a growing nationalist movement.

Camus had doubts about basic issues of Communist doctrine: "False rationalism linked to the illusion of progress, the class struggle and historical materialism interpreted in the sense of an end whose goal would be the happiness and triumph of the working-class alone" (Grenier, p. 46). This latter aspect was particularly true of the French party because of its origins in syndicalism. The narrowness of the goal meant the exclusion of a large number of people even in his own neighborhood of

Belcourt: small shopkeepers such as his uncle the butcher, or restaurant owners like Céleste in *The Stranger*, hardworking and unpretentious men who also deserved some support. As for the "illusion of progress," Camus returned to this hobby-horse in a speech delivered in Algiers on 8 February 1937, at the opening of the Maison de la Culture, an organization supported by the PCF. He proposed a new civilization for the Mediterranean basin, and added in a footnote to the printed text: "I spoke of a new civilization and not of a progress in civilization. It would be too dangerous to play with that evil toy called Progress" (*E*, p. 1327). For Camus, Progress represented one of those pseudo-idealisms inherited from the eighteenth-century philosophers and their bourgeois revolution.

In his letter to Grenier, Camus makes no overt mention of the anticolonial issue as a reason for joining the PCF. But the idea of "poison" destroying human bonds will be echoed later by his description of racism as a "stupid and criminal sickness" (*E*, p. 321). Was he in fact both intellectually and emotionally in favor of decolonization? It is significant that his membership in the PCF coincided with a drive for the "arabization" of the party, instigated by André Ferrat, a PCF instructor sent to Algiers from Paris in February 1934, a drive continued by Jean Chaintron (alias Barthel), who arrived in Algiers in September 1935 (Sivan, p. 82).

Camus sold party newspapers and put up posters, as well as working with Moslem members. "I had been assigned to recruit Arab militants and to make them join a nationalist organization (L'Etoile Nord-Africaine, which was to become the PPA). I did so, and these Arab militants became my comrades, whose behavior and loyalty I admired" (*Corr.*, p. 180).

Twenty years later, when Camus was in Algiers to promote a civilian truce, Amar Ouzegane was reminded of the abilities of the young activist: "In the particular attention he paid to the problem of organization, of technique and tactics, we caught a glimpse of the other Camus, twenty years younger, who understood the psychological effort and the mechanics needed to move, officer and guide such large masses of people" (p. 235). Like a good director, he knew how to manage his crew.

Camus spoke of problems in the party in 1935. Indeed, he maintained in a letter that he left the party that year (*TRN*, p. xxix), when the Stalin-Laval pact led to the shelving of Moslem recruitment in favor of more generalized anti-Fascist activity. However, it seems likely that the arrival of Barthel, whom Camus found likable, revived his enthusiasm. Barthel was an activist rather than a theoretician, and was impressed by Ferrat's report proposing that the anticolonial struggle be pursued as part and parcel of an anti-Fascist campaign—a quite unorthodox interpretation of the current French party line. For almost a year Barthel was instrumental in reviving the party in Algeria from setbacks suffered in the 1932 municipal elections: by January 1936, enrollment had doubled, and Moslem membership reached the highest level ever. Moslem militants were recruited and trained, and parity between Europeans and Moslems was maintained in the Central Committee and regional secretariats (Sivan, p. 86). In January 1936, a separate Algerian Communist party (PCA) was officially established, in accordance with Barthel's argument that the step would hasten the "arabization" of the organization.

The establishment of the Popular Front in France in May 1936 marked the beginning of the end of this period of successful activity, and by the end of the year a change in policy had been completed: the class struggle must be set aside to accommodate the PCF's anti-Fascist front with the SFIO (Section Française de l'Internationale Ouvrière) and the Radicals in France. The PCA had to follow directives from Paris, and Barthel accordingly disavowed Ferrat. The party toned down its anti-French slogans, and went along with the assimilationist aims favored by its partners, the Socialists and the Radicals.

This later change of policy was not wholly objectionable to Camus, for he signed a manifesto supporting the Blum-Viollette project in May 1937: the plan proposed to enfranchise some twenty thousand Moslems without loss of their Koranic statute (E, p. 1328). The thrust of the manifesto printed in *Jeune Méditerranée*, a journal put out by the Maison de la Culture, was that the left-wing intellectual's role is to defend the culture of the popular masses, and that Moslem culture cannot flourish when the people are oppressed, uneducated, and poverty-stricken. Far from harming French interests, the Blum-Viollette project would enhance the French image among the Arab population; it represented "a minimum step of the work of civilization and humanity which the new France should undertake" (p. 1329). However, Camus's emphasis on Moslem culture was at variance with assimilationist policies, which would continue to consider French language and culture of prime importance.

By the end of 1936, the change in policy had exacerbated the party's relations with the Etoile Nord-Africaine (ENA). This Arab party, which had been successful in recruiting and organizing members in metropolitan France under the auspices of the PCF, attacked the Blum-Viollette plan as an assimilationist measure, engaged in a virulent polemical exchange with the PCF, and began recruiting in Algeria. The conflict in France reached such proportions that the interior minister dissolved the party in January 1937, and the PCF refused to mobilize in its defense (Sivan, p. 96). It criticized the Messalistes—followers of the popular leader Messali Hadj—in the ENA for demanding Algerian independence at a time when all forces should be united against possible Fascist attempts to seize power in the colonies. The ENA, transformed into the Parti du Peuple Algérien (PPA), was accused of collaboration with the Fascists, to the point where verbal and physical confrontations were common occurrences (Lottman, p. 157). Moslem enrollment in the PCF fell, while membership in the PPA rose. Sivan notes that Arab members were already leaving the party in mid-1937, citing the Belcourt section of Algiers (Camus's section), although most European members were unconcerned about changes in policy toward the Moslems. "The case of Albert Camus—a party member since 1934 [sic], who seems to have left it in 1937 in protest against the anti-PPA campaign—is merely an isolated incident" (Sivan, pp. 106, 103).

Camus recounted the incident in a letter to Grenier written in 1951: "The turning point of 1936 arrived. These militants [with whom Camus had worked] were hunted down and imprisoned, their organization dissolved, in the name of a policy that the PC approved and encouraged. Some of them who had eluded the dragnet came to ask me if I was going to allow this infamy to occur without saying anything. That afternoon has remained engraved in my memory; I was ashamed; then I did what I had to" (Corr., p. 180).

Lottman's invaluable research in Algiers has now brought to light the details surrounding Camus's break with the PCF. He did not leave the party, as he stated to Grenier, but was expelled. His continued support for Moslem nationalism marked him as a dissident at a time when the Communists were allied with such moderate parties as the Radicals. A meeting of all the cells in the Belcourt section was called in order to discuss the matter. "In this far from merry atmosphere Camus rose to defend himself and to defend the dissident position. He criticized the lack of comprehension on the part of the Party's leadership of the social evolution of the Algerian people oppressed by colonialism, an evolution which he felt lacked cohesion and risked developing into radical nationalism. But there were peaceful alternatives to violence, he said, and by insisting on its own program the Party failed to take these alternatives into consideration. No one replied" (Lottman, p. 158).

At a further meeting of district leaders, to which Camus was not invited, it was decided to expel him from the party. According to Ouzegane, "No good Communist could as much as say hello to Camus" after this event (ibid.). This whole atmosphere of trial and judgment, of a vain defense followed by ostracism by former comrades, pervades Camus's work in different forms, and belies the nonchalance he affected to his friends at the time of the party's sentence. His foresight on the subject of the Algerian people shows how well he understood the possible trends of development in Moslem nationalism, and the need to avoid violent confrontation. As it was, the party continued to follow the line dictated from Moscow via Paris, with the result that it was always treated with suspicion by the Algerian nationalist movements.

This account by an eyewitness and fellow dissident points up the way in which Camus's early experience in politics was transformed into recurrent themes in his work: the impossibility of communication, the lack of dialogue, the rigidity of dogma in response to the claims of human understanding.

An almost illegible statement of Camus's position further emphasizes the extent to which he differed from his more disciplined comrades. Abbou and Lévi-Valensi discovered the text hidden in a manuscript of *The Wrong Side and the Right Side.* Since this text was published in Algiers in 1937, it is probable that these notes were written during Camus's membership in the party; they echo his letter to Grenier from the summer of 1935. The brackets indicate words crossed out in the manuscript.

> [We want a Communism.] We do not believe in Hegel, we are not materialists, we do not worship the monstrous idol of Progress. We hate all forms of rationalism, yet we are Communists. [The odds are against it. No.] Because we do not want to separate life from doctrine. And for me, Communism is much more my comrade in the party cell, worker or storekeeper, than the third volume of *Capital.* I prefer life to doctrine, and life always triumphs over doctrine. . . . I prefer an approximate truth which may involve some errors to an [absolute] truth in absolute terms in which the heart will not assuage its thirst. (*Fragments*, pp. 20–21)

Camus's scale of values is already evident: his comrades and the human heart take precedence over rationalism, doctrine, absolute truth. The metaphor of the thirsting heart, unassuaged by the search for an absolute, will be echoed in more lyrical terms in Camus's literary works, where the aridity of the desert with its distinct contours is seen as a sterile force opposing man's search for truth and justice. In his opposition to rationalism and dogma, Camus is already revealed as poet rather than philosopher.

Camus's preoccupation with the use and abuse of language may well stem from his experience within the party, where he found that lip service was paid to the neglected rights of the Arab population without any sustained effort being made to improve communication or working conditions. In August 1937 Camus wrote in his Notebooks: "Every time I hear a political speech or read those of our leaders, I am appalled that for years, I have heard nothing that sounded human. It is always the same words telling the same lies" (*CI*, p. 64). But since people never really listen, and since repetition leads to meaninglessness, they fail to detect the true meaning of the rhetoric. The Communists had to change their tactics according to the needs of international relations or of political alliances, without changing their rhetoric. Camus's vision remained within the limits of the immediate problem. Ouzegane remembers him as "the anticolonial polemicist, writing articles for Arab newspapers by putting himself inside the skin of an Arab humiliated by the alienation of his dignity . . . the Communist, the intransigent doctrinaire who refuses the tactics of the Popular Front in order to avoid fighting Fascism side by side with the Radical party, that rabble of bourgeois imperialists" (p. 235). The virulence of the latter comment probably reflects Ouzegane's own point of view rather than that of Camus, but the reference to his understanding of the dignity of man is valid; it would later constitute one of the cornerstones of Camus's opposition to the use of violence to achieve political ends.

Camus's political activities were obviously centered on improving European-Moslem relations. His adherence to the PCF coincided with its "arabization" drive, and his organizational work was among the Moslem masses. His inaugural speech at the Maison de la Culture in February 1937 reveals some interesting aspects of his vision of an ideal society in Algeria. The Mediterranean basin has a certain unity; the concept of motherland is not a meaningless abstraction, but implies a common taste for life. Camus contrasts northern cultures with that of the Mediterranean: even Fascism has a different face in Germany than in Italy. Twenty-four Western intellectuals, including Maurras, had signed a manifesto praising the civilizing mission of the Italians in barbaric Ethiopia; Camus rejects this cultural justification for colonial conquest. Yet his own view of Mediterranean culture is based on its European aspects, with no mention of the impact of Islam on the area. This is not altogether surprising, since Arabic art and literature were at a low ebb, and Europeans and Moslems alike strove for the only culture readily available and adapted to the modern world—that offered by French society and language. However, in the first issue of *Rivages*, a short-lived review of Mediterranean culture, Camus proposed to publish "living texts," with translations from Spanish, Italian, and Arabic, not coincidentally the languages of oppressed Mediterranean cultures (*E*, p. 1331). He saw the Mediterranean basin as a unique entity where East and West meet: "North Africa is one of the only countries where East and West live side by side. And at this crossroads, a Spaniard or an Italian on the quays of Algiers lives no differently from the Arabs who surround him." He goes on to base this view of Mediterranean culture on questionable foundations: "linguistic unity," based on a common Latin heritage, and "unity of origin," based on medieval collectivism—"chivalric orders, religious orders, feudal systems" (p. 1325).

The latter concept becomes meaningful in relation to Camus's next point, that Mediterranean collectivism will change and adapt Russian collectivism, just as it has adapted other doctrines in the past. In his letter to Grenier, Camus had declared that doctrines should evolve, and now he advances the statement, audacious for a party member, that "the game of collectivism is not being played in Russia" (*E*, p. 1325). Our ideas must adapt to current reality. This in no way prejudices the fate of party doctrine, which cannot be judged on past history, even if it be Russia's past. Even taking into account "the changeover from the Russification of [the party's] vocabulary to its Jacobinization" (Kriegel, p. 79), which marked the change from the strategy of the class struggle to that of the Popular Front, Camus's criticism of Russia sounds obviously deviant. "For Mediterranean men, we need a Mediterranean political system. . . . Within the framework of internationalism, such a thing is feasible" (p. 1327). These words sound like a portent of the ideas of polycentrism that would be expressed in public by Togliatti in Italy twenty years later.

Despite Camus's opposition to the change in party strategy, he reflects some of the new pluralism inherent in the party's public image during the years of the Popular Front. A speech given by PCF leader Maurice Thorez in Algiers in February 1939 proclaims a similar view of Mediterranean culture. Their point in common is that they both set out "in search of a pluralist identity that would allow the European to become an integral part of the Algerian scene . . . without giving up his cultural heritage" (Sivan, p. 113). Thorez used a "melting pot" image to reassure his European constituents that an independent Algeria would be made up of a "mixture of twenty races"; neither the Fascist *colons* nor the Arab nationalists could claim to be the "chosen race." Camus viewed the fusion between East and West as a positive dynamic force; in later articles on Algeria he was to use images of "marriage," "nuptials," and finally "divorce." The terms echo the titles of some of his writings: *Nuptials* and *Exile and the Kingdom.*

There is no doubt that Camus's education led him to stress the European cultural heritage. He denounced colonialism, but he could not call for its destruction without destroying his own

identity. Close links to France were problematic, however, because the French face in Algeria was not a democratic one, but
that of a colonial regime, more closely akin to Fascism. Camus's
vision of Algeria has local roots: "in the tree, in the hillside and
in man" (*E*, p. 1327). He felt himself a part of the landscape and
the people, a feeling echoed by Daru, the protagonist of the short
story "The Guest."

If Camus failed to find the fraternal group he sought within
the rank and file of the Communist party, he found it instead in
theatrical activities. Grenier had seen a potential politician in
him, but his experience in political life led him to denounce the
hollowness of rhetoric in the political arena, and to transfer his
talents to the theater, where rhetoric—the creation of an *illusion* of reality—has a proper home. In a talk given in 1959 entitled "Why I Work in the Theater," Camus spoke of the
comradeship he found in this kind of group. People in general,
but the writer in particular, "needs the human face, the warmth
of a collectivity. It even explains most of a writer's commitments: marriage, academia, politics" (*TRN*, p. 1723). Again the
idea of nuptials is linked with political commitment. And in a
statement that echoes the "askesis" he had hoped to achieve in
the Communist party, Camus asserts: "The theater is my convent. The frenzy of the world dies out at the foot of its walls, and
within that sacred enclosure, over a two-month period, a community of working monks,[5] snatched from their century, dedicated to a single meditation and directed towards a single goal,
prepare the service that will be celebrated one evening for the
first time" (p. 1722). This extended image suggests that thought
must not succumb to the violence of history; it needs a retreat,
albeit a short-lived one, in order to produce something original
instead of repetition.[6]

Camus's Théâtre du Travail was founded in 1936, and included "young revolutionary intellectuals, academics or students, more or less deeply imbued with Marxism, artists,
painters, sculptors and architects . . . workers and petty-

bourgeois, usually militant in a party or political movement"
(*TRN*, pp. 1689–90). The aim was to produce popular revolutionary theater for the masses. And when Camus broke with the
party in 1937, he put together the Théâtre de l'Equipe within a
few months. What attracted him to the theater initially remained a constant throughout his life. In 1959, after political
differences had led to personal but widely publicized battles and
Camus's estrangement from the main left-wing literary and intellectual circles in Paris, he explained:

> The theater offers me the community I need. . . . Alone, the artist
> reigns, but over a void. In the theater, he cannot reign. What he
> wants depends on others. The producer needs the actor who in
> turn needs him. This mutual dependence, when accepted with
> the appropriate humility and good humor, is the basis of the soli-
> darity of the profession and gives substance [*un corps*] to everyday
> comradeship. Here we are bound to each other without losing our
> individual freedom, at least more or less; isn't this a good formula
> for the society of the future? (*TRN*, pp. 1723–24)

The statement underlines Camus's lack of interest in power: he
has no taste for hierarchy, whether it be the colonial structure or
the Communist International structure. Equality is expressed
in the fraternal gesture rather than the paternal, and there is a
singular lack of father figures in Camus's work. Only the theatrical group seems to guarantee the freedom of the creative
individual within the group; in *The Plague* too we see how
fraternal solidarity can lead to creative freedom.

The theater troupe is the ideal form of collectivity because its
aims, though limited, are attainable at a fixed point in time.
"This collectivity is so closely knit only because of the prox-
imity of the goal and the stakes. A party, a movement, a church
are also communities, but the goal they pursue is lost in the
darkness of the future" (*TRN*, p. 1724). The last phrase implies
an ironic jibe at the common attitude towards the future found
in parties and churches, where the prevailing image is one of

light. The limitations imposed by the theatrical profession are accepted as a mutually beneficial necessity; there is no ambiguity as to the ends pursued, and there is no hierarchy.

Camus admits that the theater helps him to escape from the "abstraction that threatens every writer" (*TRN*, p. 1724). As a young left-wing student in Algiers, he had recognized the stigma attached to the notion of the intellectual, the recluse in his ivory tower, blamed for causing revolutions without bloodying his own hands. Camus felt that the intellectual's role in history was overrated. "It is not his job to alter the world. Whatever people say, revolutions happen first and the ideas come later" (*E*, p. 1326).

This flight from abstraction into some form of play—whether sport or the theater—arose from a need to exert the body as well as the mind. The theater is "a profession in which the body is important" (*TRN*, p. 1722). Camus enjoyed every aspect of the theater, the nuts and bolts of a production, "and when I worked in journalism, I preferred page-setting on the stone to writing those sermons called editorials" (pp. 1724–25).

The team as a social unit might work well in microcosm; whether it can be successfully applied to mass society is another question. It was certainly never given any chance in Algeria, although Camus's initiation into journalism aimed at abolishing the rigid pyramidal structure of the colonial hierarchy. Just as he had rejected the idea that one culture might be superior to another, so he rejected the principles of colonialism. The old myth that justified colonial oppression by the need to save the souls of the infidels was merely a distortion of a valid faith (*E*, p. 801). In the same way the Communist party had distorted the ideal of collectivism by positing tactical necessity as a justification for neglecting its ultimate goals. Attacking the PPA did nothing to improve the lot of Arabs relegated to the bottom of the class hierarchy by a colonialist regime.

Camus's journalistic activities, outside the confines of the Communist party, allowed him to address himself openly and

unambiguously to the needs of the oppressed. The colonial experience is central to his thought and to his physical being. In
1955 he wrote to an Algerian socialist, Aziz Kessous, "I am sick
in the Algeria within me, just as others are sick in the lungs"
(E, p. 963). The reversal of the attribution of sickness is significant: Camus in fact suffered from lung disease. But *his* Algeria
was being stifled by its own sickness, racism. He recognized
that as a French Algerian, he shared that sickness, but for him it
took the form of a recognition of difference that was not antag-
onistic but creative, a possible marriage. In June 1952 he declared that while others had abandoned the anticolonialist fight
for tactical reasons, he had "never actually engaged in any other
political struggle but this one" (p. 747). Colonialism was the
archetype of the oppressive regime; Fascism and Stalinism were
merely variations of the same fundamental evil.

The colonial structure is even more pernicious than the basic
class structure: both form a pyramid, but in the former, the
masses who form the base of the pyramid are divided into antag-
onistic racial groups, so that there is conflict not only from top
to bottom but also on a horizontal plane. A Communist party
official in Algiers considered that Camus did not understand
"the nature of the class struggle." He did understand racism,
however, and the fact that it belonged to both the vertical and
the horizontal planes of the colonialist pyramid.[7]

With his political activity, Camus was seeking a way to
change the established order of the society in which he lived.
But personal commitment did not resolve the problems involved in finding acceptable channels for that commitment.
The Communist party turned away from the claims of the
Moslem population, whose political and social situation under
colonial rule represented for Camus a fundamental violation of
human dignity; and the rigidity of party discipline conflicted
with those anarchic tendencies which Camus liked to attribute
to his Spanish heritage. The dogmatism and abstraction of ideology, which reflected a structure of authority that Camus

found unacceptable, contributed to his rejection of party discipline. And the way in which language was used and twisted by politicians offended the poet in Camus; as a creative writer, he felt a responsibility to bear witness, to communicate his vision of the world and its realities, and always to speak the truth. The ambiguity of his commitment to art and life thus stemmed from internal dilemmas as well as outside factors. Indeed these outside factors, mostly beyond his control, exacerbated his misgivings rather than allaying his doubts.

One result of these early political experiences in Algiers was an unwillingness to join any group that was based on a hierarchical rather than a fraternal "team" structure. Thus Camus never again joined a political party, and his activities as journalist, actor, producer, and resistant all fell within the sphere of the team effort: when outside forces imposed structures, he withdrew his participation. On an intellectual level, he denied allegiance to any literary or philosophical movement, declaring that he had too little faith in the power of reason to adopt any one system. His early writings reflect the tensions between poet and activist inherent in his thought.

2

The Pursuit of Happiness

Une oeuvre d'art qui
retracerait la conquête du
bonheur serait une oeuvre
révolutionnaire.
—*Carnets I*

The fundamental ambiguity evident in Camus's commitment is reflected in the title of his collection of essays published in Algiers in 1937, *The Wrong Side and the Right Side* (*L'Envers et l'endroit*). This image recurs throughout Camus's work: the two faces of a coin, or the light and dark created by the sun and the shadows it casts. In his fiction it extends to the sphere of judgment: Meursault in *The Stranger* and Clamence in *The Fall* each present two versions of reality, the "right" one and the "wrong" one. Between them they compose whole cloth. This tendency to eschew a single point of view, and to doubt the truth of words, is hardly compatible with an ideology. And yet Camus's first novel, written between 1936 and 1938, portrays a character whose life is based on an ideology.

The publication in 1971 of *A Happy Death*[1] (*La Mort heureuse*) was greeted with criticism in some quarters. It was felt that a manuscript unpublished during the author's lifetime should not have been published as a novel but as an unfinished manuscript, particularly since Camus was so scrupulous and demanding about his texts. The fact remains, however, that Camus never threw the manuscript away; as a document it provides valuable insights into the confusion of his literary and political views during the crucial formative period of 1935 to 1938. Despite the many questions it raises, the text of *A Happy Death* is in some ways more transparent than those published later in his career. And even though the effort was unsuccessful as a novel, it was nevertheless the means by which Camus worked his way through a difficult phase in his life and put it behind him.

Some of the questions raised in the text will reappear in different contexts: his notion of the Absurd, violence and its justification, withdrawal and commitment, a writer's obsession with sterility. The changes in the text from one manuscript to another reflect Camus's own changing commitments. His failure as a political activist led him to concentrate on his needs as a writer, his own self-fulfilment. The subsequent failure of the novel, both in terms of literary excellence and philosophical clarity, was due to this strongly autobiographical element. Camus's hero had to be discarded because his chosen route led to sterility.

Patrice Mersault, an office worker of little means, meets a crippled man, Roland Zagreus, who recounts the story of how he made a fortune which he could never enjoy because of an accident that cost him both his legs. Mersault is convinced by Zagreus's claim that money guarantees freedom, and that it is the right of every man to fulfill his potential by any means available. Mersault then kills Zagreus, stages the murder to look like a suicide, and steals the victim's fortune, thus freeing himself from the restrictions of work. He catches cold on the way home, so that his subsequent trip to Europe is spoiled by illness and the desire to return home to the sun. He lives for a while with three young women in a house above the bay of Algiers, the "House before the World," but finding that human company intrudes on his consciousness and diverts him from his chosen path, he moves to a remote house on the North African coast at Chenoua, where he finds happiness in solitude, in communion with the sun and sea, and dies a "happy death."

Camus's preoccupation with death is not surprising: the diagnosis of tuberculosis in his late teens had made him acutely aware of his own mortality, and led to the development of his notion of the Absurd. The arbitrary nature of the world without God, in which a person's life and work can be made meaningless by the ultimate certainty of death, makes ambition of questionable value. The gap between our aspirations and their possibilities alienates us from the world, even while it forces us to create our own meaning, and to live life to the full. In exile one must forge one's own kingdom.

In his reading notes in 1933 Camus remarked: "One might maintain that just as there is a need for unity, there is a need for death, because death allows life to form a single block, by their opposition" (*EJ*, p. 204). This notion of life as an opposition becomes a permanent theme in Camus's work, and culminates in his theory of metaphysical and political revolt. At this stage, however, it was Caligula's observation that men die and are not happy that preoccupied him. In an early version of "The Wind at Djémila" (*Nuptials*), Camus proclaimed hypocrisy the source of unhappiness; our life is a sham that avoids the reality of death. "There is something heroic in the way we blind ourselves about death. We screen it with the scenery of our factories and our daily tramrides. Getting three meals a day, faking love, trying to enjoy life, choosing a career, having ideas—these are all ways of cheating which allow us never to think about death" (*E*, p. 1352).

A lucid opposition to death is the answer. In the final version of the same essay (published in 1938), Camus wrote: "I really feel that the true, indeed the only progress of civilization, the one to which a man devotes himself once in a while, is to create conscious deaths. . . . To create conscious deaths is to diminish the gap that separates us from the world" (*E*, pp. 64–65). This passage elucidates the titles of the two parts of *A Happy Death*: "Natural Death," that of Zagreus, and "Conscious Death" which is the hero Mersault's aim. The reversal of conventional attitudes of hypocrisy is a major element in the work. The title itself questions the usual attitude towards death, which sees it as an inevitable tragedy, but one which should be evaded, camouflaged, ignored as long as possible. As Sarocchi points out in his introduction to the novel, the proverb "Money does not bring happiness" is turned around, and the story demonstrates that happiness is impossible without money. The title of the first part of the novel, "Natural Death," furnishes another example: a violent death at the hands of a murderer with a gun is precisely the opposite of what is normally considered a "natural death." Only in relation to its counterpart, "Conscious Death," does the meaning of "natural" become clearer: Zagreus dies with tears in his eyes, without eradicating hope, and this is the way most people die. Mersault, however, by facing death constantly, dies happily, with no involvement in tomorrow to cause him regrets. The usual meaning of the word *monde* is also reversed. In English too, but particularly in French, the "world" denotes people, human society. But Camus uses the word *monde*, both in his essay and in the novel, to mean the world of nature, the cosmos, whereas people are called "man" (*l'homme*).[2]

The text of "The Wind at Djémila" makes the point explicitly: "In the presence of this world, I do not want to lie or be lied to. I want to keep my lucidity to the last and watch my end with the full abundance of my jealousy and horror. I fear death only insofar as I separate myself from the world and join the destiny of men who are living instead of contemplating the enduring sky" (*E*, p. 65). Mersault will transform into a daily creed what Camus had already envisaged as a constant dialectic between solidarity and solitariness, between compassion and self-fulfilment.

Self-fulfilment is Mersault's aim in life. He rebels against the strictures imposed by the daily routine of work by making himself rich through a criminal act. One of the most significant aspects of *A Happy Death* in relation to Camus's later writings is the place accorded to violence. Mersault murders Zagreus in cold blood for his money. Both the crime and the cover-up are carefully planned; and although Mersault does not use his riches to live lavishly, he spends the requisite amount to enable him to set the scene for the attainment of his own happiness. He needs freedom from economic problems to assure him the time and the setting for a systematic search—and askesis is impossible in the setting of a "normal" social life and a forty-hour week. As Zagreus asserts, "Having money means being free of money" (p. 79). Mersault feels no remorse; Zagreus had justified violence. "He had messed up his life, for sure. But he was right: everything for happiness, etc. violence" (*MH*, early text, p. 218).

This violence is justified in early versions of the manuscript by three factors: the paramount needs of the writer, the injustices of bourgeois society, and the uselessness of political involvement. Obviously these reasons reflect Camus's own concerns, both as an aspiring writer and a disillusioned political activist. He was frustrated in his creative activity during this period by a chronic shortage of money. His writing had to be done in the evenings after a dulling day of office work (*Corr.*, p. 29). In October 1937 he wrote: "To create or not to create. In the first case, everything is justified. Everything, without exception. In the second case, it is total absurdity. All that remains is to choose the most esthetic form of suicide: marriage + forty hours or a revolver" (*CI*, p. 89). It is not surprising that in his fiction, Camus could conceive of turning the weapon on a wealthy man.

His hero Mersault sets the stage for the realization of his desires through a pattern of violence–withdrawal–askesis–happy death. In early versions of the manuscript, there is a close relationship between death and writing that becomes less explicit in the final manuscript, where the reference to Mersault's need to write is omitted. In a notebook entry, Mersault tells his friend Catherine: "I know now that I am going to write. . . . I must bear witness. . . . I must write, just as I must swim, because my body demands it" (*CI*, p. 25). This version allows Mersault to "write," that is, he relates his whole story to his friend

Bernard, the village doctor. But in the final version, he cannot confide it: "His work would henceforth remain secret" (*MH*, p. 184).

This change in emphasis leads to some confusion. For example, in the last chapter, Mersault feels a strange detachment from his own story, as if it were "a favorite book . . . that someone else has written" (*MH*, pp. 191–92). This passage is more relevant to the earlier version where Mersault tells all: detachment coincides with a successful creative act rather than with the inability to share his secret. The descriptions of the landscape around Chenoua in this last chapter also seem out of place; they stress the fruitfulness of the world in which Mersault is integrated, but his death makes him a "stone among the stones" (p. 204), silent and immobile.

This lack of coherence stems from Camus's hesitation with regard to the idea that "everything is justified" in the cause of writing. His own political activity during the period contradicted this assertion. For if a work of art represents a lasting act of revolt against the Absurd, it must be successful in order to justify the means required to attain that goal.

A Happy Death is an experiment in ways and means. Mersault justifies the murder of Zagreus by the assertion of his own needs. If others cannot understand his action, it is because they are too conventional to accept his special status. Mersault evades the judgment of society, however; that is why he arranges the murder to look like suicide. To avoid questions about his newfound wealth, "he had staged the outward setting of his life . . . he had made a large investment in German pharmaceutical products, paid an employee to manage his holdings for him, and thereby justified his absences from Algiers and the independent life he was living. . . . Indeed one need only offer the world a demeanor it can understand" (*MH*, p. 153). Mersault looks back on his past life as "a degrading farce" (p. 123), yet in his new life he feels obliged to set up the scenery that will allay suspicion. He is hypocritical in the manner in which he safeguards his freedom. By not confessing, he remains dependent on a society that thinks differently from him, but whose system is not challenged (Hirdt, pp. 342–43). The use of violence has not made him a successful revolutionary.

Just as he attenuated Mersault's needs as a writer, so Camus watered down early references to society as a justification for violent opposition. Early versions of the text, written during Camus's membership in the PCF, contain direct references to the ills of bourgeois society (MH, pp. 217–18). In Zagreus's long lecture to Mersault he says: "Since it is a certain stage in our civilization that puts us in this position, we should have no scruples about means. Since the demand for happiness is the most noble aspect of a man's heart, it justifies everything, even evil acts. A pure heart suffices" (p. 217). In the final version, Zagreus says at one point that for "a man who is well born, being happy is never complicated" (p. 75). Later he remarks that "for a certain class of beings, happiness is possible" (p. 79). Zagreus recommends joining the elite, rather than attempting to change the system of privilege.

This indictment of a certain stage in the course of civilization is played down in the final version, which dates from 1938. But when Bernard declares he despises a man who is pushed by self-interest and the desire for money, Mersault, in seeking anew some justification for his actions, evokes the ills of poverty, the misfortune of birth: "This sordid revolting curse, which means the poor end in poverty the life they have begun in poverty, he had rejected it by fighting against money with money, opposing hatred with hatred" (MH, p. 184). He might have added "violence with violence."

In his Notebooks Camus used the same word, sordid, to describe "the condition of a working man in a civilization based on men working" (CI, p. 106). This reaction against the work ethic, against the idea that any work is ennobling and that a lack of productive occupation is immoral, reveals the strong influence of Mediterranean values in the young Camus, values that insist rather on the noble virtues of leisure. Catherine's friends lament the eight wasted hours she spends typing each day. Mersault resents his dull office job. But no one is willing to accompany Catherine to the offices of the CGT to lobby for a forty-hour week. Camus wrote in his notebook in June 1938: "People talk a great deal now about the dignity of work, about its necessity. . . . But it's a hoax. The only dignity in work is in work accepted freely. Only idleness is a moral value because it can be used to judge men. It is only fatal to the mediocre. . . . Work on the other hand crushes men equally. It is not the basis of a judgment. It sets up a metaphysic of humiliation. In its current form of slavery that the society of right-thinking men gives it, the best of men succumb to it" (p. 115). Work as a form of slavery is what Camus is attacking here, and as a journalist he had witnessed it in Algeria: he proposes reversing the classical order and making work the fruit of leisure. "There is a dignity of labor in the little barrels made on Sundays. Here, work and play come together again, and play that accepts the discipline of technique attains the dignity of a work of art and of creation itself" (p. 115).[3]

Withdrawal marks the next stage in Mersault's quest. He can attain self-satisfaction and self-justification only through a steadfast attachment to his own particular brand of "work." This involves a concentrated and systematic askesis. The body must be disciplined: it must be detached from the world and yet in tune with the rhythm of the natural world, "nothing before him but himself" (MH, p. 159), without social masks or social roles. On the way back to Algiers after his journey to northern Europe, Mersault "realized that he must not sleep but be on his guard, against friends, against the comfort of body or soul. He had to create his happiness and its justification" (p. 122, my emphasis).

In the communal life of the House before the World, he begins his task of building a new life. But it is too comfortable, it offers "days . . . woven of that luxurious fabric of laughter and simple gestures" (MH, p. 146). And there is the risk of emotional attachments, restraint on his liberty, for he fears Catherine is in love with him. He cannot afford to be sidetracked from his goal: "Man diminishes man's strength, the world leaves it intact" (p. 132). The house at Chenoua is isolated, and he plans to live there alone. But once the small jobs in the house are finished, Mersault finds himself in the ironic position of having time weigh heavily. This is the test of mediocrity. At first he spends many of those long hours sleeping; then "the memory of that wasted day embittered him" (p. 160). "He was seized with anguish when he realized the disproportion between the act that had brought him to this life and this life itself" (p. 161). He returns to the simple expedient of self-discipline. "The conditions of the uncommon happiness he sought were rising early in the morning, taking a regular swim—a conscious health program . . . to harmonize his own breathing with the deepest rhythm of time and life" (p. 167). His morning swim, "this first act," sets the tone for the rest of the day. "He attuned the pounding of his blood to the violent pulsation of the sun . . . his days were organized according to a rhythm . . . he had no glimpse of eternity nor of superhuman happiness outside the curve of the days. Happiness was human, eternity ordinary. The main thing was to learn to humble himself, to conduct his heartbeat in time with the days instead of making their rhythm conform to the curve of human hopes" (p. 169). He must begin anew each day in his search for happiness.

This routine resembles that which Camus later declared an imperative for himself as a writer, and indeed he compares this stage with the point at which the artist should stop work on his creation, exercising a "determination not to know." Accord, harmony, rhythm: all these terms imply a contradiction to the dissonance inherent in the concept of the Absurd, and they can also apply to the aesthetics of poetry.

The difference between the lucid ascetic and the unhappy man is that one lives for the day only, the other is hampered by past guilt and vague hopes for the future. Mersault maintains

that everything is forgotten sooner or later. "Everything is forgotten, even great loves" (*MH*, p. 162); in an earlier manuscript,
the phrase "even the most indelible crimes" was added (*MH*,
p. 228). The question remains whether it is possible for an intellectual, or an artist, to ignore the future. When he creates a work
of art and finishes it, by offering it to other men he is commu-
nicating something, he is bearing witness, starting a chain reaction that can only take place in future time. But Mersault is
advocating a passive and solitary happiness, what Zagreus calls
an "ideal of the pebble" (p. 71).

Pérez, the one-armed fisherman, seems to fit this idea of the
pebble most easily. He has trained his body to overcome its
disability, his movements are perfectly coordinated with the sea
and the fish; and he shares a simple meal in silent companionship with Mersault, surely a stranger in his world. Mersault
"became part of a life in its pure state, he rediscovered a paradise
given only to the least intelligent or the most intelligent of
animals" (*MH*, p. 171).[4]

Purity is a dominant aspect of Mersault's ideology. He enacts
the lesson that Zagreus has taught him, that for the pure in
heart, everything is justified. Certainly the images evoked in the
opening chapter, where the murder scene takes place, suggest
innocence and purity, a kind of frigid clarity: and at one point
where Mersault is forced to question his motives, the phrase "in
the innocence of his heart" is repeated like a motto, a comfort-
ing reminder that his cause is just (*MH*, p. 186). But changes
between the first typescript and the revised version again reveal
that Camus was less convinced than his hero. Mersault's friendship with Zagreus is portrayed as deep and warm in the earlier
text; he was happy to be close to "a man he loved" (p. 216). This
crippled man is "the only person who could still listen to him
and understand him" (p. 222). The later version of chapter four
omits any mention of Mersault's affection, and dwells upon his
uneasiness in the presence of "this body that was only half alive"
(p. 68). Mersault listens to Zagreus's life history and philosophy,

but his reaction is not one of warmth and appreciation: "A rag, Mersault thought, a zero in the world" (p. 79). It would have been more difficult to construe the murder as pure and innocent if Mersault had killed a friend, a friend who may frequently contemplate suicide because of his infirmity and the degradations it entails, but who nevertheless still clings to life and hope.

Sarocchi raises the hypothesis that by choosing the name Zagreus, Camus intended the story to have a symbolic meaning. Zagreus was one of the names attributed to Dionysos, who was torn apart and eaten, and then reborn as a new god who became an inspiration to the Orphic poets. The death of Zagreus is thus a sacrificial act which enables Mersault to live up to his heroic potential. However, in the end it is the aspect of Zagreus that is linked with the underworld, with the world of rocks, that inspires Mersault. Dionysos has more than one face, and the presence of ambiguity undermines the professed certainty of the justness of Mersault's cause.

Though Mersault attains one goal—happy death—he fails to communicate his ideology to others. What accounts for this failure, this ultimate sterility? The major reason is his neglect of one side of the coin: he concentrates on beauty to the total exclusion of "the humiliated." Indeed his revolt and his aim in life are self-centered. His sense of fraternity is gradually effaced: his feeling of respect in the presence of his neighbor Cardona's wretchedness gives him the necessary impetus to take action to avoid a similar fate, but arouses no desire to effect any change in the other man's life. Mersault's gradual withdrawal from human society—retreat from the House before the World, companionship with Pérez and Bernard, occasional visits from Lucienne—is marked by a growing silence. The long philosophical conversations with the three women are given up in favor of people who speak with their bodies. Silent communication can establish authentic bonds: "The pleasure . . . of giving . . . a light— a complicity, a kind of freemasonry of the cigarette" (CI, p. 134).

As Mersault closes himself off from human dialogue, he opens himself to an even more intense dialogue or communion with the real "world," the silent world of nature. The only man he sees as he nears death is Zagreus: there is a silent visual fraternity, born of bloodshed and violence. It is like a bond between revolutionaries, and this was to be a "revolutionary work" (*CI*, p. 106). But even though Zagreus and Mersault act out a revolt they consider legitimate, the end is silence rather than a lasting achievement: Zagreus is reduced to life in a wheelchair, and Mersault's withdrawal from verbal intercourse finally inhibits his ability to profess his creed. (Jonas, the artist at work, also loses inspiration when he is cut off from human society.) In an early manuscript, Bernard admits that he can understand withdrawal from the world of men if it is done to accomplish some "great project." To which Mersault replies, "For me, what seems great is the withdrawal." And he adds, "All the rest is politics" (*MH*, p. 229).

What exactly Mersault means here by "politics" is not clear. It is possible that it encompasses all that is impure and tactical in human intercourse, behavior that hides one's motives, the "degrading farce." It could mean the rhetoric of politicians talking of justice when their real aim is power. It means submission to social convention, and implies a criticism of modern capitalist society that demands production, input, profit. It is all part of the game that Mersault, and the Meursault of *The Stranger*, refuse to play.

But politics also means people in society. Mersault has eliminated the tension between the demands of human affairs and of his work. In order to elucidate ambiguity, he must destroy a human life, and ignore society.

Indeed, Mersault specifically rejects any involvement in local politics, although he does mingle with the local people. He decries the injustice of a society that condemns the poor to remain poor, and declares the need to revolt against it; but his own wealth is not used to help Cardona, or to allow Catherine to give up her tedious job. He sets up Lucienne in an apartment and has her stop work, but only so that she can be available to him whenever he needs her. He merely replaces one kind of enslavement with another. Camus commented in his notebook in April 1941, "In Greece, there were free men because there were slaves" (*CI*, p. 234). It is proposed that Mersault run for mayor against the incumbent, who had been in office for ten years, "and this semi-permanent position led him to regard himself as Napoleon Bonaparte" (*MH*, p. 172). One day the mayor shows off his new house complete with elevator: "From that day on, Mersault developed a profound admiration for the mayor. He and Bernard wielded all their influence to keep him in the office he so richly deserved" (pp. 172–73).

Mersault's willingness to allow this brand of *colon* (whom Camus criticizes so fiercely in other texts) to continue his rule unimpeded points up one of the contradictions in his professed ideology. Obviously, the *colons* are perfect examples of the hypocrisy and the comedy of social and political life, and as such they serve to justify Mersault's withdrawal to authenticity. But his withdrawal cannot be total; he still relies on that society for support services—on the hotel boy for meals, on Bernard for medical attention, on the three students for intellectual companionship, and on Lucienne for sexual fulfilment.

"Solitude, luxury of the rich" wrote Camus in September 1937 (*CI*, p. 84). Is this luxury a legitimate part of askesis? Camus, in his response to Barthes, maintained that the evolution from *The Stranger* to *The Plague* marked a move from a preoccupation with solitariness to solidarity (*TRN*, p. 1974), but it would be more accurate to say that this change occurred between *A Happy Death*, which was rejected as unsatisfactory, and *The Stranger*.

Mersault began as an opponent of bourgeois convention, of hypocrisy and of the fear of death. He followed a systematic route towards his ultimate goal—a happy death, a life in tune with the natural world and untrammelled by the demands of others. In "The Wind at Djémila," Camus declared that one devotes oneself to such a project only once in a while: Mersault devotes all his time to it, and in so doing demonstrates the impossibility of individual happiness as a solution to man's absurd fate. An equation of one murder to one happy person is an untenable proposition. Mersault achieves a certain happiness at the expense of human solidarity, but it is an admittedly sterile happiness. Withdrawal constitutes one side of the cloth of life, solidarity the other: neither is "right" or "wrong" in the moral sense, but each one must be interwoven with the other to produce a whole.

During this period (1936–1938) Camus was searching for a rational system: he grappled with the problem of happiness and creative freedom in *A Happy Death* and in his play *Caligula;* he sought a way to achieve social change by joining the Communist party and by his journalistic work for the local organ of the Popular Front, *Alger-Républicain.* But by 1946, in response to critics who placed him in the same existentialist mold as Sartre, Camus declared, "Although I recognize the historical importance of this movement, I do not have enough faith in reason to become part of a system" (*TRN*, p. 1746).

The system devised in *A Happy Death* was obviously unworkable. It is true that Mersault dies a happy death, a lucid passage to the state he seeks, "stone among the stones" (*MH*, p. 204). Yet the path he takes seems to make life synonymous with death: by approaching the state of death in life one may avoid the anguish of the absurd, but at some cost. In *Nuptials*, Camus states that Tipasa, the experience of being one with the natural world, is only possible for a day (*E*, p. 59). That is enough time to live: "There is a time for living and a time for bearing witness to life. There is also a time for creating which comes less naturally. For me it is enough to live with my whole body and to bear witness with my whole heart. Live Tipasa, bear witness and the work of art will come later. There is a freedom in that." Mersault lives Tipasa every day, and falls silent. In his own mind, murder was justified, but to the end he fears a different judgment of his act, and only Zagreus knows the secret bond, the "blood brotherhood" of violence.

Mersault, together with Caligula, whom Camus created during the same period, reveals the course of a system followed to its logical conclusion. "We sense that an external necessity controls the murder, the behavior and the thought of the hero Mersault. A necessity with metaphysical, moral, social and political facets: an ideology" (Abbou, "Débutant," p. 3). As such, it requires self-discipline, singleness of purpose, commitment. Mersault, like Caligula, rejects the opinion of society; the twitterings of the senators—"We are the party of honor and cleanliness. And we must defend the sacred principle of order and the family" (early ms. *TRN*, p. 1764)—represent what Mersault despises as prejudice and stupidity. By 1938 the violence initiated by Mersault had been multiplied by Caligula: "He is transforming his philosophy into corpses," says Cherea (*TRN*, p. 35). The use of the imperfect tense in the relation of the murder of Zagreus could be construed as denoting an unfinished deed, one that might be repeated or become habitual. But Caligula comes to the conclusion that killing is not the solution; and Mersault, in his withdrawal from society and his refusal to combat social issues except insofar as they impinge on his personal desires, became irrelevant to his author. Mersault's moral situation "made him cumbersome. He represented the refusal to yield to the legal norms of a deceitful and hypocritical society. But at the time of Munich, and of the political struggles of *Alger-Républicain*, the response had to come from a more profound commitment and in a more scathing form" (ibid., p. 3).

Mersault is one kind of rebel. Initially, Camus had stressed the social origins of his revolt—the poverty, enslavement, degradation. But in later versions of the text it becomes clear that Mersault has no desire to change society, merely to evade its strictures. His commitment to the attainment of happy death has no consequences. Such a commitment was ethically invalid at a time when evil was threatening to engulf the world. So Camus set his hero aside.

A Happy Death is the expression not of an ideal, but of a temptation. Paul Raffi, who knew Camus well during this period, remarked that the temptation to become an aesthete was a strong one, and that it was perhaps repressed in face of the obligations entailed by his journalism. In his letters to his friends with whom he shared the Maison Fichu (the source of the House before the World), Camus expressed doubts about this work, about fear of failure and a consequent loss of justification. By the time he had finished the novel, he had overcome or moved beyond these temptations; the manuscript remained as evidence of this phase, and of his release from it. As *The Stranger* began to take shape, the revolt against the conventions of bourgeois society came more clearly into focus, and personal experience and autobiographical details were assimilated and moved to a more discreet distance.

Despite the use of the third person and the simple past narrative tense, Mersault remained too close to his author.[5] Camus's rearrangement of chapters and episodes points up his attempt to blur the relationship between his fictitious character and his own life, while retaining some narrative logic and continuity. Camus felt uncomfortable at revealing experiences or relations that were too close to him. He was not a man of confidences, and sought the kind of objectivity he admired in Stendhal. In his own early work, he noted that "the part where I tried to hide my need to weep is the best" (*EJ*, p. 202). "The true work of art is the one that says less" (*CI*, p. 127).

The process of assimilation and distanciation from personal experience was accomplished as a result of direct participation in the affairs of the world. Camus's activities as a militant journalist widened his vision and cast new perspectives on his thought.

3

Alger-Républicain

Je comprends maintenant
que si j'ai un devoir, c'est
de donner aux miens ce que
j'ai de meilleur, je veux
dire essayer de les défendre
contre le mensonge.
—*Correspondance*

In 1955, commenting on his return to journalism, Camus declared that "journalism has always seemed the most pleasant form of commitment for me, providing one can say everything" (*E,* p. 1840). This condition had certainly not been met in Algiers in the late thirties, when Camus made his first forays into journalism.

Camus worked in a technical capacity for a politically moderate newspaper, *L'Echo d'Alger,* in 1937. It was one of several jobs that allowed him the free time he needed to pursue his writing while providing him with a livelihood. In October 1938 Camus was hired by Pascal Pia and joined the staff of *Alger-Républicain,* first as a literary critic and reporter of minor incidents—*les chiens écrasés,* as such articles were called—and later as a political commentator. *Alger-Républicain* was founded as an independent newspaper with the aim of supporting the socialist elements of the Popular Front. It was a unique enterprise in that it constituted "an attempt to build up a cooperative form of journalism, independent of financiers and political allegiances." The aims of the newspaper were spelled out in its editorial of 6 October 1938: "We plan to struggle against the exorbitant privileges of certain 'families' which unfortunately number more than two hundred; against an anti-Semitism 'made in Germany'; against the social conservatism which plans to keep our indigenous friends on an inferior level." Injustice—economic, social and ethnic—was the target of the newspaper's attack.[1]

Camus's contributions to the newspaper show that he became an extremely able journalist. The confusions and ambiguity revealed in *A Happy Death* have no place in this writing: the moral judgments are clear, the language stripped of unnecessary ornamentation, the commitment to human solidarity unquestioned. Freed from the bonds of party dogma, his activism was no longer impeded by internal contradictions and misgivings. His needs as a writer were also fulfilled at least in part: *Nuptials*, a collection of lyrical essays, was published in 1939, and *The Stranger* was completed in May 1940.

One of the most salient features of Camus's articles—on the administration of the Algiers city council, on trials in other towns, on local and international politics—is humor. The reader is left with the impression of a tireless and conscientious observer, who never misses an opportunity to show up the ridiculous aspects of the Algerian social and political system. Monsieur Rozis, "the regrettable mayor of Algiers" (*Fragments*, p. 151), was the object of daily satire; his oppressive and reactionary policies were criticized by other, more moderate dailies too. In 1936 Rozis had been responsible for the ban on Camus's production of *Revolt in Asturia*, a cooperative venture of the Théâtre du Travail, and it was doubtless with some enthusiasm that Camus revealed the arbitrary nature of his administration.

On several occasions Rozis dealt unjustly with municipal employees. On 7 December 1938, Camus reported on the dismissal of seven employees, "guilty, not of going on strike on November 30, but of intending to do so on the 29th" (*Fragments*, p. 171). Rozis's hostility towards the trade unions led him to try to balance the city budget at the expense of the workers. "At all events, Monsieur Rozis, like many men today, is very careful not to oppose social legislation. He too merely makes it flexible. He changes only commas. So, for instance, far from wishing to abolish paid vacations, he merely substitutes unpaid vacations" (p. 176). Camus accuses the administration of ignoring the concrete results of its repressive policies: unemployment means hunger for a whole family, a gas explosion leaves dozens of people bereft and homeless. "Politicians cannot imagine just how difficult it is to be simply a man. To live, without being unjust, a life shaped by iniquities, with 1200 francs a month, a wife, a child, and the certainty of dying without being mentioned in history books" (p. 235). This lack of imagination on the part of politicians is a theme to which Camus was to return in later indictments of those in power. In 1950 he characterized men in power as "those who have failed in happiness: that explains why they have no compassion" (*TRN*, p. 1720). Camus follows the chain from the policy decision down to the individual it affects. His reaction to a convict ship moored in the Algiers harbor furnishes an example. While his fellow-journalist for *La Dépêche algérienne* (a right-wing newspaper) merely commented that he was pleased to see only four Europeans bound for the penal colony, Camus entitled his article, "These Men Expunged from the Human Race." Camus saw all the men as human beings in a cage, "men reduced to a less than human condition" (*Fragments*, p. 362). He expressed his horror at the "smell of solitude and despair," at a system that can condemn a man, without appeal, to an inhuman existence and oblivion.

It was in his coverage of trials that Camus proved most effective, and his satire most biting. Abbou has analyzed the brilliant style of his articles, and the perfection of "the parody of the judiciary." "Camus's language, through its multiplicity of signs and its semantic disjunctions, is a perfect reflection of this 'trompe l'oeil' world, this cascade of contradictions and surprises" (*Fragments*, p. 563). A more exact term might be "trompe l'oreille," aural rather than visual deception, for again Camus is concerned with the abuse of language. During the 1939 trial of Michel Hodent,[2] which no other newspaper covered, Camus followed events meticulously, mixing public protest with satirical barbs. Verbatim accounts of testimony are interspersed with such laconic statements as "M. Garcia José speaks Spanish, but will be interrogated in Arabic" (*Fragments*, p. 397). During the appeal that followed the harsh sentence of the "Auribeau incendiaries," the prosecution referred to the *gourbis*, in reality rough straw huts, as "dwellings," one of which was "inhabited," since it was later learned that a shepherd had spent the night prior to the fire in one of the huts. A protest in 1939 over starvation wages was blown up into a revolutionary act, prompting Camus to entitle his first article on the subject "The Story of a Crime; or, How a Crime is Thought Up for the Purposes of a Criminal Charge" (p. 512). This could have been a subtitle for *The Stranger*. Confessions had been extorted under torture, which Camus described in detail. "No free man can be assured of his dignity in the face of such procedures" (p. 517).

Abbou remarks on the skill with which Camus exposes "the grotesque nature of the linguistic structure, and the pernicious logic on which the faking of felonious deeds was based" (*Fragments*, pp. 553–54). His use of irony, of indirect speech in his coverage of the El Okbi trial will reappear in the trial scene of *The Stranger:* "The writer obviously polished his poetics in the course of his commentaries, which were for him so many stylistic exercises" (p. 546). In the novel, however, the writer is the defendant, and the polemical intent must rely solely on language and style to make its impact: as a journalist, Camus was able to be increasingly outspoken in his polemical arguments.

His exposure of judicial corruption was no less damning than his reports on the social injustice of the colonial system. In June 1939 he went on a fact-finding mission to the mountainous area south of Algiers inhabited by Kabylians, a people of Berber

stock, the last group in Algeria to surrender to the French conquerors. They grew figs and olives for the market in exchange for
grain, but underproduction, combined with a rapidly growing
population (due in part to the introduction of European medical
services), and an inept or even corrupt administration, had led to
a desperate state of poverty and malnutrition.

In December 1935 the *Echo d'Alger* had published a series of
articles on Kabylia. It stressed the picturesque qualities of the
region, and was aimed at encouraging tourism in the area. In
1938 another series commented on the backwardness and poverty of the region, but attributed these facts to the Kabylian
mentality (*Fragments*, pp. 267–72). Camus's "Poverty in Kabylia"[3] started out from a different viewpoint, that of questioning the assumption that French colonial rule had had only a
positive impact on the area.

Camus describes a situation that has been met with short-
term palliatives and a rigid resistance to change. Restrictions
on emigration allow no easing of the population pressure
(*E*, p. 906). The forestry code forbids the gathering of firewood,
and charcoal cannot be transported to town without a permit
(p. 911). Public works are organized to give some employment,
but the workers have back taxes deducted from their meager
wages; with bitter irony Camus points out that a nominally
charitable enterprise cloaks a situation that is tantamount to
slavery (p. 913).

The Kabylian peasant faces not only a rigidity in the colonial
administration, but also insidious political constraints. Distribution of grain is often subject to clientelistic intrigue, and in
one area at least those people voting for the PPA were denied
grain altogether. Obviously democracy for the indigenous population did not extend to secrecy at the ballot box.

These problems are compounded by the underlying attitude
of superiority "that we know well in Algeria" towards the Kabylian people. Excuses are made for current conditions by citing
the Kabyl "mentality," which means that "these people do not

have the same needs as we do" (*E*, p. 914). Camus denounces these stereotypes and prejudices: even the president of the Republic, "if given 200 francs a month to live on, would adapt to life under the bridges, to the filth, and to the crust of bread scavenged from the garbage can" (p. 914).

The *colons* (European settlers) look down on the Kabylian worker as inferior. "It is true, of course, that on local work sites one can see workers tottering about, unable to lift a pick. But it is because they have not eaten. And we are faced with an abject logic that says that a man is weak because he has no food, and is paid less because he is weak" (*E*, p. 918).

The paternalistic regime attempts to maintain the myth of the benevolent ruler by placating its rebellious subjects with symbolic gifts—handouts of food that satisfy only a day's hunger, or medals for war veterans.[4] Equally showy and useless are some of the school buildings erected in rural areas, obviously intended to impress "tourists and commissions of enquiry. . . . They sacrifice the elementary needs of the indigenous people to preconceived notions of prestige." A symbol of this absurd policy can be seen in the Aghrib region: "There, in the middle of this desert landscape without a living soul in sight, stood the luxurious school of Aghrib, the very image of uselessness." Camus advocates more schools at a third of the cost to accommodate the needs of a people eager for education and conscious of the advancement it can bring. He returns to his earlier parent-child interpretation of colonial policy, a policy "that consists of giving a thousand-franc doll to a child who has not eaten for three days" (*E*, p. 922).

This gap between the colonial myth and reality is what Camus is trying to expose in his articles. As a series of photographs demonstrates, the reality is hunger, exploitation, enslavement; Camus has facts and figures to prove it. And he undermines the myth by revealing the emptiness of the rhetoric, the futility of its symbols. The style of the articles is terse, and only occasionally does Camus resort to emotional appeals.

Perhaps the most salient feature of the style in these articles is the predominance of one conjunction, the disjunctive *mais*. It seems to enclose the Kabylian peasant, and the reader, in a rigid circumscription. Whichever way the peasant turns for escape from his intolerable situation, he is met by an implacable "but," until it becomes clear that there is no way out without a radical change in the structure of his world. The colonial regime surrounds him with a protective prison wall.

Camus uses the same syntactic measure to undermine the complacency of the colonial image: schools are built *but* they are inappropriate, food is distributed *but* it is insufficient and of low quality, jobs are created *but* they are akin to slavery. However, Camus offers some solutions for a possible way out. Naturally enough, education provides a way: for Camus himself, education in the French school system had opened up a new world and allowed him to escape the confines of an illiterate lower-class family background. Not that he rejected the positive qualities of his childhood environment; he merely recognized the dulling effect of poverty. "The Kabyls are demanding schools, just as they demand bread. But . . . the problem of education has to undergo a reform." Camus states that he received a unanimous response from the Kabylian people: they will have more schools "when the artificial barrier separating the European education system from that of the indigenous population has been abolished, when in the same classroom, two peoples destined for mutual understanding will begin to get to know each other" (*E*, p. 923).

In the light of a bloody revolution and a painful settlement in Algeria, this view seems both naïve and utopian. But Moslem education was mainly limited to Islamic schools, and did not provide training for jobs in an increasingly technological society. Camus was mistaken in believing that the barrier was merely an artificial one; in fact, in 1955 he spoke of "natural barriers"—cultural—and "artificial ditches"—dug by colonialism (p. 1866). His view of the dynamic effect of the meeting of

Eastern and Western cultures, expounded in his speech at the opening of the Maison de la Culture, was an optimistic one. The article on the Blum-Viollette plan suggests that Camus was aware that Moslem culture must still be allowed to flourish: whether it could do so within the French school system is a moot point. According to Ouzegane, Camus was not in favor of assimilation, hence his refusal to associate with the radicals in the Popular Front. And in this article on education in Kabylia, Camus is careful to dissociate himself from the policy. "If one really wants assimilation, and wants this worthy people to be French, one must not begin by separating them from the French people." The French text emphasizes the impersonal: *l'on* and *il*. Camus himself goes no further than a "mutual acquaintance. . . . All that is required, as I know from recent experience, is a hand stretched out in sincerity. But it is up to us to knock down the walls that separate us" (*E*, p. 923).

Walls, barriers, separation: if Camus is not clear about who created them, he is certain of who should remove them. Drastic measures are not necessary. It is unrealistic to suppose that the *caïdat* system of indirect rule can immediately be replaced by a democratic one.[5] The aim should be to make its administration more flexible (*E*, p. 926). There is no reason to suppress the Kabyls' way of life, but wiser investment in the area could provide technical and professional training, and modern agricultural techniques could improve production of the same commodities. Finally, Camus advocates renewed emigration possibilities for unemployed workers. Thousands of Italian immigrants are leaving France to return home, and Kabylian peasants could replace them and colonize the underpopulated areas in southern France. It should be remembered that apart from a brief stay in France in the summer of 1937, Camus had little experience of society in metropolitan France, and seemed unaware of the cool reception Kabylian peasants would encounter if they "colonized" parts of rural France! By 1947, however,

Camus had lived in France long enough to recognize racism there too, and to denounce it as a "stupid and criminal sickness" (*E*, p. 321). But from the Algerian viewpoint, France embodied the ideals of democracy, and Camus looked to France for enlightened reforms, knowing that it was not in the interests of most *colons* to instigate any change. "A regime that separates Algeria from France is responsible for the misfortune of our country" (p. 935).

The words *notre pays* ("our country") are significant in that they indicate a sharing of Algeria between European Algerians and indigenous Algerians on equal terms. The colonial regime stands between an outdated system of administration and an enlightened democracy. Camus continued to assert that Algeria could only remain loyal to France if France set a good example of justice. "People say: 'Be careful, a foreign power will seize [Algeria].' But those powers that actually could seize it have already been judged before the world for their cynicism and their cruelty" (*E*, p. 936). Implicit is the comparison between the Fascist regimes that could take over the country and the colonial regime in power. France should offer a more attractive alternative to Fascism than that displayed by the current oppressive administration. In 1945 Camus reiterated the need to reform the colonial system; France should "implant democracy in Arab countries. . . . True democracy is a new idea in Arab countries. For us, it is worth a hundred armies and a thousand oil wells" (p. 1428).

Camus sums up the meaning of his investigation: "If colonial conquest could ever find a justification, it is in the extent to which it helps the conquered people to retain their personality. And if we have a duty in this country, it is to allow one of the most proud and humane populations in the world to remain faithful to itself and to its destiny. The destiny of this people is, I believe, both to work and to meditate, and thus to give lessons in wisdom to us uneasy conquerors" (*E*, p. 938).

In this passage, Camus unequivocally places himself in the

ranks of the colonial conquerors. The fact that he qualifies that position as "uneasy" *(inquiet)* separates him from the firmly established *colons*, but in the division between conqueror and conquered he has no choice. By virtue of his birth, education, and language, he is a conqueror. The investigation points up the difference, the distance that separates colonizer and colonized. Camus sees his task as constructing a bridge across that gap. Facts and figures must convince his readers of the rationality of his contentions—"a collection of facts that can forego literary rhetoric" (*E*, p. 936). Once again the notion is raised of rhetoric as camouflage, and it is rejected. But since he believes that "some progress is made every time a political problem is re-placed by a human problem" (p. 937), he expresses these human problems in a more flowing lyrical style than is typical of the major portion of the articles. The evening is a time of exceptional lucidity, and Camus records two such evenings during his stay in Kabylia: both represent the sequence of the outstretched hand followed by the consciousness of an unbridgeable difference.

The following passages also crystallize the oppositions between the poet and activist within Camus. The opposition between solitude and solidarity, between the beauty of the world and the search for justice, are perfectly expressed, and contrast sharply with the one-sided philosophy expressed by Mersault. At this point Camus seems to have come to terms with duality.

> On one occasion, with a Kabyl friend, I had climbed up to the heights overlooking the town. There we watched night fall. And at that hour when the shadows coming down from the mountains over that radiant land bring some relief to the heart of the most hardened man, I knew that there was no such peace for those who, on the other side of the valley, were gathered around a cake of poor oatmeal. I knew too that it would have been sweet to give oneself up to such an unusual and magnificent evening, but that the wretchedness reflected by the reddening fires before us im-posed a kind of ban[6] on the beauty of the world. (*E*, p. 909)

The article ends with an unvoiced feeling of sympathy between the writer and the Kabyl: "Shall we go down? said my companion" (p. 909). This is the Camus whom Ouzegane remembered, who could put himself "inside the skin" of a humiliated Arab.

Evening is a time of "melancholy truce" (*TRN*, p. 1135), when hostilities cease, when Camus feels he understands the country and its people. "On one such evening, . . . a few of us were wandering through the cemetery of gray stones and contemplating nightfall over the valley. At that hour between day and night, I did not feel *my difference* from these people who had sought refuge here to regain some measure of themselves. But I was forced to feel that difference a few hours later, when everyone should have been eating" (*E*, pp. 937–38, my emphasis). The true meaning of the sickness within him becomes clear: Camus can freely overcome class barriers, the horizontal barriers that divide men. But good will alone cannot overcome the vertical walls of that criminal sickness, racism. He was not advocating "a ridiculous sentimentality that mixes up all races in the same fond confusion. All men are not alike, it is true, and I know well the depth of traditions that separate me from an African or a Moslem. But I also know what unites me with them, and that there is something in each one of them that I cannot disdain without degrading myself" (p. 323). These words appeared in *Combat* in 1947, but they apply equally well to the *Algerian Reports*.

The imagery of walls, barriers, and moats evokes the impression that colonial society is besieged, surrounded by fortifications, rather as the crusaders were in earlier colonial times. Camus's aim is to undermine those fortifications, to bridge the gaps established between Westerner and Arab. His only weapon is language, a medium fraught with its own problems and shortcomings. Membership in the PCF, which should have provided a vehicle for action, had proven ineffective, in part because words did not necessarily coincide with the realities they denoted. The

mystification of language in politics became one of Camus's
bêtes noires; it was particularly evident in the ideology of the
dominant class, but it was also obvious in the ranks of a party
dedicated to the eradication of colonialist oppression and con-
sisting of members with a racist attitude to the most oppressed
among them.

Journalism combines political action and writing, "the two
faces of one and the same revolt against the disorders of the
world" (*E*, p. 404). The choice of topics shows where Camus's
political sympathies lay, but in "this world in which all words
are prostituted" (p. 1672), language can create as many barriers
to understanding as bridges. In an essay on Brice Parain published in 1944 (in *Poésie 44*), Camus poses the problem: whether
our language is falsehood or truth. The world needs a dictionary.
Parain asks "whether such a dictionary is possible, and above
all, whether it is conceivable in the absence of a god to give its
meanings" (p. 1672). Camus criticizes set formulae that serve to
"camouflage heart-breaking experiences." But Parain's question
is even more imperative, "for the problem is to know whether
even our most exact words, our most successful cries are not
empty of all meaning, whether language in the end expresses
only man's definitive solitude in a silent universe" (p. 1673).
This theme was explored further in Camus's play, *The Misunderstanding.*

Thus Camus stood between the two sides in Algeria in 1939.
He had rejected the definitions of two possible gods on the European side—the language of colonialist ideology and that of the
Communist party.[7] But he could not speak the language of the
Berbero-Arab side; he knew he must be viewed as one of
the colonizers, albeit the "colonizer who refuses" (Memmi,
pp. 19–44). His situation became impossible when the colonial
administration pulled up the drawbridge across the moat that
Camus was attempting to ferry. Perhaps he was fortunate, since
many of his erstwhile comrades were interned or imprisoned by

the end of 1939 (Sivan, p. 117). The recurrent phrase in Camus's work, "there is no way out," reflects the political impasse evident at this point.

With the benefit of hindsight, critics suggest that Camus could have found a way out by advocating the abolition of colonial structures, decolonization, whereas he proposed reforms within the framework of a French presence. He certainly could not have *published* calls for decolonization, and it seems unfair to expect of a *pied-noir*, even an enlightened one, a political stance that not even Algerian Moslems or the PCA had taken up. In a sense, what Camus advocated was decolonization, in that he called for the abolition of a power structure in which Moslems were always at the bottom of the hierarchy. To him, as a man who had never lived anywhere but Algeria, colonialism was a power structure, not a conflict between European and Moslem: the system could be changed without the eviction of inhabitants.

Camus's brand of journalism met with increasing opposition from the government. By July 1939, military censorship had been imposed, and *Alger-Républicain* displayed more and more blank spaces on its pages. Its financial situation was desperate: readership fell, newsprint was scarce, and workers had to be laid off. Pia launched a new afternoon paper, *Le Soir-Républicain*, which could be distributed by street-hawkers (Lottman, p. 210). He and Camus devised all kinds of tricks to hoodwink the censors, but it was a losing battle and both men knew it. They were faced with the choice of bowing to the strictures of censorship and deceiving their readers, or of continuing to defy the censors by asserting their opinions, an option that was bound to end in the death of the newspaper. Pia and Camus chose the latter course: "Camus . . . made a choice and went down a dead-end path" (*Fragments*, p. 743). Some of the shareholders were critical of this decision, and felt that the paper should have been maintained as an anti-Fascist organ, rather than being scuttled.

Pia was already planning a move to Paris. But why did Camus

choose journalistic suicide? Following up on the symbolism of his 1941 article "To Prepare for the Fruit" (*Fragments*, p. 738), Abbou suggests that one of the conditions for bringing about a new order, or better fruit, might be the destruction of weeds and thinning of plants—in this case, "the scuttling of a newspaper that people wanted to pervert or to reduce to an unworthy role" (p. 743, n. 1). Certainly the moral role of journalism was of paramount importance to Camus: "The press constitutes a terrible weapon in our time. . . . It can make or break public opinion" (p. 733). Without freedom of the press, the truth could be twisted, and faithful readers deceived. So during the last weeks of publication, Pia and Camus dissociated themselves from any former political ties, and expressed their views as individuals. "We speak here as individuals devoted to liberty, and not as party members. . . . Today, when all the parties have betrayed us, when politics have degraded everything, man is left with nothing but the awareness of his solitude, and his faith in human and individual values" (this "Profession de foi," suppressed by the censors for *Le Soir-Républicain*, was first published in *E*, p. 1387). This defiant humanistic line was followed to the end and led to the suspension of both papers. Camus found other possibilities of employment in Algeria blocked (Grenier, p. 171), and he followed Pia to Paris in March 1940 to work with him at *Paris-Soir* until the German occupation.

Camus's early career in journalism was meteoric. Within eighteen months he rose from a little-known reporter of minor events to a major contributor to public opinion, and a constant thorn in the flesh of the colonial administrators and the military government. His fall from grace was equally rapid and precipitated by his own actions. His experience with *Combat* (from 1944 to 1947) would follow the same parabola: it is as if once he had made his position clear, repetition could not enhance it, and it became subject to distortion and misunderstanding. Changes in the historical situation called for a flexibility and a readiness for compromise that Camus rarely displayed. Subversive writing proved easier to publish in occupied France than in "free" Algeria.

Apart from moral conviction, and the long-term view proposed by Abbou, the temptation to despair in the power of the individual also played a role in Camus's decision to abandon the newspaper in Algiers. The Notebooks of the period refer frequently to despair: his "Letter to a Man in Despair" (*CI*, pp. 178–82) is an attempt to convince himself that "despair is an emotion and not a condition" (p. 179). A few months later, he expresses the desire to withdraw from participation in human affairs: "More and more, in response to the world of men, the only reaction is individualism. Man is an end unto himself. Everything one attempts for the general good ends in failure. Even if one wants to try in any case it is advisable to do it with the requisite scorn. Withdraw altogether and play one's own game" (p. 203). The sentiments expressed in this entry echo the theme of *A Happy Death:* the word *idiot* was scrawled across it, which suggests at least a partial explanation for the shelving of his first novel. Now his advice to the person in despair is to play a part first, and then, "when you have done everything you should in your area, on your ground, stop and despair as much as you please. You must understand that one can despair of the meaning of life *in general,* but not of its specific forms, of existence, since one has no power over it, but not of history, where the individual can do everything" (p. 181).

It was through journalism that Camus made his individual contribution to the course of history, and it was in this occupation that he felt the least tension between life and art. His commitment to truth and justice, and to the end of oppression, was unambiguous, and language could adequately express his thoughts. His skill as a polemicist is evident; his impatience with mystification and false rhetoric helped him to reveal the lies perpetuated by those in power. Writing served the oppressed.

However, the success of a journalistic enterprise can also be judged objectively, by its results. Camus's campaign against injustice in Algeria had little lasting effect: a few individuals who benefited from his actions on their behalf remember him with gratitude, but nothing was changed in the structure of colonialism in Algeria. In the foreword to his *Algerian Reports*, published in 1958, Camus evaluated his struggle against the poison of racism and fanaticism. "I have attempted this work of detoxification as best I could. Let us admit that up to now the results have been worthless: this book is also the story of a failure" (*E*, p. 899). This admission of failure can be heard in *The Fall*, where the voice of the prophet crying in the wilderness reminds the reader of the satirical humor of Camus's early journalistic work.

Camus's preoccupations during this period leading up to World War II reveal the direction that his thought and work would follow throughout his life. The themes that stand out in his journalism are constantly echoed in his novels and short stories. Language as a tool of ambiguous purpose—for communication, for the creation of beauty, for oppression or camouflage—is treated in *The Stranger*, *The Fall*, "The Renegade," and "The Adulterous Woman." The opposition between solidarity and solitude, the often conflicting demands of reformism and humanism, are most strikingly portrayed in *The Plague*, and then surface again some ten years later in "The Silent Men" and "The Growing Stone."

Camus's desire for a side-by-side, rather than an adversary, relationship between European and Moslem Algerians is reflected in his later conception of the team or the theater troupe as the ideal social organization, a mutually dependent rather than a competitive unit. But with regard to oppression, direct opposition remained the only possible tactic, and one to which Camus clung in spite of its political consequences.

Now, gagged by the censors in Algiers, Camus turned to a more subtle brand of subversion, and succeeded at the same time in creating his first successful novel. *The Stranger* marks the culmination of these apprentice years and launched Camus as a successful writer on the Parisian scene.

4

The Stranger

Je ne suis pas d'ici—pas
d'ailleurs non plus. Et le
monde n'est plus qu'un paysage
inconnu où le coeur ne trouve
plus d'appuis. Etranger, qui
peut savoir ce que ce mot
veut dire?
—*Théâtre, récits, nouvelles*

The Stranger, which grew out of the experiment of *A Happy Death* and was nourished by Camus's political experiences, constitutes an attack on the accepted norms of bourgeois society. It calls into question many aspects of an oppressive colonial regime: the use of the judiciary, religion, and above all, language to maintain dominance. It is an ironic condemnation of colonialist and racist attitudes. The novel also develops a theme with variations on indifference and difference, a theme rooted in the Algerian experience, as Camus's articles in *Alger-Républicain* have shown. If the hero Meursault has a moral message—and the reference to him as a Christ figure would suggest that he has[1]—it is one that plays a constant role in Camus's thought; there are no absolutes to which one can adhere, only limits, and the vital nuances are played out within those limits. Total indifference and apathy allow others to act without limits. Meursault develops from an acquiescent figure who admits no limits to a combatant who claims the right to be different.

The story has a simple plot. Meursault, a clerk in an Algiers shipping office, attends his mother's funeral at an old people's home in Marengo. The following day he goes swimming, meets an old friend, Marie, takes her to see a Fernandel movie, and initiates an affair with her the same evening. With another friend, Raymond, he spends a Sunday on the beach with Marie, where they encounter three Arabs, one of whom has a grudge against Raymond. In the ensuing confrontation, Meursault shoots one of the Arabs.

The second half of the novel relates Meursault's trial and conviction, and his growing self-awareness during the months in prison. After being sentenced to death, he affirms his own system of values and rejects that of established society.

When *The Stranger* was first published in 1942 the aspect that evoked the most interest among critics was the use of the *passé composé*, the compound past tense, since the traditional tense used in literary narrative is the *passé simple*. Sartre, in his review of the book, comments that the effect of the *passé composé* is to isolate each sentence, to avoid giving any impression of cause and effect. Meursault's experience is a succession of presents. During the transition from Mersault to Meursault, Camus changed the form of the narrative: an omniscient author using the *passé simple* and the third person was replaced by a first-person narrative in the *passé composé*. The author leaves his hero in a situation where he is dominated by the power of language rather than in control of it; language is equivalent to destiny.

Renée Balibar has analyzed the ideological implications of this use of the *passé composé*, and finds that Meursault's narrative is almost a parody of an elementary school exercise ("Passé composé," p. 112): hence the tendency of those in power to treat him like a child. His inability to make himself understood in a situation that brings him into conflict with the dominant class leads to his subjugation. His interrogators find him suspect because of the apparently naïve articulation of his motives.

Camus's concern with language is evident in *The Stranger*. In his essay on Parain he cites the need for "honesty and baldness" in a renewed language, the need to "turn our back upon attitudes and oratory" (*E*, p. 1681). The style of *The Stranger* reflects an attempt to attain this simplicity. John Cruickshank has analyzed the reasons for "lapses" into a more rhetorical and metaphorical style, drawing his example from the description of the murder of the Arab on the beach, the climax of part 1, where the sustained use of imagery is most striking.

> Camus's temporary use of rhetorical prose, far from suggesting failure to sustain the sobriety that otherwise marks his use of words in *L'Etranger*, is in strict accordance with his attitude to language elsewhere in the novel. This attitude is dictated by a distrust of rhetoric and the belief that it obscures the real nature of experience. He is therefore being entirely consistent when he uses rhetorical phrases to convey a confused state of mind— Meursault's momentary and fatal failure to distinguish between reality and phantasy. The point at which Meursault's language becomes fanciful and metaphorical is also the point at which he wrongly interprets experience—as distinct from simply failing to understand it—and becomes a murderer. (*Literature of Revolt*, p. 158)

Thus the use of language beyond his mastery reveals an intellectual confusion that stems from the limits of his education. It is true that Meursault was once a student; but in rejecting ambition, he also rejected the value of an intellectual life. Rational thought is not worth the linguistic effort involved. Ironically enough, misinterpretation is not limited to Meursault. The French authorities misinterpret too.

"Literature" obscures the true nature of reality: like the Communist defined by Parain, Meursault is someone who has "given up language and replaced it with *actual revolt*. He has chosen to do what Christ scorned to do: to save the damned—by damning himself" (*CII*, p. 110). Viewed in this light, Meursault's deliberate firing of four more shots into the dead body is an act of revolt, a defiance of the society in which he lives. Meursault, who places no reliance on language, throws down the gauntlet but fails to justify his action in the eyes of the world.

As early as 1937, Camus had written in his notebook: "Story—the man who refuses to justify himself. He prefers the idea others have of him.[2] He dies, alone in his awareness of what he really is—Vanity of this consolation" (*CI*, p. 46).

An inarticulate rebellion is doomed to failure in the short run; Meursault exults in a sense of victory at the end of the story, but his individual action has changed nothing. However, in a longer political perspective, Meursault's revolt should serve as a warning to the unheeding ears of those who hold power, for sooner or later rebellion will find a voice. And the parallel with Christ suggests the initiation of a wider movement. Camus does not present the Arabs in this story as the only oppressed people, but they are aware of their oppression while Meursault is not, at least not in objective terms. In 1937 Camus had warned the PCF in Algiers of the consequences of not listening: in his preface to *Algerian Reports* he reiterates the same theme to attack French nationalism: "If France alone should reign in Algeria over eight million mutes [*muets*], she will die there" (*E*, p. 896). The Arabs in this story are silent.

Camus's indictment of an oppressive class system is widely applicable and reflects his concern with Fascism, but in *The Stranger* the specific elements of colonialism are singularly evident. Most commentaries on the political aspects of the work have centered on Camus's (or Meursault's) presentation of Arabs, the role they play in the story, and the author's or narrator's attitude towards them. Two examples are Pierre Nora's view that Camus voiced fears typical of the *petit blanc* in Algeria, and Conor Cruise O'Brien's that he unconsciously upheld the status quo of French jurisdiction and domination of the Arab population. To test the validity of these opinions, the narrator's perception and presentation of French society in Algeria should first be examined.

Several critics have pointed out that Camus observes with an ironic eye the representatives of the State, the Law, and the Church. All of these characters attempt to persuade Meursault to fall into line, to anticipate and respond to the norms of French society. These men are paternalistic: Meursault is regarded as a child who needs the gentle guiding hand of a father. The director of the old-age home calls him "my dear child" and even regards the old people in his care as children;[3] the feeling between Madame Meursault and Pérez is "a little puerile" in his view (*TRN*, p. 1134). The priest at the mortuary addresses Meursault as "my son." And although he wants to see his mother immediately upon his arrival, he is prevented from doing so by the necessity of first seeing the director and being subjected to a speech. "I wanted to see Mother at once. But the concierge told me I had to see the director first" (p. 1128). The use of a conjunction is rare and therefore all the more forceful, while the use of the French *il fallait* instead of *je devais* expresses the statement of an impersonal ironclad rule rather than an optional courtesy.

The director's main concern is that the daily routine remain undisturbed; any exception "makes things difficult for the staff" (*TRN*, p. 1128). His link to the French administration is symbolized by his ribbon of the Legion of Honor, which makes up for his lack of uniform. It is his behavior that is heartless, not Meursault's: the abrupt telegram with its meaningless clichés, the priority of efficiency over grief, the speed with which he dashes to the cemetery, leaving the unfortunate Pérez to limp across the fields.

The examining magistrate displays a similar paternalistic attitude, addressing Meursault with the familiar *tu*, and reminding him that he must become like a child to have God's forgiveness. He tries to persuade Meursault to revere the Cross. The gesture has little meaning for Meursault, and it echoes the moment during the El Okbi trial when according to Camus's article for *Alger-Républicain* (24 June 1939), Monsieur Vaillant, the examining magistrate, "expounds on the crucifix which he has shown to the accused," a Moslem (*Fragments*, p. 454). By refusing the possibility of judgment and acquittal by God via the magistrate, Meursault commits himself to the judgment, and prejudice, of men.

He has the impression when the magistrate and the lawyer are discussing his case that he has very little to do with it. No one is unkind to him. Everything is orchestrated so that he has "the absurd impression of being 'one of the family'" (*TRN*, p. 1176). The Law will try to woo its prodigal son back to the path of duty, to the role assigned to him in the hierarchy.

Another example of the gap between Meursault and the representatives of the State and Church is symbolized by the director's refusal to react to physical discomfort on the way to the funeral service in the village. It reflects not only his belief in his own representation of the French state, but also a denial of normal physiological reactions. Meursault responds without shame to each and every physiological stimulus, and it is the ease with which he falls into a sexual liaison that will appall his judges later. This refusal to recognize the demands of the body is a contributory factor in the ambiguous attitude of the authorities toward the old-age home, which Meursault's lawyer brings out in court: a paternalistic state provides funds for the care of the aged, yet it discredits these very institutions because they allow young people like Meursault to enjoy sexual and economic freedom without the inhibiting burden of a watching parent.

Meursault's confrontation with the priest in prison follows a similar pattern: the priest's paternalistic attitude is made even more offensive by his denial of the validity of the body's needs. This time Meursault loses his temper, because he finally understands that a conflict exists. Despite the priest's assertion that it is an informal rather than an official visit, his dress underscores his identity as representative of the Church. He too attempts to divert Meursault from the earthly to the mystical, but Meursault can only acknowledge what he knows physically: rather than seeing a divine image in the darkness of his cell, Meursault sees a face with "the color of the sun and the flame of desire: it was Marie's face" (*TRN*, p. 1209). The inanimate rhetoric of theology has no meaning for the stranger.

Other strata of French society in Algiers viewed through Meursault's eyes provide examples of the hierarchy of power. Naturally the narrator's viewpoint is limited—to the building where he lives, to the street below his balcony in a European neighborhood, to Céleste's café and his place of work. The policeman who comes to investigate the fight in Raymond's room is a stereotype of the low-level public official in a Fascist administration as portrayed by Wilhelm Reich (p. 47). Rather than feeling any solidarity with his fellow citizens, he identifies with the government whose authority he represents. The policeman who kicks Cottard at the end of *The Plague* is of the same ilk. While Fascism and colonialism have different political aims, in that the former seeks to mobilize the masses for change while the latter strives to maintain apathy and the status quo, they have other aspects in common: a strict paternalistic structure and similar psychological motivation. Raymond's policeman first reduces him to the level of a child with his condescending use of *tutoiement*, the familiar form of address, and establishes his authority by giving him a hard slap in the face for continuing to smoke in his presence. Raymond is unable to respond to the insult, although on the tram his reaction to such an affront was quite different. The use of force replaces dialogue. Raymond knows the score; he must submit to this petty official, but will later manipulate the bureaucracy to his advantage.

Raymond displays many of the qualities ascribed to the typical *petit blanc* in French colonial society. He wants full control of his mistress, both financial and sexual, to compensate for his marginal role in the power structure. Because he is a pimp, his attitude toward women is sadistic and demeaning, but he shows due respect for Meursault's mother and for Marie. He is deeply concerned with his image as a *man*, and is uneasy that Meursault witnessed the humiliating scene with the policeman.

Meursault makes no judgmental comment on Raymond's actions, although it is clear that Marie dislikes him: Meursault merely mentions a physical repulsion to Raymond's white skin. "His forearms were very white under the black hairs. I was a little disgusted by it" (*TRN,* p. 1160).

Even Salamano's relationship to his dog reveals Camus's preoccupation with domination and power, and reminds us of Raymond with his mistress. Each one is engaged in a permanent battle for control, although in Salamano's case old age and loneliness make him a less despicable character. His name—"dirty hand"—emphasizes the squalor in which he lives. He rejected a career in the theater for a job on the railways, as a government functionary with an assured pension; but he vents his frustrations on the dog he acquired after his wife's death, since he has no one else under his control. In the outline of the same relationship in the notebooks, the dog is an adopted child. Paternal love becomes cruel and stifling: the father "considers himself master of the child and of a magnificent kingdom under his control. He bullies him" (*CI,* p. 159). The story offers a microscopic image of the oppressive state.

The bourgeois family viewed from Meursault's balcony is almost a parody of convention. Parents and children are dressed in their Sunday best for an afternoon walk: the boys are dressed in uniform—sailor suits—and are physically restricted in their stiff clothes; the little girl's hair is tied in an enormous pink bow, to prevent it from blowing freely in the wind. On the way back from their imposed walk, the children are crying or being dragged along, still learning the lessons of discipline and self-control. The contrast with the groups of young people is striking—the young women laughing and flirting with the young men with sleek hair and fashionable clothes.

How does this French society relate to the indigenous Arab population? Far from propagating the colonial myth, as O'Brien suggests, Camus presents it in its true light and shows up its inherent injustices. The policeman handles Raymond roughly for causing a breach of the peace, but at the police station Raymond has no difficulty in brushing off the Arab girl's accusations, and Meursault's statement is not even questioned. Only when the prosecution wishes to prove Meursault a sordid underworld figure does Raymond appear to the authorities as a reprobate.

The fact that Meursault is condemned to death for murdering an Arab has been criticized as unrealistic; although a European would be condemned for such a deed, it is unlikely that he would be sentenced to death in these circumstances. Why then is the victim an Arab? Both the aesthetic and political necessities of the novel require the effacement of the victim in the eyes of the court, so that the full absurdity of the judicial system, rather than the crime itself, can be emphasized. Everything has to support the fact that Meursault is condemned not for murder, but for subverting the status quo. A European victim could not be so easily dismissed from the mind of the jury. The Arab victim is obviously forgotten, and of course no Arab witnesses are ever called.

The fact that Raymond's mistress is an Arab is also a logical necessity of the plot, since her brother dies avenging her disgrace. Nothing else in the text makes her ethnic background significant, for Meursault's point of view tends to blur races. It might be pointed out that she is a typical victim of colonial exploitation, and that Raymond describes her as too lazy to work, a common racial slur. But Raymond would treat any woman in the same way, regardless of race, and if his story is true, the girl was hardly a naïve victim. Nothing in the text tells the reader that Raymond's opponent in the tram brawl is an Arab, nor that his mistress is an Arab, until Meursault sees the name while addressing the letter. The terse "I wrote the letter" that follows this discovery is given the sense of an implicit "nevertheless" by the juxtaposition of a revealing adverbial phrase: "I wrote it rather haphazardly" (TRN, p. 1148).

There is no discernible hostility in Meursault's attitude toward Arabs in the novel, but there is a feeling of difference, of separation. Meursault's reference to the watching Arabs who stare silently "in the special way they have" is not a hostile colonialist's comment (O'Brien, p. 23), but an observation of fact, an attribution of difference. The hostility lies rather on the Arab side, a justified but still latent hostility that will grow stronger and explode outside the confines of this novel. The sentence ends, "as if we were nothing more than stones or dead trees," which makes "in that way they have" an objective statement. A key word in the sentence is *silently:* there is no dialogue between Arabs and Europeans. Meursault turns around at the bus stop and remarks that "they were still in the same place, gazing with the same indifference at the spot where we had been" (*TRN,* p. 1161). In an article published in *L'Express* (23 July 1955), Camus drew the same portrait: "The Arabs, uprooted from their past, with no future prospects, paralyzed in a perpetual present, have no other choice now but silence or violence" (*E,* p. 1873). Camus's fictional hero is in the same position, and the text clearly shows that in part 1, Meursault is naturally akin to the Arabs in his silence and indifference; his act of violence and the recognition of responsibility for it produce in him an awareness that can eventually be expressed in part 2. While Mersault killed in order to be able to write and ended in silence, Meursault follows the same path in reverse: the catalyst is violence, but its results are different.

In his study of indifference in the works of Camus, Claude Treil suggests that it provides a means of avoiding suffering (p. 65). Meursault in part 1 is indifferent to the society in which he lives. He sees no difference in people except in physical terms, and therefore makes no moral judgments. He also feels that it makes no difference whether he views his mother's body or smokes a cigarette during his vigil, whether he marries Marie or continues a pleasurable liaison. In his indifference to difference, however, he opposes the mores of French society. Such an equalizing vision presents a threat to a strictly hierarchical structure where fathers rule and sons obey. Meursault is a marginal person, for he refuses to fit into the slot specified for him. The indifference shown by the French authorities is selective: Raymond's violent attack on an Arab girl and the murder of an Arab on the beach are seen as episodes of little consequence.

At one significant point in part 1, Meursault feels integrated in his immediate society. He is at Masson's small beach house, and the atmosphere is relaxed and jovial. Masson's wife and Marie are laughing together, there are plans for a summer spent at the beach with shared expenses, a kind of House before the World. Meursault comments: "For the first time, perhaps, I seriously considered the possibility of getting married" (TRN, p. 1162). The group exerts a certain attraction, but Meursault's commitment is short-lived, for he soon finds the effort of verbal exchange too demanding, and avoids the company of the group in order that he may return to a silent and indifferent state.

Once more his affinity with the Arabs becomes apparent, in the sharing of "maternal values" (cf. Van-Huy, pp. 10–14). The maternal values emphasize the natural and biological aspects of human beings, a link with the earth that stresses harmony and annuls difference. Paternal values, inherent in French colonialist society, emphasize the mental and the rational, and the predominance of the superego; hence the sense of guilt evoked by the gap between the demands of authority and reality. (Meursault experiences these vague feelings of guilt in the presence of authority figures—his boss and the old people at the wake.) The sun, symbol of the male principle in nature, attacks both Meursault and the Arabs, and turns the sea from a caressing liquid state into a steely mass ("molten metal," TRN, p. 1167). But the difference between Meursault and the Arabs is revealed, too, and suggests that despite their deeper affinity, they are culturally separated. Meursault's skin may be tanned to the same color, he may feel no hostility towards Arabs, but he cannot truly be integrated. He has not adapted to the climate. The only occasion when the sun is beneficial to him is when he is swimming in the sea, or watching the sky from the shelter of his apartment or prison cell.[4] At other times the heat, the dust, the blinding light make him acutely uncomfortable, to the point where he is unaware of anything but his physical needs. In an earlier manuscript, the phrase "still hatless" was crossed out, as an obviously over-self-conscious detail in Meursault's narration of events. Arabs of course adapt themselves quite differently to the climate: rather than stripping off their clothes and lying on a beach at high noon, they wear more clothes and stay in the shade, or wear a protective head covering. When O'Brien says that Meursault is indeed a stranger on the Algerian beach, he is not far from the truth. The European maintains a precarious foothold in Africa and needs to be close to the sea to withstand the heat. The Arab, however, has little use for the sea and recognizes rather the supreme importance of fresh water. So it is not surprising that the two Arabs wait in the shade of the rocks beside a little spring. "The Arabs slithered behind the rock"— this is their Algeria. Meursault links the sounds of the flute and the running water with silence: "sunlight and this silence, with the murmur of the spring and the three notes," "the murmur of the water and the flute amid the silence and the heat," "the two-fold silence of the flute and the water" (*TRN*, p. 1166). Everything is so perfectly in tune that it has the same tranquilizing effect as silence.

Meursault's experience is more like the clashing of cymbals. He approaches the spring in his desire for cool water and silence, to escape the heat and the salt water—of women's tears, of the sweat clouding his eyes, and of a sea turned to molten metal. "I kept thinking of the cool spring behind the rock. I wanted to hear once more the murmur of its waters, wanted to flee from the sun, the effort of movement and women's tears, and to regain the shade and tranquility" (*TRN*, p. 1167). This desire for shade is significant in a man who is "in love with the sun that leaves no shadows" (preface to American edition, *E*, p. 1928). It highlights the dangers inherent in a total lack of differentiation.

Meursault understands the notion of choice most poignantly during his final outburst to the priest in jail—"It is better to burn than to disappear" (*TRN*, p. 1927, omitted in final version). He feels the pressure of the heat behind him and takes a few more steps toward the spring. There is an obstacle, however (expressed by a rare conjunction, *but*), in the presence of the Arab. This man fails to recognize a fellow "natural" man in Meursault, because he has all the outward appearances of a European, and is therefore classified as an enemy. The Arab draws his knife to protect himself and, symbolically, his territory; he remains passive only so long as the European stays on the shoreline, where he can be regarded with as little passion as if he were a stone or a dead tree.

Under the influence of the sun, Meursault becomes the perpetrator of violence. He is trapped between his past—the force of all the paternal values—and his future, the desire for harmony. In firing the shot, he realizes at once that "I had destroyed the *balance* of the day, the exceptional *silence* of a beach where I had been happy" (*TRN*, p. 1168, my emphasis). What had been in harmony is now out of tune—absurd—and unattainable. Meursault is aware of his responsibility ("*I* had destroyed"). Ironically, if he had refused responsibility, his action would have been acceptable to the state, but his first active move is to fire four more shots into the inert body. He remarks on the indifference of that body to the impact of the bullets (Treil, p. 57): "The bullets went in without leaving any trace" (*TRN*, p. 1168). The use of the imperfect tense where one would have expected the perfect underlines the progression of its impact on the usually indifferent Meursault. Awareness that he has reduced a human life to this state of indifference, a state in which the body is insensible to pain or pleasure, marks the beginning of his acquaintance with unhappiness. He learns to differentiate to a degree.

In contrast to Mersault in *A Happy Death*, Meursault blurs the concept of happiness, and defines only a sense of not being unhappy (Hirdt, p. 340). After passing through the "door of my unhappiness" (*TRN*, p. 1168), Meursault is obliged to face up to the assaults of joy and sorrow. His indifference will survive with regard to the meaningless discussions of sin and social duty, but his place as a human being, as a brother in a fraternal system, will enable him to recognize the value of life itself.

Meursault understands that he has committed a crime and that he is being punished for it. The judges, however, find him guilty of the wrong crime: that of being different, and indifferent to their beliefs. The prosecutor declares that "I had no place in a society whose basic principles I disregarded" (*TRN*, p. 1198).

So Meursault is removed from the society to which he feels so little affinity, a society that is indifferent to the death of an Arab. Ironically, it is the defending lawyer who bursts out in exasperation to remind the court that Meursault has in fact killed a man (*TRN*, p. 1193). The lawyer could have used the word *Arab* without jeopardizing his client's case, but the court has forgotten that the victim was a man. Meursault jeopardizes his safety in prison by doing the reverse: he tells his fellow-prisoners (mostly Arab) that he killed an Arab rather than that he killed a man. One might imagine that Meursault would be in danger in a big prison cell at night where the Arab prisoners could seek revenge. They laugh when he comes in, as if enjoying the discomfiture of a Frenchman brought down to their level. "Then they asked me what I had done. I told them I had killed an Arab and they remained silent."

This is obviously a tense moment. "*But* presently night fell. They explained to me how to lay out my sleeping-mat. By rolling up one end, you could make a sort of bolster. All night long, bugs were crawling over my face" (*TRN*, p. 1177, my emphasis). The conjunction *but* appears at a point where one might expect no connective; and the opposition it implies seems to make little sense. But nightfall effects a change from silent and even hostile distance to comradeship. Both at the beginning and the end of the novel, Meursault refers to the evening as a time of "melancholy truce." This truce comes into effect in the prison cell, where Meursault appears to the Arabs as a man of courage and simple words. They understand violence because they are oppressed, and it creates a fraternal bond. The simplicity of such silent fraternal relationships is expressed in the Notebooks where Camus talks of the "freemasonry of the cigarette" (*CI*, p. 134). It is also evoked in the steadfast gaze of the journalist at Meursault's trial, and in the helpless gesture of Céleste. But this truce among equals is broken by the prison authorities; after a few days, Meursault is moved to a private cell with a plank-bed, a latrine bucket, and no bedbugs. Difference and distance are reestablished, to reflect the norms of a colonialist order that accommodates prisoners according to race rather than to the gravity of their crime.

The scene where the prisoners see their visitors reiterates the predominance of Arabs in the prison, and their difference. Their posture is different: they squat down. "Most of the Arab prisoners and their families had squatted down facing each other. They did not shout. Despite the din, they managed to hear each other while speaking very softly. The murmur of their voices . . . created a kind of *basso continuo* to the conversations going on above their heads" (*TRN*, p. 1178). Europeans have to shout to communicate. This orchestration of noise which stuns Meursault as he enters the room reflects the colonial situation in Algeria: the monotonous murmur of the Arabs close to the ground is undisturbed by the shrill tones above them; it is a permanent but not necessarily passive accompaniment. Even after the Arabs leave, the European woman continues to shout. Only the young man and his mother communicate silently, rather as one may imagine Meursault communicated with his mother when they lived together.

A parallel situation is depicted in the scene where the two Arabs await the second confrontation with Raymond. As far as they are concerned, the score is even; it is Raymond who seeks revenge. One of them is playing a flute, repeating three notes that seem in tune with the sound of running water at the spring.

The monotonous sounds are like the *continuo* of the murmuring Arab voices in the prison, and as Meursault says, "Our coming changed nothing" (*TRN*, pp. 1165-66).

On only one occasion is there a dialogue between Meursault and the Arabs, and it leads to a truce in an overcrowded prison cell. On the beach, the silence and repose both parties seek is obscured by a hostility, evident in the knife and the revolver, which overrides any verbal communication. The Arabs are silent because that is their accustomed state, and Meursault because he is seeking the avoidance of speech.

Henri Kréa's assertion that Meursault exhibits the typical racial prejudices of the colonial *petit blanc* seems without foundation in the text. The attitude of the French government authorities is pointed up quite sharply, however, and leads to an Arab expectation of hostility that Meursault is in fact far from feeling. But his mere association with Raymond marks him as an enemy in a situation where appearances are the sole criteria available. The Arabs have no legal recourse against aggressors, but are forced to take the law into their own hands. They are obviously treated as second-class citizens in the prison, where they outnumber Europeans, and the death of an Arab is not considered an unforgivable offense. But nowhere is it clear that Meursault shares these attitudes.

Indeed, it is obvious that Meursault is in conflict, albeit unconsciously, with all the norms of the French system; in response to his narration of events, the reader's sympathies lie with the Arabs defending their honor rather than with the unsavory Raymond. Meursault refuses to play the game, to be part of the family. The authority figures are all predisposed to be kind to Meursault: the soldier on whose shoulder he falls asleep on the bus, the director of the old-age home, his employer, the examining magistrate, his lawyer, the priest. It is only when he says no that they begin to resent him: he declines to view his mother's body, he turns down a promotion that would take him to Paris, he refuses to recognize the Cross, or to misrepresent the details of his case. When he says yes, it is to the "wrong" things: to a cup of coffee, to a Fernandel film, to Raymond's sordid plan. (The ridiculous aspect of the way in which the prosecutor blows up Meursault's acceptance of a cup of coffee into a proof of a criminal personality is brought out by the fact that all the mourners are later served, and accept, a cup of coffee.)

So although his interrogators are at first ready to view his case sympathetically, it soon becomes clear that there is no communication between the two parties. Meursault fails to understand the concept of sin: in jail he responds to the priest "that I did not know what a sin was. I had merely been taught that I was a guilty man" (*TRN*, pp. 1208–9). Because he is different he is a suspicious character. It is the fact that he is *not* representative of a social class that makes him dangerous, (Girard, p. 519), whereas Raymond is easily typed and dealt with accordingly. Racism is founded on a fear of difference. At the El Okbi trial in June 1939 a defense lawyer summed up the reasons why the Arab defendant was considered a public menace: "Akacha was one of those little Arabs that we meet on winter evenings crouched in doorways, while we are in our dinner jackets and our wives in evening dress—that is what makes him a menace to public safety" (*Fragments*, p. 492). People resent being disturbed by otherness. The examining magistrate believes that a man who refuses to recognize the Cross can be nothing less than an anti-Christ: "He seemed . . . to have classified my case" (p. 1176).

During the trial, it becomes clear that Meursault is being tried not for his action, but for his attitudes. The ironic presentation of the prosecutor's arguments, in which the narrator's use of free indirect discourse shows up the emptiness of the rhetoric, makes the trial seem farcical. Indeed one could assert that Meursault is innocent with respect to the invalid reasons for guilt attributed by the prosecution: "I accuse this man of burying a mother with a criminal heart" (*TRN*, p. 1194). The implications of "the void in the heart that we find in this man" are enlarged to the scale of "an abyss into which society could sink" (p. 1197). Girard states that Camus disapproves of the verdict (p. 519), but it is the manner in which that verdict was reached that is presented in an unfavorable light. Meursault is accused of two crimes which he has not committed: burying his mother with a criminal heart (although psychoanalytical studies of this text have concluded there is some basis for his feelings of guilt at her death), and killing a father, since the prosecutor affirms in a flourish of rhetoric that he is responsible for the crime that will be tried in court the following day.

Bearing in mind the trials in Algeria that Camus covered as a journalist, one could conclude that the parodic deformation is mild, for in many of those cases the charges were politically motivated, the witnesses bribed, and the verdict a foregone conclusion. It is true that Meursault makes no effort to defend himself; but it is because he does not understand the ideas behind the verbiage, nor the consequences of his own words and deeds. Eleven months of *instruction* fail to clarify the issues for him, and in court he has the impression that "they seemed to be excluding me from the proceedings" (*TRN*, p. 1195). The courtroom is like a club where everyone else knows the ropes: Meursault has "the odd impression . . . of being *de trop* here, rather like a gate-crasher" (p. 1185). He might be watching a drama in which everyone else knows the dénouement. He has no voice; his lawyer speaks for him, to the point where he says "I" when speaking of his client. The same mannerism is repeated when the judge announces "in some weird formula that I would have my head cut off in a public square in the name of the French people" (p. 1201). The "weird formula" refers to the euphemisms employed to camouflage the savagery of the fact of execution from the people who are supposed to sanction it—an acquiescence of the French people in the delivery of court verdicts that was denounced by Camus as a lie (*Fragments*, p. 523). The words used do not express reality, but Meursault and his friends are unable to counteract the force of their intent. They are verbally ill-equipped. The prosecutor, however, rejects such a defense before it is voiced. "This man is intelligent. . . . He can answer. He knows the value of words" (*TRN*, p. 1196). In a sense, this is true. Meursault refuses to use words that do not precisely translate his feelings, words like *love, guilt, shame*. Society is accustomed to euphemism and lip-service.

A limited mastery of language can be compensated to some extent by gesture, which is more direct and marks a deeper sense of human solidarity. Camus describes such men in "Summer in Algiers":

> I really think that virtue is a word without any meaning throughout Algeria. Not that men lack principles. They have their own ethic, and a very special one. You don't let your mother down. You make sure your wife is respected on the street. You show consideration for pregnant women. You don't fight two against one, because it's 'dirty pool.' [Meursault and Raymond observe this principle.] If anyone fails to observe these elementary rules, 'he's not a man' and that's all there is to it. It seems fair and convincing to me. A lot of us still observe this street code *unconsciously*; it's the only one I know that's *unprejudiced*. But at the same time, shopkeeper morality is unknown. I have always seen faces full of pity when a man goes by surrounded by policemen. And without knowing if the man is a thief, a parricide, or simply a nonconformist, they say 'poor fellow.' (*E*, p. 72, my emphasis)

This code of honor, with its nonverbal system of communication, is successfully portrayed in the courtroom when Meursault's friends come to offer their support. Unfortunately Meursault is the only person to interpret this information correctly, with the exception perhaps of the journalist. But why is there a breakdown in communication between them and the other spectators, who are not sympathetic to Meursault? Although Camus's description in "Summer in Algiers" is idealized, it nevertheless expresses the solidarity of the Algiers working class. In the courtroom, this solidarity is interrupted by the intervention of distinctly bourgeois rhetoric, with all its value judgments and classifications. The breakdown in communication reveals the fragility of this solidarity by showing the damage which language can effect on relationships based on nonverbal modes of mutual understanding.

The men depicted in Camus's essay are not judges. They have no system to impose on others. Particularly in the first part of *The Stranger*, Meursault, like them, seems unaware of the meaning or significance of actions or words: when pressed to comment on their meaning (smoking in front of the coffin, Marie's question about love and marriage, Raymond's plan to take revenge on his mistress), he denies that they have any. He refuses to evaluate actions from a moral viewpoint. He has no system of classification: he hears the words *mistress* and *criminal* without relating them to Marie and himself. But he frequently has the uneasy feeling that he is *being* judged, and he responds by asserting repeatedly, "It's not my fault" (*TRN*, p. 1127), a denial of responsibility. The old people lined up at the wake seem to be judging him; ironically, he feels they are evaluating him from a moral standpoint, whereas in court, where the jurors are in fact doing this, he is reminded of people on a tram looking for something ridiculous. His fears are justified; when he succeeds in speaking, everyone in the courtroom laughs. Meursault is dimly aware of the influence of these "paternal" values, but they are meaningless. Raymond, on the other hand, when faced with authority, loses all his bravado and becomes a whining hypocrite, thus remaining in control of his destiny.

Meursault is not self-conscious, and so he is carried along by the tide of events, until the prison priest provokes an explosion by insisting on praying for him. "Then, I don't know why, something in me burst. I started to shout at the top of my lungs, and I insulted him and told him not to pray. I had grabbed him by the collar of his cassock. I poured out on him, in great surges of joy and anger, all that had been in the depths of my heart" (*TRN*,

p. 1210).[5] For the first time, Meursault affirms his values verbally: the explosion reveals to him the absurd nature of life and at the same time evokes a feeling of revolt against it. In grasping the priest's cassock, he symbolically comes to grips with a paternalistic authority which he equates with a living death. The events of his past life are indifferent to him; the natural world to which he feels such a close affinity is indifferent because death is an integral part of natural life. But Meursault hopes that the spectators at his execution will *not* be indifferent, that they will greet him with cries of hatred, so that his death will have some meaning, so that he will not be alone.

Meursault finds a voice and an adequate command of language in the final pages of his narrative. The reader is led to suppose that his execution is imminent and that his voice will be silenced: the guillotine effectively dislocates the very source of speech.[6]

Meursault, the nonconformist of part 1, presents no threat to the status quo in Algeria. He narrates the injustices visited upon the Arabs and the poor Europeans by a colonial administration as facts, without comment or conscious framework. He has not found a role for himself in attempting to alter these facts, until the act of narrating his story imposes a new awareness. Memory establishes an organization of events that had seemed disconnected. The other factor is solitude, which is here presented as a *condition* for this consciousness, rather than as the goal that Mersault sought.

Only when Meursault is seen as a threat does he become one, a kind of self-fulfilling prophecy. Emmett Parker states that the problem of Meursault's innocence is linked to the innocence of the French Algerians who asked no questions. Obviously Meursault is not politically conscious, or even self-conscious. When he does become aware of himself, he is detached, with a schizophrenic's sense of looking into a mirror and seeing a stranger. He is unable to fix himself in a given society at a given moment in history. Much has been made of Meursault's confusion over time, in that it denotes a schizophrenic's divorce from reality. However, it is only in prison that he loses a sense of time passing, a state of affairs common to most prisoners; down through the ages they have made marks on their cell walls in an attempt to divide an unending repetition of days into weeks and months and years. Indeed, Meursault learns to "kill time."

In the opening chapter of part 1, far from being vague about time, Meursault is quite exact: he has all the details as to the distance from Algiers to Marengo, the bus timetable, the time of arrival, and the number of days he needs to take off from his job. His uncertainty about the day of the funeral can be attributed to the wording of the telegram and the vagaries of the French postal system rather than to any lack of precision in his own mind. The narrative in the first part of the novel is quite specific about time (Pariente, pp. 56–58). Meursault himself states that he is always too preoccupied with today and tomorrow to have a clear memory of the past. Events are dealt with as they arise. They do not seem to form a coherent pattern. This is in part a result of daily routine, which dulls one's senses with monotony and fatigue. But Meursault seems to have deliberately chosen this routine as an escape from pressures and anguish. His policy is to avoid discomfort whenever possible. Only occasionally does he feel a sense of fraternity with another human being: with the concierge at the old-age home, with the Arab prisoners, with Céleste at the trial, with Salamano in his grief. Usually he withdraws from involvement with others because it might involve some duty that would prove tiresome.

Clearly, a complete lack of judgment can be dangerous. There is a vital difference between judgment that leads to punishment and that which precedes choice. Meursault consistently fails to evaluate the world around him, but there is a middle way between total withdrawal and the imposition of one's own values on others. Only in his final outburst does Meursault consciously evaluate other people, although still in a negative way. Camus called him "a negative snapshot" (*CII*, p. 33). "What did it matter if Raymond was as much a friend as Céleste, who *was a far worthier man?"* (*TRN*, p. 1211, my emphasis). In an absurd world, all men are equal. It is through a kind of askesis, a narrowing down of his field of vision, that Meursault reaches an initial state of awareness, just as Mersault did. But Mersault is committed to death, and Meursault is committed to life.

Meursault's affirmation of the value of life is not tinged with any political insights, for the words of politics have already been proven false or misleading by those in power. When the book was published in 1942, some critics disapproved of it for sounding a demoralizing note in the midst of defeat. "Fools who think that negation is a surrender when it is a choice," fumed Camus in his notebook (*CII*, pp. 30–31). Meursault is not a paragon, but merely a "poor naked man, in love with the sun that leaves no shadows" (*TRN*, p. 1928). The moment when Meursault realizes how words have been distorted and stripped of their true meaning is the moment when he finds he can no longer remain indifferent. He recognizes his place in the order of things, as part of a fraternal world where men are pitted together against the absurdity of human life. "It is always useless to try and cut oneself off, even from other people's stupidity and cruelty. You cannot say: 'I don't know anything about it.' You collaborate or you fight. . . . The ivory towers have fallen. Self-indulgence is forbidden, for oneself as well as for other people" (*CI*, p. 172).

Meursault reaches the limits of his "self-indulgence," or "good will," as Camus termed it (*CII*, p. 45). He can remain indifferent as long as those limits are not transgressed.

In the last paragraph of the text, Meursault talks of starting again. He understands why his mother, in her old age, "had taken a 'fiancé,' why she had played at starting again. . . . And I too felt ready to relive everything" (*TRN*, p. 1211). The theme links the work of art with the work of life.

In part 2, Meursault has rewritten part 1, or perhaps corrected it. He is ready to rewrite it again, but it will be the same life, because he believes he was right. In part 1, each chapter heralds a new start, a new day of confronting the absurdity of existence by maintaining a constant balance (Brody). That balance is shattered by the murder. In the prison of part 2, where all the diversions of daily life are withdrawn, where there is askesis, Meursault relives the experiences of part 1, but through the eyes of other people. (We are reminded of Mersault's feeling that someone else is telling his story.) These people create a different version, equally plausible, of the same facts. Indeed, lawyers and writers have the same aim: the creation of a plausible scenario (Fitch, *Narcissistic Text*, p. 54), and the reader is left to judge for himself.

Camus is playing ironically with ambiguity here, but this does not detract from the *moral* intent, to demonstrate that judgment is unjust because it is based on ambiguous data. Misinterpretation can be accidental or intentional, but in either case the consequences can prove fatal.

Metaphysical absurdity is mirrored by the social situation depicted in *The Stranger;* as Camus remarked, "*The Plague* has a social meaning and a metaphysical meaning. It's exactly the same. This ambiguity is also present in *The Stranger*" (*CII*, p. 50). The injustice of that social situation is in turn reflected and complicated by the particular attributes of a colonial society. Meursault learns in the course of writing his life that it is not meaningless, and his desire to relive it is the first positive affirmation he makes.

One aspect of Meursault's statement, which will be a constant in Camus's ideas on rebellion, is the emphasis on the concrete and the present. The prison chaplain embodies exactly what Meursault rejects: a nonphysical relationship with the world and with human beings, a passive submission to the injustices of God and society, and a dogmatic faith in a better life in the future. Meursault is solidly involved in the here and now, convinced that joy is one of the most precious of human emotions, not to be sacrificed for some abstract and hypothetical goal. He sums up, but only for his readers, his notion of happiness during the final day in court: "While my lawyer went on talking, I heard the echoing sound of an ice-cream vendor's horn. I was overwhelmed by the memories of a life that was no longer mine, but in which I had found the simplest and most persistent joys [*les plus pauvres et les plus tenaces de mes joies*]: the smells of summer, the neighborhood I loved, a certain evening sky, Marie's laughter and her dresses" (*TRN,* p. 1199). The core of Camus's arguments in *The Rebel* is here in embryo. It will be further developed during the period of the Occupation of France, when Camus once more turned from poetry to journalism as a means of fighting oppression.

5

Occupation and Resistance

On collabore ou . . . on combat.
—*Carnets I*

In June 1940, as the German army approached Paris, Camus, along with the newspaper staff of *Paris-Soir*, was evacuated to Clermont-Ferrand, and later to Lyon, where the newspaper was published until December 1940. The manuscript of *The Stranger* had been completed, but remained unpublished until 1942. Camus remained in Lyon for a short period and was remarried there. When *Paris-Soir* returned to Paris as a collaborationist newspaper, Camus returned to Oran with his wife. There he did some teaching in a secondary school which the local Jewish community had established, and which served the influx of children expelled from the state schools in accordance with the Vichy laws that the French rulers in Algeria had been quick to enact. According to his friends Emmanuel Roblès and Charles Poncet (*E*, p. 1458), in the autumn of 1941 Camus was trying to organize a resistance group that would enable Jews and political opponents of Vichy to escape to Tunisia. Madame Camus recalled that he was already in contact with resistants in metropolitan France.

Two short articles written in 1940 testify to Camus's opposition to the defeatist attitudes that were rampant after the humiliating conquest of the French army. The first of these, entitled "To Prepare for the Fruit," was published in *La Tunisie*

française of 25 January 1941 (*E,* p. 1457), and later, with significant changes, in the collection *Summer,* under the title "The
Almond Trees." It opened with a quotation from Napoleon:
"There are only two forces in the world: the sword and the mind.
In the long run, the sword is always conquered by the mind"
(p. 835). This battle for the human mind was to be taken up
again in *Letters to a German Friend.* In the 1940 essay the
emphasis is on the impossibility of ignorance or withdrawal in
the face of modern warfare. Acquiescence, as Meursault discovered, can have mortal consequences. "The painter and the
monk have been drafted—we are in solidarity with this world"
(p. 835). The end of the world is not at hand, and even if it were,
there would be a new world to build. The symbol of the almond
trees, black and silent in winter, and the first to blossom in the
spring, is used to affirm that "the winter of the world" can be
used to gather strength, to prepare the fruit of a new season.
"Like a Tow Fire," published in the same review of 24 May 1941,
was partly incorporated into the final version of "The Almond
Trees," in particular the paragraph where he expresses scorn for
those who wring their hands over the tragedy of events.
"'Tragedy,' Lawrence said, 'ought to be a great kick at misery.'
There's a healthy and immediately applicable thought. There
are many things today deserving such a kick. Let's hurry up and
deliver it. Let's learn to watch the tow burn.[1] And once we have
learned our lesson well, let us return to History with the appropriate scorn" (p. 1466).

This necessity for scorn in the face of an ever-changing world
is a crucial aspect of Camus's active commitment. "It is impossible and immoral to judge an event from the outside. Only by
remaining at the heart of this absurd misfortune can we legit-
imately despise it" (*CI,* p. 172). Malraux had called the 1930s
"the era of scorn," a time when human rights were disdained in
favor of power and efficiency, and Camus was aware that one
must sometimes use the same weapons as one's adversary—
"resemble him a little," as Rieux says of the plague (*TRN,*

p. 1293). The idea of contagion in *The Plague*, and of complicity in *The Fall*, are inherent in this need, and Camus recognized the dangers it entailed: only through a conscious detachment or indifference could one *use* scorn as an attitude without allowing it to become a permanent facet of one's outlook.

Striking the right balance was not always easy: belief in the effectiveness of individual action wavers and the desire to withdraw and pursue one's own interests is hard to dismiss. After being rejected for military service on the grounds of ill health, Camus must have felt a strong temptation to withdraw; but the role of spectator was untenable. One of the main characters in an early version of *The Plague*, Stephan, reflects this penchant for despair and disengagement, and hangs himself after the plague has disappeared. After 1945 he was dropped from the text altogether. The only man who despairs in the final version is Cottard, who has been viewed as the "collaborator": Camus's concerns had gone beyond the limited role of the intellectual in wartime.

Camus remained in Oran until August 1942, when a recurrence of tuberculosis made it advisable for him to return to France for a cure in mountain air. During this period he finished *The Myth of Sisyphus* (21 February 1941), which he felt completed the Cycle of the Absurd, in conjunction with *Caligula* and *The Stranger*. "Beginnings of liberty," he commented (*CI*, p. 224). When the essay was published by Gallimard in December 1942, it was suggested by some critics that a philosophy based on the absurdity of the world must lead to despair, and was therefore ill-timed at this moment of French history. This was not Camus's intention, although he was aware of that temptation. In a letter to Francis Ponge dated 27 January 1943 he wrote, "One of the ends of absurd thought is indifference and total withdrawal—the state of the stone" (in *E*, p. 1665). But in a letter to Pierre Bonnel (18 March 1943) he stated: "The profound thought of this book is that metaphysical pessimism in no way leads to a point where one must despair of man—on the contrary. To take a precise example, I believe it quite possible to link an absurd philosophy to a political thought that is concerned with the improvement of man's lot and that places its optimism in the relative. The absurd has more links with good sense than people think" (p. 1423).

This idea of the relative, as opposed to absolutes, is one of the keystones of Camus's political thought. In an interview with the journal *Servir* (20 December 1945), in which he dissociated himself from the streams of existentialism exemplified by Kierkegaard and Jaspers on the one hand and by Hüsserl, Heidegger, and Sartre on the other, Camus commented: "I can understand the advantages of the religious solution, and I am especially aware of the importance of history. But I do not believe in either of them, in the absolute sense. I examine my own beliefs, and I would be very disturbed if I were forced to choose absolutely between Saint Augustine and Hegel. I have the impression that there must be a tolerable truth between the two" (*E*, p. 1428).

When Camus left for France in August 1942 he planned to stay for about three months before returning to Algeria to continue his writing. His wife, a mathematics teacher, returned to Oran in September, but the Allied landings in North Africa made Camus's departure impossible. "November 11. Like rats!" (*CII*, p. 53). There are two possible interpretations of this cryptic note: either he felt trapped like a rat, or the movement of German soldiers into the "free" zone of France was compared to an invasion by rats—*la peste brune* ("the brown plague"), as the Nazis were dubbed. It is not clear whether Camus had any role in Resistance activities at this point, but he already had contacts with active participants, and the Notebooks reveal a frustration with the written word and a desire for more concrete actions. "That struggle through poetry and its obscurities, that conspicuous revolt of the intellect is *the one that costs least*. It is ineffectual, and the tyrants know it" (*CII*, p. 31). Impatience with armchair revolutionaries and inconsequent politicians grows with his experience of life in occupied France. "The life of silence and despair that all France endures while waiting . . . the dreadful straits of those lives. And the others are making speeches" (*CII*, pp. 38–39). Rhetoric is used to mask impotence.

The years of World War II, despite their toll in terms of physical and emotional stress, were years of relative serenity for Camus. The moral choices were clear and simple: Nazism was an evil that had to be conquered. Camus's writing is unambiguous, and his journalistic talents propelled him into the limelight in France after the Liberation. However, the post-Liberation years brought back to the surface the ambiguities that had been temporarily suppressed. As the choices became less clear-cut, Camus was once again forced into opposition against the left as well as the right.

History produces anomalies that Camus found morally unacceptable. In the 1930s the official left had been against anticolonialism; now in the 1940s an advocate of liberty was viewed as a bourgeois lackey who had abandoned the workers' struggle for justice.

Camus's contributions to the clandestine Resistance press began in 1943 with his *Letters to a German Friend*, which were first published as separate epistles.[2] Camus later described them as "a document of the struggle against violence" (*E*, p. 219). The first letter (July 1943) compares the reaction of a young German and a young Frenchman to the absurdity of a world without meaning. The German believes he has found meaning in the destiny of his country, and that he should sacrifice all to it. At this point Camus already parts company with him: "I cannot believe that everything must be subordinated to a single end. There are some means that cannot be excused. And I want to be able to love my country and still love justice" (p. 221). The key words are clear; the end does not justify the means, and no end can be so absolute as to require the total surrender of self. Camus equates Germany's idea of destiny to a firing squad: many Frenchmen "have already faced the twelve little black eyes of German destiny" (p. 221).

Camus admits the temptation to submit to the forces of instinct, to forgo intelligence and cultivate efficiency. France is weak, both politically and culturally, but Camus believes in objective evaluation: "This country deserves the difficult and demanding love that is mine . . . your nation, on the other hand, has received from its sons only the love it deserved, which was blind. One is not justified by just any kind of love" (E, p. 225). Love is not necessarily an absolute virtue, and neither is obedience. Both must evaluate the source. Excessive love breeds fanaticism, and blind forces demand blind love. The anti-Fascist forces are more lucid and detached. "We are fighting for nuances. . . . We are fighting for the nuance that distinguishes sacrifice from cruelty, and for that even finer nuance that distinguishes falsehood from truth, and the human being we envisage from the cowardly gods you worship" (p. 224). The emphasis on human beings as opposed to some higher spiritual force or destiny is brought up again in the second letter (December 1943). The French are fighting for greater things than mere patriotism: "friendship, man, happiness, our desire for justice" (p. 228). The Germans, on the other hand, have submerged these ideals. "Even the gods are mobilized in your country," Camus observes, and tells the story of a German priest who is accompanying a group of Frenchmen to a cemetery for execution. When a young boy tries to escape, the priest betrays him to the German soldiers (p. 231). The rather ignominious role played by the churches during the Occupation and the lack of a comprehensible policy in Rome are criticized elsewhere by Camus, but did nothing to diminish his respect for those members of the clergy who did follow their calling and take action on behalf of the martyrs.

According to Camus, it is incidents such as these that have finally aroused the anger of the French people. Theirs is not the

blind anger of hatred, but an anger that fuels the energy necessary to resist, day after day, the onslaught of the executioners. A
visceral revulsion to the torture of children led Camus to make
it a major theme in many of his works of this period. The death
of the judge Othon's son is a central event in *The Plague*, and it
fills Dr. Rieux with an uncontrollable anger, the first sign of
passion he has shown. In a speech given in 1945 Camus talked of
the meticulousness with which the Nazis did their work. "Men
like you and me, who in the morning patted children on the
head in the metro, would be transformed in the evening into
meticulous executioners. They became the bureaucrats of
hatred and torture. . . . They trampled children's bodies into
coffins too small for them, they tortured brothers in their sis-
ters' presence" (*E*, p. 314).

This sentence echoes an editorial in *Combat* of 22 August
1944 entitled "The Time for Justice," which calls for the punishment of traitors: "We had the imagination needed in the face of
thousands of reports about our brothers, arrested, deported,
massacred or tortured. And those dead children trampled and
kicked into coffins, we have carried them within us for four
years." In response to Gabriel Marcel's question as to why
Camus's 1948 play *State of Siege* was set in Spain instead of in
Eastern Europe, Camus reminded him of Guernica, "where, for
the first time, Hitler, Mussolini and Franco demonstrated to
children the meaning of the totalitarian technique. . . . The
blood of innocence flowed amid a loud chatter of pharisees"
(*E*, p. 392). It is the presence of the archduke's children in the
carriage that prevents Kaliayev from throwing his bomb in *The
Just Assassins*. In *The Fall* Clamence mocks his erstwhile role
of defender of widows and children.

Camus's reaction to the starving children in Kabylia was the
same as to all forms of violence perpetrated on the innocent. In
his Notebooks he commented that all philosophies are self-
justification: it might be said that his own philosophy was a
justification of his body's revolt. This almost primitive aspect of

his thought is expressed in the third letter to a German friend (April 1944), which begins with a discussion of semantics, and ends with an expression of faith that echoes "The Almond Trees." The words that are understood differently by the Germans and the French are *homeland* and *Europe*. The French see Europe as a living body: "mutilated," "wounded to the quick in our very flesh," "despoiled." For the Germans, Europe is merely a piece of real estate, "an expanse encircled by seas and mountains, dotted with dams, gutted with mines, covered with harvests. . . . But for us Europe is that fertile soil of the mind that for the last twenty centuries has fed the most amazing adventure of the human spirit" (*E*, p. 234). The lines are drawn between abstraction, the view of efficacy, and the physical link with the earth that nourishes the mind and spirit. By this time, there is a sense of hope in Camus's letter, "for all these landscapes, these flowers and ploughed fields, this most ancient of lands, prove to you every spring that some things cannot be suffocated in blood. . . . I could not do without the earth. The weapons that the European mind can muster against you are the same as those of this land, constantly reborn with harvests and blossoms. The struggle we are waging is bound to be victorious because it has the obstinacy of spring" (p. 236). Camus bases his optimism on the power of repetition: Sisyphus will triumph.

The fourth and last letter of July 1944 links the struggle of the mind and the body. Camus recalls the point at which he and his German friend began to differ:

> You accepted willingly enough the injustice of our condition to resolve to add to it, while it seemed to me that man should support justice in order to struggle against eternal injustice, create happiness as a protest against universal unhappiness. In a word, you chose injustice, you sided with the gods. . . . I chose justice, on the other hand, to stay faithful to the earth. I still believe that this world has no higher meaning. But I know that something in it has meaning, and that is man, because he is the only creature who demands it. (*E*, pp. 240–41)

The ideas expressed in this passage are somewhat obscure, and assume a knowledge of Camus's philosophical thought. He opposes divine injustice, that is, the gods' cruel imposition of the human condition, to human justice. The Germans, in following their theories of national destiny, placed themselves on the side of the gods and inflicted further injustices on humanity; Nazism is associated with the Absurd, in that it suppresses the human spirit and leaves us with no alternative but despair (Werner, p. 101). The resistants, on the other hand, have sided with men and women in their absurd condition, and have chosen the earth in preference to heaven. Man's link is with the earth, source of life and regeneration; it is the human body that can define justice, for "the body . . . shows us our limits" (*CI,* p. 90).

Amidst the debris of Europe, Camus held up the idea of man as the basis for a better future. The human condition has not changed; but the events of the past years had proven that we do not deserve such injustice, that we are not lonely creatures to be disposed of as an abstract mass. "Hundreds of thousands of people executed at dawn, the terrible walls of prisons, a Europe whose earth is steaming with millions of corpses that were once her children—it took all that to pay for two or three nuances that perhaps will have no other function than to help a few of us die more nobly" (*E,* p. 243). The vast scope of the destruction in Europe made it almost impossible for the mind to grasp the meaning of numbers. The limits of conception are evoked with a humorous tone in *The Plague* when Rieux considers the death toll in past epidemics of plague: "A dead man is of no consequence unless you have seen the dead body" (*TRN,* p. 1248). On the other hand, if a rat measures thirty centimeters, forty thousand rats placed end to end—and imagination ceases to function.

This lack of imagination for the reality of flesh and blood inspires Camus's article "Not Everything Is Working Out," which appeared in the clandestine journal *Les Lettres françaises* in May 1944 (reprinted in *E*, pp. 1468–70). The incident in question is the death sentence passed on Pierre Pucheu, the notorious minister of the interior during the Occupation. He was the man who set up the special Police for Jewish Questions and the Anti-Communist Police Service, who chose the hostages to be executed by the Germans, and who helped to make the Gestapo an efficient organization in France. For the first time, Camus has felt no revulsion at the execution of a man, and he asks himself why. His conclusion is that Pucheu is guilty not only of treason and murder, but of having no imagination. He thought that government had not changed, "that he was still in that abstract administrative system he had always been in" (*E*, p. 1469). He failed to understand that words had a new and mortal meaning; he failed to see the carnal connection between the signifier and the signified. "Those laws that he signed in everyday surroundings, in a comfortable anonymous office—he did not have enough imagination to see that *in reality* they would be translated into a dawn of agony for innocent Frenchmen who would be put to death." This abstraction, or withdrawal from physical reality, must end. The greatest crime of such men "is that they have never approached a *body*, tortured like that of Politzer [a Resistance fighter executed in Paris on 23 May 1942] with *the eyes of the body and the notion of justice that I shall call physical.*" (ibid., my emphasis). Pucheu opened his eyes only when his own body was threatened in Algiers, "in a land of flesh and blood." And the lesson to be learned from his death is that we can accept the execution of certain individuals, that we can judge our erstwhile judges without hatred, but without pity.[3]

In 1943 Camus became a close friend of René Leynaud, the regional leader of the Combat group in Lyon. It was early in that year that he had met with the local group of the CNE, and in the autumn he joined the team working on Combat's clandestine journal in Paris, where Pascal Pia was editor-in-chief. Camus took over that job when Pia was assigned to other duties. Most of his work was apparently routine; but as other members of the group were captured and deported or executed, the dangers became more acute. Camus frequently spent the night with friends after his own apartment became suspect. An old friend from Algiers, Paul Raffi, recalls that Camus often stayed with him in mid-1944 because his apartment had an escape route through a back window.

Combat clandestin was first published in December 1941, with Georges Bidault as its editor. There were usually two editions per month: different printing presses were used and sometimes the paper was mimeographed. The symbol on the masthead was the Cross of Lorraine with a C between the two horizontal bars; it continued to be used after the Liberation. The Cross of Lorraine had been adopted by General de Gaulle, who enjoyed the support of the Combat group; his speech of May 1942 was printed in full. By February 1944, Combat claimed that the total circulation of the underground press was well over one million. This number did not represent total readership, however, since the papers were passed from one person to another. As the Occupation forces became more ferocious, more French men and women were drawn into the Resistance, often to escape forced labor in German factories. In July 1944 there appeared an editorial on torture entitled "The Great Fear of the Assassins," and though it was unsigned, it reflects Camus's ideas on torture, a technique that has become a refined political tool of the twentieth century. It is a dehumanizing process that attacks the body in order to subvert the mind, to reduce man to an animal whose physical needs overwhelm his spiritual ideals. Camus's deepest sympathy went out to those men who died after betraying their comrades, in a terrible solitude.

Camus always played down the role of the writers of the Resistance, particularly in comparison with the men who had engaged in armed struggle and who also carried the moral burden of the inevitable death of hostages as a result of their actions. On the other hand, the Resistance taught writers a good deal, as

Camus later remarked: "Risking one's life in any way, just to get an article printed, is to learn the true value of words. . . . And the writer, discovering suddenly that words are loaded, is led to use them judiciously: danger makes one classical" (E, p. 1490). Camus's preference for simple and direct language, his mistrust of rhetoric and euphemism, found its justification in the needs of clandestine journalism.

Camus was always critical of the majority of French newspapers, with their banner headlines and rabble-rousing tactics. In *Paris-Soir* he found "a contemptible shop-girl mentality" (CI, p. 212), and in 1959 he declared in an interview: "With one or two exceptions, sneering, banter and scandal provide the content of our press" (E, p. 1564). The aim of Pia and Camus in Algiers had always been to remain independent of any sponsors except their readers, and it was in the same spirit that *Combat* was launched as a daily newspaper on 21 August 1944. At this time people of different political affiliations were still united in their struggle to evict the Germans and to forge a new and rejuvenated French government. And one of the sources of respect for *Combat* was that it remained independent, rather than voicing the current line of political parties or factions. Its sympathies were most closely aligned with the Socialist party, and gradually withdrew support for de Gaulle. Alexander Werth described *Combat* as the newspaper that "expressed more brilliantly and coherently than any other paper, the hopes, anxieties, disappointment and growing frustration of the non-Communist elements of the Resistance, who had hoped and believed that a New France would really be built on the foundations laid by the CNR charter" (p. xxx). This charter had been drawn up by the Comité National de la Résistance in 1944, and it was "not a revolutionary programme; it represented a sort of New Deal, or what Bidault, the President of the CNR had called . . . 'la révolution par la loi' " (ibid., p. 223). Revolutionary or not, it caused Camus some delay with immigration officials in New York when he arrived on a lecture tour in 1946.

In 1950, Camus published a selection of his *Combat* editorials in *Actuelles I*. In the preface he stated that he no longer held all the opinions expressed in the articles, but that the account of those years could not conceal the errors and doubts. The articles appear under different rubrics rather than in chronological order; the selection gives an idea of what Camus considered to be the major themes of his editorials and his response to the different problems of the period, but they fail to give a sense of the day-to-day experience of those frenetic years. Roger Quilliot has made up for this distanciation in some measure by including a large number of additional articles in the latter section of his Pléiade edition of *Essais*, but there are other articles omitted that bear closer scrutiny.

The editorials published in the euphoric days of August 1944, when Paris was liberated, speak in terms of renaissance. "This dreadful travail will give birth to a revolution" (in *E*, p. 256). The definition of this revolution will undergo some changes: in the unsigned article headed "From Resistance to Revolution" (*Combat*, 21 August 1944, p. 1, attributed to Camus by Quilliot), the members of the Resistance are described as aiming at revolution. "We want to bring about without delay a truly popular workers' democracy. . . . We think that any policy that excludes the working class is useless. France will be tomorrow whatever her working class will be. . . . It is possible that [the revolution] can be achieved with order and calm." These people can forge a new kind of politics: "The collusive solidarity of the politicians has been submerged by the comradeship of a struggle in which each person threw in his lot wholeheartedly. . . . Politics is no longer separate from individuals. Politics is the direct address of man to other men. It is an accent" (p. 1524). The word "collusive" (*complice*) implies a dishonest association in which the individual could conceal himself behind a curtain of political rhetoric, unreachable and immune to the reaction of the people he represents. Camaraderie, on the other hand, denotes an open association among equals. The new men commit themselves entirely: their relationship with the people is face-to-face, "direct address." An accent rather than a mode of discourse distinguishes them. A new order of things is a necessity that has nothing in common with "that mediocre and tainted bunch represented by M. Chautemps, M. Chichéry and many others"—the men of the Third Republic. "These men of the past, who now inspire only indifference or scorn, can always keep themselves busy writing Memoirs that no one will ever read" (p. 1525).

By mid-September, however, *Combat* was defining its position as more and more distinct from the Marxist conception of revolution. The Resistance had constituted a revolt, "that is, the total rejection—obstinate, almost blind at first—of an order of things that would bring men to their knees. Revolt is first and foremost the heart" (in *E*, p. 1526). This blindness, with its physical and metaphysical implications, is paradoxically the attribute of people of vision, of those who react instinctively. The invisible leader of the Resistance, the rebel incarnate de Gaulle, formed a nation without ever being seen. "This man, whom we suddenly recognize without ever having seen him, became close to us merely by the miracle not even of a language, but of a word. That word was the word 'no'" (*Combat*, unsigned, 26 August 1944). The reaction of revolt is not necessarily rational. "But there comes a time when it moves into the mind, when feeling becomes idea, when a spontaneous outburst ends in concerted action. This is the moment of revolution" (in *E*, p. 1526). It is significant that this progression—feeling–idea–action—is the reverse of that propounded by Camus in his speech at the Maison de la Culture in Algiers in 1937, when he was playing down the intellectual's influence on revolution. "Revolutions are made first and the ideas come later" (p. 1326). But four years of struggle have brought insight to the resistants. "Here we do not believe in definitive revolutions. All human effort is relative. . . . In fact, we believe in relative revolutions" (p. 1527).

A relative revolution is obviously no revolution at all to a

Marxist. However, Camus at this point admits the inevitability of violence: "Revolution is not necessarily the guillotine and machine-guns, or rather, it is machine-guns only when necessary" (*E*, p. 1527). Camus fails to elaborate here on the point at which machine-guns become necessary, nor on who makes the decision, but other articles suggest self-defense as a legitimate motive and moment.

This separation from the Communist faction of the Resistance did not mean that the Communists should be excluded from the government. A *Combat* editorial of 30 September 1944 criticizes the Americans for putting all the resistants in the same Marxist basket: there may be disagreements between the different factions, but they represent the new France, and "they must be accepted as a unit, with General de Gaulle and with the Communists." The following day, Camus's editorial describes the Combat group's aims in a new society. Basically, they hope for the conciliation of liberty and justice. "Justice for us . . . is a social state in which each individual gets every opportunity from the start, in which the majority of the population is not oppressed by a privileged minority. And liberty for us is a political climate in which the human person is respected in what he is as in what he expresses" (*E*, pp. 1527–28).

The balance between justice and liberty is hard to maintain. Camus cites the Scandinavian countries as examples of systems that have been successful, but realizes that they have achieved their state in relative isolation. "A collectivist economy and liberal policies" are two more factors that must be kept in equilibrium, for "in this constant and cautious balance lie not human happiness, which is another question, but the conditions needed to ensure that every man can be solely responsible for his happiness and his destiny. It is simply a question of not adding an injustice of human origin to the profound wretchedness of our condition" (*E*, p. 1528). And Camus reiterates the need for a true popular democracy. The introduction of the right to the pursuit of happiness recalls the revolutionaries of 1776, and Camus might be considered somewhat outdated in 1944. Indeed, his own thought had moved beyond such a demand. But he believed that the human creature has been denigrated throughout the Christian era: "We are the outcome of twenty centuries of Christian imagery. For two thousand years, man has been offered a humiliated portrait of himself. The results are obvious. But who can say what we might have been like if those twenty centuries had seen the persistence of the classical ideal with its beautiful human face?" (*CII*, p. 16). Camus was not so naïve as to believe that a social system could ensure human happiness; but any oppressive, abstract regime certainly removed all possibility of the freedom necessary to achieve such happiness.

In another criticism of the Marxist method, Camus states: "We do not believe in political realism. A lie, even one made with good intentions, is what divides men, and plunges them back into the most fruitless solitude" (*E*, p. 1529). Camus was criticized for his vague Scandinavian model of democracy; but the fact was that he had no absolute answers. He was always amazed and frightened by the certainty of ideologues. His opposition to their strictures can be linked to that distaste for moral conventions which he voiced so clearly in *A Happy Death, Caligula,* and *The Stranger.* Rigid lines of demarcation often conceal motives of self-interest, or a lack of imagination, and the political affiliation of their proponent is immaterial.

On 7 October 1944 Camus responded to what he termed "misunderstandings" with his Communist comrades. The Combat congress had affirmed that their movement had adopted the formula "anti-Communism is the beginning of dictatorship" (*E*, p. 272). Camus abided by this formula, because "even though we do not agree with Communist philosophy nor with its practical ethics, we energetically reject political anti-Communism, because we are well aware of its sources and its unstated goals" (p. 273). The last clause is significant, since Camus obviously recognized anti-Communism as a weapon of the right, designed to break up the alliance forged during the Resistance. His aim was to agree to disagree, particularly on means. "We share most of the collectivist ideas and the social program of our comrades, their ideal of justice, their disgust for a society in which money and privilege are all-important. It is just that . . . they find in a very coherent philosophy of history the justification for political realism as the foremost method for accomplishing an ideal shared by many Frenchmen. It is on this point, very clearly, that we part company with them. We have said this many times, we do not believe in political realism" (p. 273). It should not be forgotten that Camus had had first-hand experience of the practice of political realism in the PCF in Algiers, where policy was altered frequently to meet the current needs of the party's strategy. Moral obligations and past loyalties held little sway against orders from the Central Committee. As Werth wryly comments, "the Communist party line did not become clear until after the German attack on the Soviet Union, which transformed the 'imperialist' war into an 'anti-Fascist' and 'anti-imperialist' war" (p. 149). And Camus in his Notebooks tells the story of "Robert, a conscientious objector with Communist sympathies, in '33. Three years of prison. When he gets out, the Communists are in favor of war, the pacifists are for Hitler. He no longer understands anything in this world gone mad. He signs on with the Spanish Republicans and *goes to war*. He gets killed at the Madrid front" (*CII*, p. 187). Sartre used the same theme as the basis for his play *Les Mains sales*.

Lottman cites another, more immediate reason for Camus's hostility toward the Communists. In May 1944 "an anonymous tract was circulating in Paris attacking existentialist writers as 'pseudo-resistants.' The four writers cited and thus exposed to the attention of the French police and the German occupying forces were Sartre, Camus, Lescure, and a poet named André Frenaud. At least one of the writers thus targeted [Jean Lescure] had reason to believe that the tract was written and secretly distributed by the Communists, who used this tactic to expose and thus eliminate potentially troublesome opponents" (p. 312).

Camus admits that the experiment supported by Combat may not work: their members are at a disadvantage because their world died in 1940, whereas the Communists adhered to the same doctrine then as they do in 1944. This position vis-à-vis the Communists was at odds with other factions in the Resistance movement which aimed to keep the Communists out of any further government; and so Camus and his colleagues were squeezed into a narrow ideological space between the left and the center, with an uncertain experiment in orderly and "relative" revolution on their hands, while their American allies were sponsoring those elements bent on bourgeois reconstruction.

Critics of Camus's political stance have scored his naïveté in believing that a progressive French government could be born of the Resistance. Claude Bourdet, a member of the permanent steering committee of the CNR, who worked on *Combat* with Camus and took over the newspaper in 1947, thought that Camus threw himself into politics without realizing the scope of the problems involved; having played no part in the direction of any of the Resistance groups, he knew little of the political infighting that was rampant well before the Liberation. There was strong opposition to the Communists' attempts to take over the leadership of the different groups and to politicize the Resistance (Werth, p. 150). On the other hand, the Communists were the toughest and most experienced fighters, and suffered far more inhumane treatment in captivity than their non-Communist comrades-in-arms.

Camus had his critics on other issues. His public debate with François Mauriac over the organization of the purge of Vichyites and other collaborators shows him in an unusual stance. Mauriac protested in the *Figaro* that the Resistance tribunals were excessive and arbitrary in meting out justice: as a Catholic he felt that mercy should be exercised, since divine justice would ultimately prevail. Camus did not advocate the private settling of accounts, but he did believe, with the passion of his "physical idea of justice," that some crimes were beyond pardon. Such men as Pucheu, who had been directly responsible for the death of so many of his compatriots, and the French *milice*, without whose enthusiastic diligence the Gestapo would have been virtually ineffective, deserved no pity. Fresh in Camus's mind were the executions of such friends as Leynaud and Velin (the pseudonym of a young *Combat* director). "Whenever we are tempted to dwell on the generous sacrifices of the war rather than face the dark tasks of justice," he wrote in *Combat*, "we need to remember the dead, and the unbearable memory of those amongst us who were turned into traitors under torture" (in *E*, p. 1534).

His rejection of mercy earned Camus the nickname of St. Just; but by early 1945 he was appalled by the uneven way in which justice was applied. Werth comments, "It is significant that the most famous trials after the Liberation were not those of the economic profiteers of the Occupation, but of the men who supported the Germans on the political and ideological plane. . . . It was a curiously French tribute to the power of the pen, to the prestige of the intellectual" (p. 120). Camus was more skeptical of the power of the pen, and felt that the literary traitors deserved scorn rather than death. He signed an appeal for clemency for Robert Brasillach, and in 1948 he declared in public that Mauriac had been right on this point (*E*, p. 372). Camus was really anxious for the purge of bigger fish: the leaders in government and industry who had sold out. Significantly, the only "black" character developed in any detail in *The Plague* is Cottard, who welcomes the plague because he fears discovery of past illegal actions, and becomes a successful profiteer in the black market.

Camus's traditionally antibourgeois stance is reflected in his indictment of Louis Renault, and of the Parisian bourgeoisie in their ignorance and indifference. An unsigned series of articles in *Combat*, 26–28 September 1944 (attributed to Camus by

Quilliot, but not reprinted in *Essais*), emphasizes the extra responsibility of the ruling class. Renault "ought to have rebelled even before the masses." The Vichy fiction must be destroyed, and the nationalization of the Renault works would be a good step, hitting the moneymakers where it hurts them most—in their pockets. During the Liberation of Paris, the lack of barricades in the bourgeois *arrondissements* was noted with bitterness. As Camus commented on 1 December, "All the Liberation of France meant to them was a return to their traditional meals, their cars and *Paris-Soir*. Let liberty come quickly so that we can be mediocre and powerful in comfort!" (in *E*, p. 1542). An editorial of 13 December attacks the control of the banks over industry: "What terrible madness to think that precious blood is today being spilled on the ground in the East, while some men are calculating interest and [financial] policy." On 7 December the front page of *Combat* ran one article by François Bruel maintaining that despite the demise of Vichy, the bourgeoisie was still running the country, and another article by Camus attacking the black-marketeers, and criticizing the fact that luxury restaurants were allowed to get extra supplies. Camus's hostility to the bourgeoisie had not waned since his first encounter with the Lyonnais in 1936. In an unpublished letter to a friend in Algiers, he stated how he detested their hypocrisy and mediocrity, their well-fed complacency. On the way to New York in March 1946 Camus talked on the boat with some French businessmen who agreed that "the only problem these days is money." "Ugly mugs, rotten with cupidity and impotence," was Camus's comment (*JV*, p. 27).

Greed and complacency were not the only aspects of the bourgeoisie that Camus found repugnant. The political power wielded by its older members endangered the renewal of France and threatened to annul the possibility of any kind of social reform. On 4 December 1944 Camus comments in *Combat* on the fact that in the Constituent Assembly, only 40 out of a total of 225 members were present. "I doubt whether we can escape this awful old age which has befallen our administrators and our habits, unless each one of us makes up his mind that he will never be tired"; on 20 December he refers to the "senility of the administration." The recurrent reference to old age reflects Camus's concern with time. In his notebooks he remarked on each decade of his life with a rueful comment on how little he had achieved thus far. In *Nuptials* he described how quickly men in Algeria became burnt out before their time, passing from exuberant youth to old age with scarcely any intermediate stage. The words *old age, tired, senility* point up Camus's sense that time was running out for a successful change in the structure of society; if old men were returned to power, then apathy and dilatoriness would lead to a return by default to prewar politics, where the leaders dreaded change.

Camus's disdain for the clique of old men in power is exemplified by an ironic anecdote in his notebooks: "The deputy for Constantine who is elected for the third time. The day of the election, at noon, he dies. In the evening people come to congratulate him. His wife comes out on the balcony and says he is a little tired. Soon afterwards, the corpse is elected deputy. Just what we needed" (*CI*, pp. 140–41).

But the left in France shared some of the characteristics of the right: lethargy, mediocrity, cupidity. In 1942 Camus noted: "The Frenchman has remained accustomed to the idea and the traditions of revolution. All he lacks is the guts: he has become a bureaucrat, crass and petty bourgeois. . . . He reshapes a world without lifting his backside out of his armchair" (*CII*, p. 13).[4]

The bureaucrat creates structures that lead to an often paralyzing stasis, making change an impossibly complex task. This growing tide of bureaucratization attained gruesome proportions in Camus's vision: with biting irony he raised the subject of the strikes of 1947, when even the public executioner of Paris stopped work. It was natural that he should demand a bonus for each execution performed, but his major demand, Camus observed to an international group of writers, was that he should have administrative status, "the only tangible honor that a modern nation can bestow on its faithful retainers. Thus, beneath the weight of history, one of our last liberal professions was snuffed out" (*E*, pp. 400–401). It was this resistance to the restrictions of government and financiers that made *Combat* such an unusual paper, and Camus left it when it could no longer survive as an independent publication. Claude Bourdet took over on 2 June 1947 and ceded fifty percent of the shares to a Tunisian businessman, Monsieur Smadja. Ill health as well as disappointment and loss of faith in the efficacy of his journalism have been cited as reasons for Camus's departure, yet the progressive disillusionment of the post-Liberation years might be summed up in Werth's description of *Combat's* slogan, "From Resistance to Revolution," "printed . . . in smaller and smaller characters, and finally in almost invisible type" (p. 229).

It is no wonder that Camus responded with such acrimony to the accusations that greeted his series "Neither Victims nor Executioners," accusations that dismissed him as merely a bourgeois lackey. "Anguish at the thought of doing those articles for *Combat*," wrote Camus in his notebooks (*CII*, p. 183). "There are times when I don't think I can endure the contradiction any longer." The contradiction lay in the choice Camus faced between retiring from the political arena without making more enemies, and speaking out against Stalinism and its concomitant terrors. He knew that any criticism of the left would be interpreted as a gesture in favor of the right. Yet to remain silent would constitute a betrayal of the ideals of freedom that had inspired the Resistance movement.

> How can one remain on the sidelines and not denounce the lie that is poisoning everything? Everyone is afraid, lying low and keeping quiet. . . . And I myself, am I so sure? If there are no eternal values, then Communism is right and nothing is permitted, we must build human society at any price. If it is wrong, then we must follow the Gospel and Christianity. This dilemma has never seemed more distressing and insistent than it is today. And

men like me, who dream of an impossible synthesis, who reject violence and lies without necessarily justifying their opposite, yet who cannot help shouting out, we are in a state of madness. (*Corr.*, p. 119)

Camus's notes during his visit to the United States in the spring of 1946 reveal his deep misgivings about the political situation, with France caught between two opposing giants and still unstable because of continuing internal strife between parties vying for power. His optimism of late 1944, when he could claim that "the activities of the Resistance will remain above prejudices or personal ambitions" (*Combat*, 8 October 1944) had waned. De Gaulle had revealed his true conservative colors, and the lines were being drawn in Eastern Europe. The hope that something could be done "for man's happiness without causing bloodshed" (6 October) had died with the unleashing of the atomic bomb: "The machine civilization has just reached its greatest degree of savagery" (8 August 1945). This abstraction *par excellence* seemed to imply for Camus that we could no longer afford realistically to believe in ideology. "Our age marks the end of ideologies. The atomic bomb prohibits ideology" (*JV*, p. 50).

Camus realized that he was out of step with his contemporaries: "Collective passions are taking precedence over individual passions. Men do not know how to love any more. What interests them today is the human condition, and not individual destinies" (*CII*, p. 151). Camus had no faith in either Marxism or bourgeois capitalism: "As for the notorious optimism of Marxism, allow me to scoff at it. Few men have driven distrust of their fellows to such a degree. Marxists do not believe in persuasion or in dialogue. You cannot turn a bourgeois into a worker, and in the bourgeois mentality, economic conditions are more terrible fatalities than divine whims" (p. 159). Yet Camus could not remain unmoved by the desire to improve the lot of the underprivileged: "I have a taste for freedom. And for every intellectual, freedom ends up being confused with freedom of expression. But I am perfectly well aware that this is not a number one problem for a great many Europeans, because only justice can give them the minimum they need to survive, and rightly or wrongly, they would willingly sacrifice freedom for this fundamental justice" (*CII*, pp. 141–42; the story of "The Guest" points up the moral ambiguity of this choice).

Justice and liberty: were they mutually incompatible, and must one necessarily choose between them? "Political antinomies. We are in a world where we must choose between being the victim or the executioner—and nothing else. That is not an easy choice" (*CII*, p. 141). Once again, Camus felt the urge to turn back to art, to sit out the match. "As a non-Christian, I must go all the way. But all the way means choosing history absolutely, and with it the murder of man if the murder of man is necessary to history. Otherwise, I am only a witness. That's the question: can I be just a witness? In other words, do I have the right to be just an artist? I cannot believe that" (p. 155). "Neither Victims nor Executioners" showed that Camus had rejected the role of passive witness, as well as the necessity of choosing one of the two absolutes. Once more his instincts provided him with a political affirmation that opposed the inevitable logic of history.

The first article is entitled "The Century of Fear." Fear may not be a science. "We have seen men lie, degrade, kill, deport, torture," yet all these actions were perpetrated in the name of an abstraction, "that is, [by] the representative of an ideology," a person who is deaf to protest. We live in a world of offices and machines, "of absolutist ideas and of unadulterated Messianism. We are suffocating among people who believe they are absolutely right" (*E*, p. 332). Deafness, muteness, stifling: physical maladies familiar to Camus describe the force and consequence of ideas. He wants to propose an alternative to those who doubt that socialism will be realized in Russia, or liberalism in America, but who recognize the right of those countries to pursue their goals without imposing their beliefs on others. In "Saving the Body," Camus notes that he was accused of utopianism because he could not accept any truth that obliged him, directly or indirectly, to sentence a person to death. His response is that killing has become less immediate in the modern world. "Just as people make love over the telephone, and work by machine rather than on the material itself, so today people kill and are killed by proxy. It makes for neatness, but reduces awareness" (p. 334).

Obviously murder cannot be eliminated from human society—but it should never be legitimated. He considers the notion of utopianism more applicable to Marxist and capitalist ideologies, both of which are based on the idea of progress, and are convinced that their programs will inevitably lead to justice and a comfortable life for all. Camus seeks a more modest philosophy, "freed from any Messianism, and free of nostalgia for an earthly paradise" (E, p. 335). In "Socialism Mystified" he sees this moral problem as the current dilemma of the French Socialist party: does the end justify all means? But the Socialist party in its eighteenth congress in August 1946 failed to choose: some believed that one could not be revolutionary without being Marxist, others that one could not be Socialist without being Marxist; but they could not necessarily accept all the consequences of Marxism.

Camus's response is to propose a new definition of the word *revolution*. The traditional concept is no longer valid. "1789 and 1917 are still dates, but they are no longer examples." "For one thing, taking power by violent means is a Romantic idea that has been made illusory by the modernization of weaponry" (E, p. 339). Uprisings in Eastern Europe in the 1950s certainly vindicated this view. Secondly, a country would have to be isolated from the rest of the world to achieve a successful revolution. "We are not free, as Frenchmen, to be revolutionaries" (p. 339), since economic as well as political factors are involved.

The only possibility is the extension of a successful revolution: "It is something that Stalin has understood perfectly, and it is the kindest explanation one can give of his policies: the other is to refuse to allow Russia the right to speak in the name of revolution" (E, p. 340). With the enormous increase in the destructive power of human weaponry, the available means would jeopardize the end; utopia would be a mass of rubble. Some kind of international parliament should be established, in which emerging nations would participate. Petroleum, coal, and uranium should be placed under international rather than national control and distribution. "Everywhere, in fact, colonized peoples are making their voices heard. In ten years' time, in fifty years, the preeminence of Western civilization will be challenged again" (p. 345). It is certainly a Camusian irony that by the late 1970s the advanced technology of the Western world relied on supplies controlled by countries that have rejected Western domination.

Camus declares a need for a new social contract. Peace must be restored so that vital human needs can be met. Domestic politics are secondary, and internal administrative problems should be dealt with provisionally, until such time as an orderly change in society can be achieved on the international level. An international code of justice should be drawn up, and have as its first article the abolition of the death penalty. Communication, dialogue is required between nations rather than threats and hostility. "Henceforth, the only honorable course will be to take up this formidable wager, which will decide once and for all whether words are more powerful than bullets" (E, p. 352). Again Camus opposes human contact to the abstraction of remote weapons: human speech versus a mechanical means of murder that has neither eyes nor ears.

Camus was the object of attack from Communist writers soon after the Liberation. Action and Les Lettres françaises accused him (somewhat paradoxically) of vacillation and an excessively critical viewpoint. But it was not until the republication of "Neither Victims nor Executioners" in November 1947 (the

month of widespread strikes that saw the creation of the Corps
Républicain de Sécurité, or CRS), that Emmanuel d'Astier de la
Vigerie undertook a specific criticism of his articles. D'Astier was an outstanding leader in the Resistance, a Communist
sympathizer, and director of the journal *Libération*. The titles of
his response to Camus, "Snatch the Victim from the Executioners" and "Pontius Pilate with the Executioners" mark the
theme of clean hands that was to become a permanent aspect of
all leftist criticism of Camus's political views. Camus was identified with his character in *The Plague*, Tarrou, a kind of lay
saint. His response was as virulent as the attack. He was convinced that violence should never be legitimized; the truth
about Stalin's camps had now been revealed to the outside
world, and the tactics that had formerly been associated with
Nazism were now irrevocably linked with Communism. Abstraction, with its concomitant aspects of lack of realism and of
humanism, has led to the Gulag phenomenon; the Gulag crys-
tallized the focus of Camus's opposition to the ideologies of his
time. "One cannot be on the side of concentration camps"
(*E*, p. 356). He rejects the excuse of historical necessity: "There
is no reason in the world, historical or no, progressive or reactionary, that can make me accept the phenomenon of the concentration camp" (p. 365).

Camus's next target was what he called the *philosophes-
spectateurs*, or "armchair philosophers" (*E*, p. 357). "I abhor
comfortable violence. I abhor those whose words go farther than
their deeds. It is here that I part company with some of our great
minds, and I shall cease to scorn their calls to murder only when
they themselves are part of the firing-squad" (p. 356). All too
often theoreticians have no immediate conception of the physical results of their words. Camus alienated a good portion of the
left-wing Parisian intelligentsia with this sally, but he had not
finished with them. A colleague of d'Astier had commented
that Camus had not learned about liberty in Marx. "It is true: I
learned about it in poverty. But most of you do not know what

the word means," Camus responded (p. 357). It was the first time
he had mentioned class distinctions publicly,[5] and only then in
response to the portrait of bourgeois lackey that had been created by his opponents. *"Just this once,* I must remind you that
most of you Communist intellectuals have no experience of the
proletarian condition, and so it is not for you to treat us as
dreamers ignorant of reality" (p. 364). "With a single sentence,
he set almost all the left-wing intellectuals against him": Jean
Daniel's comment (*Le Nouvel Observateur,* 27 November 1978)
on a sentence from Camus's preface to Guilloux's *La Maison du
peuple* is equally applicable to his second response to d'Astier.
The tone gives some idea of the bitterness of polemic during the
period of the cold war.

Once more Camus found himself at odds with both sides. His
intransigent opposition to the right, coupled with his decision
to place human needs above the abstract requirements of history, placed him in what appeared to be a fence-sitting position.
It was an unenviable position, yet he felt he should have taken it
up even earlier. "One thing I regret is having sacrificed too much
for the sake of objectivity. Objectivity is sometimes self-
indulgent. Today things are clear-cut, and we must call that
which is tainted by the concentration camp by its real name,
even socialism. In a sense, I shall never be polite again. I strove
for objectivity, against my nature. Because I mistrusted liberty"
(*CII,* p. 267). In a speech delivered in November 1948, Camus
compared the role of the artist to that of the politician: artists
are "witnesses of the flesh, not of the law," and the flesh "tran-
scends any history" (*E,* p. 406). In the last interview accorded
before his death, Camus was asked what he felt French critics
had neglected in his work. "The dark side, that which is blind
and instinctive in me," he replied. "French critics are interested
primarily in ideas" (p. 1925).

Doubtless Camus felt obliged to organize his ideas in *The
Rebel,* but the instincts that spawned those ideas were already
fully expressed in his journalistic articles. In the face of such

organized criticism from both ends of the political spectrum, the creative work served as a means of self-assurance. Perhaps the outsider always has a clear perspective, and after the integrated phase of the Resistance, Camus once more found himself on the outside. "I continually have the feeling that I have broken one of the rules of the clan" (*TRN*, p. 1723).

"From the right and from the left, blows rained down and scorn lashed him; there were no holds barred in those cold war years. Was not Camus's only fault, apart from being too widely read, that he was right too soon?" (Poirot-Delpech in *Le Monde*, 5 August 1977).

6

The Plague:
A Totalitarian Universe

La vérité n'est pas dans
la séparation. Elle est
dans la réunion.
—*Essais*

Camus's work on *The Plague* coincided with his active participation in political affairs. His longstanding opposition to fascism had overriden his pacifist leanings; his commitment to the aims of the French Resistance and to its postwar goals were unambiguous, and clearly expressed in his journalism. His growing disenchantment with the Communists and the Gaullists was exacerbated by sectarian attacks against him, and when he left *Combat* in 1947, he was already reassessing his motives and beliefs.

The Plague, like *The Stranger*, was completed at the end of a period of active involvement, in 1947. While *The Stranger* is primarily concerned with the fate of the individual in an absurd society, *The Plague* deals with individual action that can alter that society. There is no single hero, but a group of men, drawn together by the historical situation. This progression reflects Camus's view, not only of the nature of his own contribution to the improvement of the human lot, but also of the value of group action as opposed to that of the individual. The solitary rebel has little impact: the second part of the credo, "I rebel, therefore we are" (*E*, p. 432) comes to the fore in *The Plague*, and expresses

[120

the stance of solidarity that Camus always sought to maintain.

The transposition of a political and metaphysical experience into a work of fiction revealed many of the problems underlying Camus's commitment, as well as the problem of writing itself. Journalistic articles are usually written against a deadline and openly express immediate current responses; fiction demands a more carefully polished text. *The Plague* is remarkable for its reiterated self-reference. The narrator constantly draws the reader's attention to the difficulties of writing, to the danger of betrayal, of saying too much or too little (cf. Fitch, *"La Peste"*). The complexities of *The Plague* throw light on Camus's political thought at this moment in his life.

The book can be read on three levels: as a straightforward narrative, as an allegory of the Occupation, and as a symbolic representation of the problem of evil in an absurd universe. The most obvious level is the story of a city suffering from an epidemic of plague, and the response of its citizens to the crisis. The plot is simple. Oran, an important city on the North African coast, falls victim to an outbreak of bubonic plague. It is then isolated from the rest of the country to prevent contagion. Dr. Rieux, together with his friends and associates, organizes a group to combat the disease, to set up quarantine camps, and to dispose of the dead. The disease runs its course, the city is reopened, and life returns to normal after the celebration of freedom and reunion.

The narrator claims to be presenting an objective chronicle, based on historical data, his own experience, that of other witnesses, and other documents to which he has access, in particular the diary of Tarrou, an erstwhile left-wing militant now living in Oran. The identity of the narrator is only revealed at the end of the book, although several clues lead us to suspect that he is Dr. Rieux. The story is told in a generally dispassionate and monotonous style, with only occasional passages of heightened tension and emotion. It is the style of the responsible journalist.

A second level of interpretation is one in which the plague represents the Nazi occupation of France. This reading is supported by Camus's own comments, and reflects many of the attitudes expressed in his journalism. His aims are clearly stated in his notebook: "I want to express by means of the plague the feeling of suffocation we have endured, and the atmosphere of menace and exile we have been living in" (*CII*, p. 72).[1]

Why did Camus choose Oran as the setting, rather than a French city such as St. Etienne, where he had seen the effects of the Occupation at first hand? Obviously, the reality of the city is irrelevant to a work of fiction, and Camus claimed that it could be any city. His sister-in-law suggested, perhaps only half in jest, that he chose Oran because his wife's family lived there. It might also be considered another example of ironic reversal of his own experience: he left Oran to go to the mountains for treatment of tuberculosis, leaving his wife behind, only to be cut off in the wake of the Allied invasion of North Africa. If so, then Oran is France, and Dr. Rieux and his colleagues represent the French resistants.

But the choice of Oran was not a random one. Camus's reactions to the city are made explicit in *The Minotaur*, written in 1939 and first published in 1946. It is a city of lassitude because it lacks any attribute to stimulate the soul. It is a totally unpoetic environment. "The mineral sky of Oran, its streets and trees in their coating of dust, all serve to create this thick and impassive world in which the heart and mind are never diverted from themselves" (*E*, pp. 819–20). The Oranais themselves have contributed to this leaden milieu, and have turned their back on the natural beauty of the site: "Forced to live before a glorious landscape, the people of Oran have triumphed over this formidable ordeal by covering the city with exceptionally ugly buildings. You expect a city looking out over the sea, cleansed and refreshed by the evening breeze. But apart from the Spanish quarter, the town turns its back on the sea, and is built up turning in upon itself, like a snail. Oran is a great yellow circular

wall, beneath a hard sky" (p. 818). The contrast with Algiers is
obvious, and Camus gives a humorous account of the rivalry
between the two cities in his description of the boxing-match
between Amar, "the tough Oranais" and Pérez, "the Algiers
puncher" (p. 821). But Oran, a far more European city than Algiers, typifies modern isolation from the natural world. Camus's
description at the beginning of *The Plague* emphasizes this aspect: ". . . a city without pigeons, without trees and without
gardens, where one never encounters the flutter of wings or the
rustling of leaves, a neutral place" (*TRN,* p. 1219). Even the sea-
sons are glimpsed by way of the commercial life of the town;
spring is heralded by the baskets of flowers on sale, "a spring that
is sold in the marketplace" (p. 1219). The central preoccupation
of the Oranais is making money. Their life of utter mediocrity
makes an ideal setting for the monotonous drama of the plague,
since it is to all appearances neutral, neither better nor worse
than any other modern city.

Despite our growing sympathy for the plight of the Oranais,
we are never invited to imagine them as anything more than
mediocre. As a portrait of France before and during the Occupation, the impression of Oran conveyed by Rieux reflects
Camus's inveterate scorn for the bourgeoisie. Its lack of collective consciousness in normal times continues unchanged
through the crisis. "What they lack is imagination. They settle
down in the epic mode as if it were a picnic" (*CII,* p. 68). Black
marketeering, violent attacks on guards at the city gates, an
irresponsible press and local government: a general policy of
every-man-for-himself prevails. And Camus's assertion that the
plague is absolutely just in its indifference is tempered by an
injustice that arises because of the social organization of the
town. The poorer neighborhoods are hardest hit in the beginning. "The plague, in view of the efficient impartiality of its
ministry, ought to have reinforced the spirit of equality among
our fellow-citizens, but on the contrary, because of the usual
interplay of selfish interests, it sharpened the sense of injustice

that men felt in their hearts" (*TRN*, p. 1413). Equality does not necessarily entail justice: "It has not been understood in politics that a certain kind of equality is the enemy of freedom" (*CI*, p. 234). Because of the black marketeers, the poor are hungry while the rich lack for nothing. For the duration of the plague, most people are concerned with the problem of survival. Only when the city gates are opened is a true fraternity widespread, and then it is fleeting. "For the time being, people of very different backgrounds rubbed shoulders and fraternized with each other. The equality that had not actually been realized by the presence of death was now being established by the joy of release, at least for a few hours" (*TRN*, p. 1464).

The combination of liberty, equality, and fraternity is short-lived. "Moral of the plague: it has led nowhere and served no one. Only those touched by death directly or through their loved ones have learned something. But the truth that they have earned concerns only themselves. It has no future" (*CII*, p. 68). The old asthmatic knows that nothing has changed: a monument will be erected to honor the dead, "and there will be speeches. . . . I can hear them now: 'Our departed ones . . . ,' and they'll go off for a meal" (*TRN*, p. 1473). It was precisely this lack of innovative energy that Camus decried in postwar France, and the reality of events during that period, in which the country slipped back into prewar molds, is accurately reflected at the end of *The Plague*. It is a realistic view of history, and is consistent with the views Camus expressed in *Combat*. If Rieux chooses to plead the case of the Oranais, it is because, during the course of his experience, he has acquired a greater measure of human kindness, of which his mother is surely the personification.

If there is little action and scant dialogue in *The Plague*, it is because in this stifling atmosphere time stands still, each day resembles the next, and even the words at one's disposal lose their impact. "While in normal circumstances the Oranais had used past experience to formulate and legitimate their plans, with yesterday coloring tomorrow, now for the first time they found themselves in the position of those who have only an unusable past on which to base the rest of their life" (*TRN*, p. 1963). For the duration of the plague, people merely mark time. Authentic emotions are reduced to the level of banality for lack of renewal, or to the few formulae allowed in a telegram: "After a time those very words that had at first been a spontaneous expression of heartfelt anguish were emptied of their meaning" (p. 1961). The expression of passion is degraded to a "sterile and stubborn monologue." Thus the narrator insists on a detached, dispassionate account of events in a situation where suffering and death are a daily occurrence, and the rise and fall of the death toll a mere curve on a statistical chart.

It is this plodding aspect of the action, a day-to-day experience in which the protagonists are aware of danger but so accustomed to it that they barely notice it, that perhaps best depicts Camus's experiences as a resistant during the Occupation. Indeed, only a minority of resistants actually engaged in dramatic acts of heroism. Most were like the clerk Grand, who meticulously carries out his assignments without the gratification of seeing immediate results. In this respect too they were not subject to the same moral dilemmas inherent in violent resistance. John Cruickshank points out that these "moral dilemmas . . . are almost entirely absent from this symbolic representation" ("Art of Allegory," p. 70); the usual example of such dilemmas is the foreknowledge of reprisals, the shooting of innocent hostages in response to acts of sabotage. But it should be remembered that Camus only wrote of what he knew, and insofar as the plague is symbolic on one level of the German Occupation, it reflects Camus's experience of it. In fact Rieux is faced with some painful moral dilemmas, such as experimenting with a vaccine on prisoners, brutally separating plague victims from their families, allowing workers in his organization to risk infection. Picon commented that the notion of risk does not exist in *The Plague,* but the risks are in fact mortal.

The plague as symbol of the Occupation has been found inadequate. "There is a disturbing moral ambiguity present in such products of human agency as war, oppression and injustice, but this ambiguity is entirely absent in *La Peste*, because, by his allegory, Camus places the origin of suffering in a phenomenon existing outside the scope of human responsibility. . . . The plague . . . covers human wretchedness but ignores human wickedness" (ibid.). Cruickshank is partly right: the plague symbol fails to take into account human responsibility in the origins of human wretchedness.

But Camus is more concerned with another kind of evil, that of human response to suffering. The plague brings about a separation, an atomization of society: people become even more selfish, more self-contained; passivity gradually overcomes the majority of the population. Paneloux, in his first sermon, stresses the divine nature of the scourge and thus encourages this attitude; it reflects that of the Catholic Church, which, after Germany's victory over France in 1940, promulgated the line that this was in fact a visitation from God, a chastisement for the moral decay into which the French people had fallen.

In "The Wind at Djémila" the young Camus had denounced illness as "despicable." "It is a remedy against death. It prepares you for it" (*E*, p. 64). So the plague is accepted by some as an answer to the problem of life, as a relief from the stress of independent thought and action. The man who spends his hours transferring peas from one pot to another offers an ironic example of preparing for death by renouncing life. It is against this kind of evil, an inducement to passivity and conformity, that Rieux fights, and it is in this sense that he embodies the credo of the rebel: "I rebel, therefore we are." His task is to fight the cause of human suffering and to restore human solidarity in the wake of the subsequent effects of separation and alienation.

As Camus stated in a letter to Barthes, on a manifest level *The Plague* speaks of "the struggle of the European resistance against Nazism," but "in one sense, [it] is more than a chronicle of the Resistance" (*TRN,* p. 1973). On a third level, *The Plague* deals with the problem of evil too.

The association between Nazism and evil was not new. In an article published in *Soir-Républicain* (11 October 1939) and signed "Zaks," a pseudonym attributed to Camus by Abbou and Lévi-Valensi, he wrote: "In my opinion, this Hitlerian doctrine, and any that might resemble it, should be flatly rejected and condemned, because it is based on a false vision of reality and on inhuman premises and goals. Both in itself and in the regime it inflicts on the German people, it seems to me one of the most abominable forms of evil in political thought and political life" (*Fragments,* p. 635). And in his *Letters to a German Friend,* Camus accused the Nazis of contributing to the inherent injustices of life by collaborating with the unjust gods who arbitrarily impose death on humankind. Their doctrine and the fury it had unleashed provided an apt representation of the metaphysical problem of evil in the world. As work on *The Plague* progressed, however, the target of Fascism per se was extended to embrace all forms of totalitarianism. Direct references to the concentration camps, and the personification of the plague in the guise of a Hitler-like demagogue, were omitted from the fictional text and published separately (viz. *Corr.,* p. 136).

The change in emphasis coincided with Camus's growing opposition to the Communists, and his realization that there were still camps filled with innocent victims. Rieux and his group fight "any terror, under whatever guise, for terror has several faces, which is why I did not name any one specifically, in order to strike at all of them. No doubt that is what people criticize me for, that *The Plague* can refer to any resistance to any terror" (*TRN,* p. 1974).

The multiple use of the symbol of the plague leads to some basic problems in its application. As an analogy of the Absurd, it has a good deal of force. It can be neither eliminated nor justified. Like death, it is inescapable. In *The Myth of Sisyphus,*

Camus had rejected suicide as not, after all, the logical response to awareness of the Absurd. In his Notebooks he quotes from Tolstoy: "The existence of death obliges us either to give up life voluntarily, or to transform our life *in such a way as to give it a meaning that death cannot take away*" (*CI*, p. 242). Rieux's choice of medicine as a profession reflects this attempt to give his life meaning in an absurd world. "In every collectivity involved in struggle, you need men who kill and men who cure. I chose to cure. But I know that I am engaged in a struggle" (*CII*, p. 107). He knows that he can never win the battle in absolute terms, but a relative victory means more than a cowardly submission to fate. He is acutely aware that in this particular struggle he faces "an unending defeat" (*TRN*, p. 1324): therefore, like Sisyphus, he must find value in the struggle itself.

Camus spelled out a plan in his Notebooks in the summer of 1942, when he was still wrestling with the form of the work. "Plague. Impossible to work out. Too many 'coincidences' this time in the composition. I must stick closely to the idea. *The Stranger* describes the nudity of man confronted with the absurd. *The Plague*, the ultimate equivalence of individual points of view responding to the absurd. It is a progression that will become explicit in other works. But in addition, *The Plague* shows that the absurd *teaches nothing*. It is the definitive progression" (*CII*, p. 36).

The lesson, then, is that in a face-to-face confrontation with the Absurd there is no lesson. At the end of *The Plague* there is a return to the *status quo ante;* people slip back into their comfortable life once the immediate danger of death is past, for they cannot maintain the struggle indefinitely. They will once again seek refuge in religious faith or in a Pascalian *divertissement*. "One possible theme: conflicts between medicine and religion: the powers of the relative (and what a relative!) against those of the absolute. It is the relative that triumphs or rather that does not lose" (*CII*, p. 69). During the plague, Christian theology is shown to be powerless to explain or justify the suffering of the innocent: the priest Paneloux exhorts his flock to have faith in the ultimate righteousness of God's punishment, but after witnessing the death agony of a child, he loses his absolute assurance and dies a "doubtful case."

As a symbol of the Absurd, the plague means both life and death, a moment in time when we all have no choice but to face up to a reality we normally avoid. "In this regard our fellow-citizens were like anyone else, they thought about themselves, in other words they were humanists: they did not believe in scourges. . . . How could they have imagined the plague that suppresses the future, travel and discussion? They thought of themselves as free, and no one will ever be free as long as there are scourges" (*TRN,* pp. 1247–48). We can never free ourselves of the physical limitation of death; only relative liberty exists, and the only just aspect of life is death, the transcendental equalizer.

The human condition is unalterable, but does our social condition have to be bound by the same limits? Dr. Rieux is limited in his ability to cure by the bounds of human physiology, yet in his work of resistance, he need not accept the status quo, but could reorganize the city of Oran in a more fundamental way. The possibilities for revolution that appear at the beginning of *The Plague* are allowed to slip away. Rieux deliberately refuses to go beyond a limited struggle.

Violence is the key to his choice. The plague, in both its real and symbolic character, attacks human beings, causes suffering, violates their right to life and liberty. The response to that violence cannot use the same methods without propagating further suffering. Violence, like the plague bacillus, is contagious. The arrest of Cottard, the black marketeer, illustrates this point; when he is brought out into the street after shooting from an apartment window, "a policeman came up to him and struck him twice, with the full force of his fists, calmly, with a kind of diligence." When Cottard is knocked down, "the policeman started kicking indiscriminately at the heap lying on the ground" (*TRN,* p. 1471). A human being is reduced to a mere heap. The abstract violence of the purge of collaborators is reflected in this scene, and it recalls the similar tactics of the policeman in *The Stranger*. Rieux responds uneasily that it is perhaps harder to contemplate a guilty man than a dead man; an impassioned assault would have been less chilling than this cold-blooded abuse. The incident underscores the insidious way in which violence, a scorn for the physical individual, becomes impersonal, or a mere habit.

In a violent situation, how can a man protect himself against habituation without abstaining from active struggle? Tarrou, the most passionate rebel in the group, declares that consciousness and will are essential: "One must watch oneself constantly in order to avoid the possibility, in some distracted moment, of breathing into another man's face and infecting him. It is the germ that is natural. Everything else—health, integrity, purity if you like—is a result of the will which must never stop functioning" (*TRN*, p. 1426). Thus the tension—between recognizing the plague as reality and asserting the rebel's need to combat it—must be consciously maintained.

Rambert maintains his equilibrium by steadfastly holding on to his links with the outside world; his commitment is temporary. With Rieux lies the responsibility of decision-making. He has to cultivate an indifference to human suffering in order to be effective: the danger lies in the force of habit, which can transform a temporary expedient into a permanently engrained feature. "A kind of temporary consent" is difficult to maintain (*TRN*, p. 1366).

During the course of their work, the members of the sanitation squads develop a measure of immunity to death and suffering; they assume aspects of the sickness they are fighting. As the numbers of dead increase, efficient disposal of the bodies leads to a total depersonalization of the process, from mass graves to mass cremation: "The progress is undeniable," remarks Rieux grimly (*TRN*, p. 1361). "They had entered the order of the plague itself" (p. 1366). Bureaucracy, once it deals with large numbers, lacks imagination: that is why the plague is so deadly, for it effaces the individual. In such an abstract system, individual lives can be destroyed by a rubber stamp, a Star of David, a bubonic ulcer.

There are obvious parallels here to the aims and dilemmas of the Resistance movement during the Occupation, and to the postwar purges. The particular danger to Rieux is that he has become a judge in his own right: "His role was no longer to cure. His role was to diagnose. To discover, see, describe, write down in the record, and then condemn—that was his task" (*TRN*, p. 1375). He must resist the pleas of family members and insist on the removal of plague victims, often by violent means. How does Rieux differ from the judge, Monsieur Othon? The reference to Othon as a "well brought-up owl" (p. 1239) suggests that the judge is a bird of prey, as well as a symbol of wisdom. Rieux is different because his power is limited, and because he is at one with the victims of the plague: in a sense, they have already been condemned, and Rieux's task is merely to protect the healthy and limit contagion.

Indeed, the activity of the sanitation squads is only permissible insofar as it is limited. If these men had taken power in the city, their methods would have assumed a sinister aspect; as it is, if they should be tempted to indulge in excesses, restraint is still possible. Tarrou had already learned that the dividing line between solidarity and complicity is a fragile one; it is frighteningly easy to assume the role of executioner if there are no imposed limits. Political violence has an aesthetic appeal, a heady comradeship that inspires moral values such as courage, loyalty, and self-sacrifice (Aho, p. 160). There is certainly a sense of this kind of fraternity in Rieux's squads, who allow limited violence to combat total violence. As Tarrou attested, "One must watch oneself constantly" (*TRN*, p. 1426).

From judge, Rieux becomes advocate (a reversal of the progression found in *The Fall*). When the plague is past, he decides to write the story of the Oranais, "to bear witness on behalf of these victims of the plague" (*TRN*, p. 1473), to reveal the physical assaults suffered by those victims. The emphasis on the physical recalls Camus's condemnation of violence in his journalism. Modern weaponry has made the executioner's job easier, for his victim is rarely seen and his suffering not witnessed. In this respect the plague, which is specifically linked with abstraction in the text, is an apt symbol of the dehumanizing process of warfare. The accusation that Camus preferred to fight microbes rather than people, thus keeping his hands clean, masks the real issue: in the game of war, people *are* objectified in this way. Camus's aim is to reiterate the concrete consequences of ideology, the human aspects of war and revolution.

The key to a successful resistance is the correct balance of human values. Each member of Rieux's team has a particular struggle. For Rambert, "abstraction was anything that stood in the way of his happiness" (*TRN*, p. 1293). He has instincts similar to those of Mersault, but he comes to ask himself if he has the right to be happy alone, a thought that never occurred to Mersault. Rieux watches in Rambert "that dreary struggle between individual happiness and the abstraction of the plague" (p. 1293). He does not condemn the desire for happiness, for it is a legitimate human aspiration.

Max-Pol Fouchet thought otherwise. Commenting on *A Happy Death*, he declared that "with this very notion of happiness, I think he avoids the duty of the true revolutionary, who does not talk of happiness but of justice. For the word 'happiness' relates to the individual person and the word 'justice' relates to the collectivity." During the genesis of *The Plague*, however, Camus steadily moved the accent from individual happiness to collective endeavor. Stephan, the unengaged intellectual, was dropped from the text to be replaced by Rambert, who temporarily puts aside personal desires in order to fight the plague. Happiness can thus be a collective endeavor too.

For Rieux, "the generous demands of happiness" are worth more than heroism: individual happiness need not exclude the

rights of others, whereas justice is at best an approximation—
"hideous, laughable justice" (*TRN,* p. 1376). Justice is an abstract idea, open to interpretations that can be murderous;
happiness is tangible, and by maintaining the tenderness in
man, it keeps humanity in perspective. In a television program
broadcast in 1959, Camus reacted to criticisms of the emphasis
he placed on happiness, and pointed out the importance of its
contribution to total health. "Powerful men are often failures in
happiness: that explains why they have no compassion"
(p. 1720).

In affirming the impossibility of absolute justice, Camus was
denying the claims of Marxist ideology. In *The Plague* he depicts
the logical results of a regime that is absolutely just—everyone
is equally vulnerable. The plague symbol is more readily applicable to the Stalinist than to the Fascist variety of totalitarianism, since Fascism, unlike Stalinism, was not random in
its choice of victims. The consequences of the regime are
imprisonment, exile, death, fear, apathy, anger, and sterility—
the death of the child, the absence of women, and the dust of the
city all denote sterility.

Criticism from the Marxist perspective of the political implications of the plague symbol has stressed Camus's failure to
account for the origins of suffering. By inferring that human
nature is inherently evil, and that the true sickness of society is
not solely the result of historical influences, Camus was ignoring the role of social injustice and inequality as well as the
specific historical events that spawned Fascism.

Reich has discussed the aspects of human psychology that
respond to the appeal of Fascism. His argument that "there is
not a single individual who does not bear the elements of fascist
feeling and thinking in his structure" is a convincing one
(p. xvi). As Tarrou remarks, "What is natural is the germ." This
assertion does not however preclude the impact of particular
historical factors on the development of Fascist thought within
the individual. Camus, both in his notebooks and in the text of

The Plague, discusses the social soil in which Fascism can thrive.

Here the choice of Oran as the setting for *The Plague* is relevant on two levels. The Oranais are smugly settled in their petty bourgeois existence, careless of moral problems and unmoved by the beauty of the world of nature. The city is thus a suitable place to experience the absurdity of the world—death, war, and pestilence being manifestations of the arbitrary nature of the universe. On the metaphysical level of the absurd, the inhabitants of Oran succumb because they have failed to maintain the necessary balance. By turning their back on the sea, and enclosing themselves in a snaillike labyrinth of stone, they have cut themselves off from the natural world and its ability to give physical meaning to life, thus making themselves vulnerable to the hostile elements of that world. The plague, with its physical mark, brings home the importance and the vulnerability of the human body.

This abstraction from the physical aspects of the world represents one of the hallmarks of modern society, and results in a "false vision of reality." "Demonstration. That abstraction is evil. It creates war, torture, violence, etc. Problem: how the abstract view holds up when faced with carnal evil—ideology confronted with the torture inflicted in the name of that ideology" (*CII*, p. 133). Nowhere is this separation from the physical more acute than in the city. "This is the era of big cities. The world has been cut off from a part of its truth, from what creates its permanence and balance: nature, the sea, etc." (p. 160). Oran, "the Chicago of our absurd Europe" (*CI*, p. 189), provides the perfect setting for the demonstration.

The Oranais are susceptible to the forces of abstraction by virtue of their detachment from human values. The plague is abstraction in the sense that the body is deprived of joy and restricted to pain. The sea is out of bounds, so that the delicate balance between physical and intellectual activity is upset. "Sea-bathing is banned. It is the sign. It is forbidden to indulge in physical joy—to be reunited with the truth of things" (*CII*, p. 112). The body, our antidote to abstraction, is put aside—a fatal separation.

"Make . . . separation the major theme of the novel" (*CII*, p. 80). In the early stages of his writing, Camus envisaged the physical separation of people as a dominant aspect of the situation brought about by the plague. Rieux is separated from his wife; Stephan the professor writes long and passionate love letters to the absent Jeanne before committing suicide. It was a typical fate for millions during the Occupation. But during the process of revision, Camus deemphasized the passionate expression of love in favor of a wider application of the theme of separation, extending it to the metaphysical and the ideological.

When he commented in his Notebooks that "people who are separated lose their critical faculty" (*CII*, p. 76), he was referring to the internal split in a personality pledged to an abstraction or an ideology. Total devotion results in a lack of balanced judgment. Thus an undiluted concentration on the battle against the plague could be just as dangerous as the plague itself. But the men in Camus's story are never totally separated from their individual passions, even though they may be physically separated from the object of those passions. All the women to whom the male characters are emotionally attached, with the exception of Rieux's mother, are outside the city, unreachable. In an early version of *The Plague*, Rieux thinks of starting a new life with his wife, even though she cannot share his experience of the plague. "But all that was good, for she was woman, that is to say, that which escapes history. She was the warmth and the flesh that he needed after the hideous abstraction of these months of plague" (*TRN*, p. 2002). The illegal swim in the sea, shared by Rieux and Tarrou, with its sensual connotations, is a refreshing reminder of that link with the earth and its natural elements, which the city of Oran has forgotten. Only during this swim are the two men briefly "freed from the city and from the plague" (p. 1429).

In an earlier manuscript version of *The Plague*, Rieux is tempted to let himself sink down into the water: "He felt its attraction and its oblivion" (*TRN*, p. 2001). But in the final version, when the men pass through an unexpected cold current, they are invigorated by it to start the struggle all over again: this reaction is quite different from that of Mersault in *A Happy Death*, for whom the cold current initiates lassitude and death. The search for individual happiness seems to have reached its appointed end; in a collective struggle, one must always begin again. The theme of separation—of man from nature, of man from woman (that is, the male and female aspects of each individual)—underscores Camus's view of the nature of tyranny, which is a separation of mind and body, a false view of reality.

One of the effects of the plague is to destroy the sense of poetry in the world. "Plague. One cannot delight in birdsong in the cool of evening—in the world as it is now. For it is covered with a thick layer of history which its language must penetrate in order to reach us. It is deformed by it. Nothing of the world is felt for its own sake, because each moment . . . is associated with a whole series of images of death and despair. There is no longer a morning without dying, an evening without prisons or a noon without horrible bloodshed" (*CII*, p. 118). The connotations have changed, and make contemplation of natural beauty almost unbearable, for death permeates the world. As Camus comments ironically in his Notebooks, "It seems that writing a poem about spring nowadays is tantamount to serving capitalism" (p. 180). It is certainly true that in *The Plague*, Camus subdued the natural lyricism of his writing in favor of a more dispassionate distance. The result did not satisfy him: "*The Plague* is a pamphlet" (p. 175). Ideology entails the suppression of the poetic: the plague silences Orpheus too.

Camus was pessimistic about our ability to create a new world, as the end of *The Plague* suggests. In 1947 he noted: "One can foresee the day when the silent creation of nature will be replaced entirely by man's creation—hideous and flashing, resounding with the clamors of revolution and war, rumbling with factories and trains, definitive and triumphant in the course of history—having accomplished its task on this earth, which was perhaps to show that all of its grandiose and breathtaking achievements over thousands of years were not worth the fleeting perfume of the wild rose, the valley of olive groves, a beloved dog" (*CII*, p. 193). *The Plague* underscores this world without beauty or imagination, which can herald the death of poetry.

Paradoxically, two characters in *The Plague* succeed in writing despite their imprisonment in the city. Grand, whose name belies his stature and his role in society, is the character proposed as the hero of the story, an "unassuming and insignificant hero who had nothing to offer but a little kindness of heart and an apparently ridiculous ideal" (*TRN*, p. 1331). His ideal, since his wife's departure, is to write a perfect manuscript, but the opening sentence holds him up. He has a mental picture of a scene that he cannot express satisfactorily, but he returns to the task every day after work, always operating within that framework. A victim of the plague, he asks Rieux to burn all his rough drafts; when he unexpectedly recovers, he starts again, succeeds in writing a letter to his wife, and finishes his first sentence, omitting all the adjectives. His recovery suggests that he has the right antibodies.

If Grand is a hero, he is more like Sisyphus than Prometheus. The major themes of separation and *recommencement* are united in this character. He resists the plague, both as part of a collective effort and as an individual, and his victory over the plague and literary sterility are linked with creativity and reunion.

Grand is a sympathetically ironic model of Camus's ideal of the writer and activist. Camus himself identifies more closely with the other successful writer, Rieux (viz. *Corr.*, p. 141), who combines the activities of Grand with that of witness. He shares Grand's acceptance of limits and his steadfast return to the task. (Indeed, all the major characters in *The Plague* share this stubborn insistence on beginning anew: Tarrou in his search for "sainthood," Rambert in his attempts to escape the city, the judge Othon in his new social awareness, Paneloux after the death of the child, the old asthmatic with his bowls of peas.) Rieux also accepts the roles of judge and advocate temporarily, but never loses sight of his true role as witness to the outside world.[2] His position and point of view are admirably supported by the complex narrative techniques Camus employed in this text.[3]

The narrator is a doctor, not a man of letters, who writes a chronicle in which he is the principal character. He disguises his identity, but lets slip certain clues. He claims to be objective, to avoid making changes for art's sake, and he uses a secondary narrator, Tarrou, whose major interest lies in the insignificant details of Oran life.

Rieux avoids writing a first-person narrative because "I" as narrator is automatically separated from the rest of the characters. "I" was an apt technique for Meursault, but not for an integrated member of a fraternal group. That the narrator be integrated, that he participate in the events he narrates is essential: his own experience, rather than reliance on outside reports, is vital to a full physical understanding of the consequences of the plague, for words do not necessarily convey the truth. Rieux's repeated references to the difficulties of writing remind the reader of the inadequacies of art and the lack of artifice in the account. Rieux is identified with the other inhabitants of Oran in his inability to express reality.

While Rieux as primary narrator reveals his naïveté, Tarrou adds a cynical outside view. Here their social origins are relevant to their development: Rieux is the son of a worker, Tarrou the son of an affluent judge. Tarrou is disillusioned: his observation of eccentricities and insignificant details mark him as an outsider. He already knows the plague and hates it, but succumbs in the end despite his growing ability to feel tenderness under the influence of Rieux's mother. His internal separation is too entrenched.

Rambert is another "moral" type from whom Rieux learns. He reminds Rieux of the need for happiness as a balance to physical and metaphysical suffering. His commitment is temporary, but nonetheless valid. If the plague should break out again, Rieux will need such men as allies.

Thus Rieux elucidates Camus's political and artistic position: he is not a didactic theoretician, he has no permanent cures, but he is committed to improving the human lot by means that will not increase its suffering any more than necessary. "Knowledge and memory" (*TRN*, p. 1459) are the only vaccines available, and unfortunately, most memories are short. But Rieux never considers disengagement as a possibility. The old man with the chick-peas provides an example of someone who has stepped outside history. He has thrown away clocks and watches that denote chronological time, and relies on the time recorded by his own circular method of measuring, which for him is an apt record of historical time: nothing ever really changes. The ironic portrayal contains a temptation, but like illness, it was rejected as being a preparation for death rather than a reaction against it.

Camus's position was criticized as defensive rather than offensive, a reaction to the effects of evil rather than to their cause (Picon, d'Astorg). "Despite Camus's contention to the contrary, rebellion alone cannot furnish us with values—the rebel acts for the sake of pre-existent norms, though they may be implicit rather than overtly expressed" (Willhoite, "Politics of Rebellion," p. 414). It is true that Camus was skeptical of "new" values. *The Plague* shows up the bankruptcy of both the bourgeois and the totalitarian systems, but fails to posit a systematic alternative. "What Rieux (I) means is that one must cure everything one can cure—until one *knows* or sees. It's a holding position and Rieux says 'I don't know.' I have backtracked a long way to reach this avowal of ignorance. One begins with a dissertation on parricide and ends up with middle-class morality [*la morale des braves gens*]. It's nothing to be proud of" (*Corr.*, p. 141). Camus's confession of ignorance explains why he reasserted basic humanistic values in the interim. In the course of the verbal duel with Emmanuel d'Astier de la Vigerie, Camus wrote: "My role . . . is not to transform the world, or man. . . . But it is, perhaps, to serve in my own way those few values without which the world, *even a transformed world*, would not be worth living in, without which a man, *even a new man*, would not be worthy of respect" (*E*, p. 368, my emphasis). His anti-Marxist position is here made clear. The price to be paid for revolutionary change is too high: violence, suffering, and death would be multiplied, and used to establish a new order whose goals would already be compromised by the means employed to attain them. *The Plague*'s message is ultimately a reunion of the three levels of interpretation: act *as if* life itself possessed all the meaning necessary, act *as if* a cure for the plague were possible and one could eliminate all unnecessary suffering, act *as if* liberty and justice were possible, but make the means to that end a value in themselves.

It is only a temporary solution. Camus never reached a definitive answer; his stance remained that of questioning and probing, of going back to the beginning and trying again, but never letting go of the values he knew to be legitimate.

Camus's entry into history had marked a period of certainty. "When one sees the wretchedness and the pain the plague causes, one would have to be mad, blind or cowardly to resign oneself to it" (*TRN*, p. 1322). Experience made him question that certainty. Perhaps the Oranais are not wholly innocent, but they do not deserve the suffering they endure. "In every guilty man, there is a measure of innocence. That is what makes absolute condemnation so revolting. People don't think enough about pain" (*Corr.*, p. 141). Camus's obstinate refusal to accept absolutes, his insistence on following the dictates of the body rather than the precepts of abstract ideology, led him into an impasse in the 1950s, when these values came into conflict with other loyalties in the Algerian war of independence.

7

The Limits of Rebellion

En raison de mon incapacité
de raisonner au-delà d'une
expérience vécue, je fais
plus de confiance à une pensée
qui laisse son avenir dans
l'incertitude au risque même
de rester un peu en-deça de
sa propre intuition.
—*Essais*

Before he had finished writing *The Plague*, Camus had reached the conclusion that he should attempt to rationalize the path he had traveled from nihilism to revolt, to trace the historical patterns, in art and politics, in a way that would explain how revolution could betray the basic principles of revolt. The task was not an easy one. In a letter to René Char dated 27 February 1951 he remarked, "Giving birth is long and difficult, and it seems to me that the child is really ugly" (*E*, p. 1627). "I am not a philosopher, and I have never claimed to be one. *The Rebel* does not pretend to be an exhaustive study of revolt. . . . But I wanted merely to retrace an experience, my own. . . . In some respects this book is a confidence, the only kind of confidence, at least, of which I am capable" (p. 743). The degree of personal anguish Camus would later suffer as a result of hostile criticism of *The Rebel* may be attributable in part to his view of it as a confidence.

141]

What led Camus to undertake such a study, and to commit so much of his creative energy to a topic in which he claimed little expertise? In an essay entitled "Defense of *The Rebel*," which evidently dates from the period after the violent polemics the book engendered, and which remained unpublished until 1965, Camus spelled out his motives. "I would not have written *The Rebel* if, during the 1940s, I had not come face to face with men whose system and actions I could not understand. To put it briefly, I could not understand how men could torture other men and continue to look at them" (*E*, p. 1702). Thus the starting point was his own experience of political systems, and the work an attempt to trace the development of those systems in order to pinpoint the moment of fatal flaw. He also must have felt a responsibility to justify his own political commitment in intellectual terms. In spite of himself, he had become by the late 1940s a writer whose works exerted a good deal of influence in many segments of society. By 1950, Camus's political position placed him in opposition to the prevailing currents in the left-wing Parisian intelligentsia; with an analysis of his own experience he hoped to clarify his position to himself and to meet his critics on their own ground.

The political situation in France during the late forties had deteriorated with the increasing chill of the cold war. In 1948 the trade union movement split, and the Communists became more sectarian and isolated as a result, while on the extreme right, de Gaulle's followers were rehabilitating ex-collaborators and Vichyites. The polarization between left and right was exacerbated by their sponsors' activities: the Communist coup in Czechoslovakia and the show trials on the one hand, and the McCarthyite witch hunts in the United States on the other. The Berlin blockade and the Korean War aroused anti-American feeling even among staunch anti-Communists. In 1951 the swing toward the right in French national elections was due in large part to increased fighting in Indo-China and growing unrest in North Africa.

Antagonisms reached new heights in May 1952, when General Ridgeway arrived to take command at SHAPE. The Communists organized demonstrations that were violently suppressed, and the Pinay government made a concerted attempt to outlaw the PCF. They failed, but arbitrary arrests, police frame-ups and illegal searches of party offices served to increase paranoia and to further demoralize the working class.

The late forties also witnessed the demise of the Third Force, as it had been envisaged by the non-Communist left after the Liberation. The Combat group and their allies had aimed at a rejuvenated socialist government that would steer a middle course between the extreme ideologies of left and right. But it rapidly became clear that the French government was dependent on Washington and had in fact established a bourgeois democracy. Once again the working class was the loser. Wages did not keep up with inflation and living standards were hardly better than they had been in the thirties.

Because of the weakness of the French government, the threat of war between the two superpowers on French soil often seemed imminent. The Americans were as unpopular as the Russians. It was hardly an auspicious moment to publish an indictment of Marxist ideology, for that constituted implicit support for Western capitalism. But Camus was more impressed by the immediate danger to Western Europe of Stalin's henchmen taking over in the Eastern bloc. Opposition to American hegemonic trends did not justify defending the interests of Communism.

The Rebel was published in the summer of 1951. It is divided into four major sections. *Metaphysical Revolt*, which Camus defines as a revolt against the human condition, follows a path that can be traced to nihilism and to his own experience of the absurd. Sade, the Romantic dandies, Dostoevsky, Stirner, and Nietzsche are all discussed, and the section ends with an analysis of Lautréamont and the Surrealist movement. *Historical Revolt* deals with revolution as the logical consequence of metaphysical revolt, that is, rebellion against the social condition. The death of kings in the eighteenth century is followed by the death of God in the nineteenth. Nihilism becomes an ideological notion with Hegel, and leads to terrorist activity in Russia. Bakunin and Netchaiev are discussed in this context, as are the "fastidious assassins" of 1905, whom Camus depicted in his 1949 play *The Just Assassins*. Finally, Fascism is dealt with in the context of irrational terror, and Marxism in that of rational terror.

A chapter on *Revolt and Art* outlines art as a pure form of revolt, because it can create a new world outside the limits of history. A concluding section entitled *Thought at the Meridian* condemns the world of organized terrorism and calls for a return to the Greek ideal of beauty and measure, of a balance between history and humanism. Camus praises the political systems of the Scandinavian countries, where socialism has been achieved without recourse to totalitarian means. Revolutionary syndicalism comes close to being an ideal manifestation of revolt, because it proceeds from the individual to the group, rather than being a mass organization that submerges the needs of the individual.

The work represents an anomaly in Camus's published writing in that it lacks the conviction and urgency of his journalistic articles, while possessing little of the polish and subtleties of his fiction. It attempts to encompass vast movements and to reduce them to convenient proportions for subsequent classification. Its criticisms are weakened by a humorless rhetorical style, where one might have expected that polemical vein in which Camus excelled. He seems curiously perverse in being so attached to a text that is generally considered to be his worst; perhaps, like Meursault, he allowed rhetoric to obscure his vision of reality. *The Rebel* is overwritten and lacks the solid theoretical underpinnings that a philosophical essay requires.[1]

The major aim of *The Rebel* is to show how the ideals of revolution have been betrayed. Marx's theories were based on the hypothesis of the perfect state attainable in the future, and are thus comparable to other myths like Christianity, which justify present sufferings with the promise of future happiness. "The future is the only kind of property that the masters grant willingly to the slaves" (E, p. 599). But Marx himself had been betrayed by Communist practice—as Camus saw it in the Soviet Union under Stalin, and in Eastern Europe during the period of the cold war. The revolutionary myth in practice has led to enslavement rather than freedom. Revolt, on the other hand, retains the value of human life as inviolable, and allows pragmatic choices based on personal convictions, whereas ideology, whether revolutionary or reactionary, ignores the individual in favor of the masses.

Camus defended his attack on Marxism as an attempt at demystification. "I thought it appropriate and useful to initiate a reasoned criticism of the one instrument [i.e., the Communist party] that claimed to liberate the workers, so that this liberation might be something other than a long and hopeless mystification. This criticism does not culminate in a condemnation of revolution, but merely of historical nihilism" (E, pp. 1708–9). Camus resolutely refused any doctrine based on faith, and maintained the artist's duty to remain independent, to serve no master but the truth, to criticize injustice at any point on the political spectrum. "The only committed artist is the one who, without refusing combat, refuses to join the regular army, I mean the *franc-tireur*" (p. 1092). The French *franc-tireur* can be translated as a "sniper" or a "free-lance journalist"; both are individualists, and it was in individual action that Camus engaged in politics after the crisis precipitated by the publication of *The Rebel*.

One weakness of Camus's indictment is that it restricts itself to a specific manifestation of Marxism—Stalinism. He never refers to the recent revolution in China, and in his attack on the mass nature of the Communist system, he fails to mention the qualitative improvements brought about by revolution, which affect vast numbers of the oppressed. Indeed, this text is unique in that Camus presents his facts in terms of black and white, and effects the kind of polarization that is absent from his fictional texts and that he abhorred in the views of others. In attempting to confront Marxists on their own terms, he fell into the ideological trap of a Manichaean division.

His text was a warning of the dangers encountered by the rebel when he puts thought into revolutionary practice. The major danger was the transformation of rebel into tyrant, of Prometheus into Caesar. His play *Caligula* had dramatized this process; *The Plague* had defined the limits of revolt and the need to maintain constant vigilance over the temptations of power.

For Camus saw both Nazism and Stalinism as branches of a common root, leading to totalitarian rule and the universe of the concentration camp. In a speech delivered in 1948 entitled "The Witness of Freedom," Camus declared that the revolutionary had degenerated into a conqueror: "What the conqueror seeks, be he on the right or the left, is not unity, which is above all the harmony of opposites, but totality, which is the crushing of differences. The artist makes distinctions where the conqueror levels" (*E*, p. 404). Yet in *The Rebel*, Camus too tends towards this process of *nivellement*. One reason for this unnuanced view was Camus's fear that with the crushing of Fascism in Europe came a widespread relaxation, a smug feeling of comfort in the knowledge of a job well done. But Camus knew that the world of the concentration camp, of torture and violence, was not merely an aberration, the creation of one madman; it was not a new phenomenon invented by Hitler, as colonial history had shown, and it represented an ominous trend for the future. The atrocities perpetrated in Algeria, Vietnam, Cambodia, and Latin America on behalf of varying political interests have since proven that Camus's fears were justified.

If not a Marxist revolution, what kind of process could Camus posit as an alternative route to the same goal? A major omission in his argument is the lack of any *practical* socialist alternative.

He deals at length with the failure of rebels to enact their beliefs in terms of political effectiveness, and who thus fall into the trap of totalitarian methods, yet he fails to formulate means for achieving rebellion in the future. "There is an apparently irreducible contradiction between the moral demands of revolt and the practical requirements of revolution" (Cruickshank, *Literature of Revolt*, p. 112). The final chapter, *Thought at the Meridian*, is an unsatisfactory piece of writing in which logic is transformed into lyricism and proofs into metaphor. In response to critics of the chapter, Camus replied: "I do not claim that Mediterranean thought [*la pensée méditerranéenne*] contains the solution . . . measure is not exclusive to the Mediterranean. Of course measure is the result of facing things squarely. It is not an attribute of particular civilizations, but the product of their greatest tension. First and foremost, it is anything but a state of comfort" (*E*, pp. 1628–29). In large part, it is a reiteration of human values in the face of totalitarian attacks on freedom. Camus stated the case much more coherently and successfully in *The Plague*.

The basic difference between the viewpoints of Camus on the one hand, and of Sartre and Jeanson on the other, has been admirably summed up by Cruickshank:

> Sartre, in his essay on Baudelaire, takes the opposite view to Camus on the question of the relative merits of revolt and revolution. The aim of the metaphysical rebel, he says, is to keep intact the abuses from which he suffers so as to be able to continue his rebellion against them. The revolutionary, on the other hand, is actively concerned to change the world of which he disapproves. He seeks future values by inventing them and fighting for them here and now (ibid., p. 103).

Camus's failure to arrive at a synthesis is due in part to his "inability to reason beyond a lived experience" (*E*, p. 1615. Cf. Gay-Crosier). In his experience, every utopia produced its opposite, which in turn demanded renewed revolt. Rather than transcending that opposition and venturing into the unknown, Camus returned to basic moral principles and retraced the path again. But there was no way out, as long as he refused to go beyond the limits of his knowledge. He was well aware of the banality of "middle-class morality"; but even the temporary waiving of moral principles engendered too high a cost in human pain and risked the permanent abolition of such principles in political action. As for Sartre, he may have found the gulag repulsive, but he was equally disgusted by the glee with which the right welcomed the news of their existence (viz. his letter to Camus in *Les Temps modernes*). Camus, however, could not place human suffering on the same level as political opportunism.

Camus's moral position contradicted his social instincts. Injustice creates unhappiness, to which Camus's answer was rebellion and the freedom to pursue happiness. It was in this action that people developed solidarity with their fellows, but it could not change the structures that cause injustice. Nonviolent reform had not worked in postwar France, although admittedly outside influences played a major role in determining the course of events. But fundamentally, Camus was less interested in theory than in praxis. He wanted to see conditions improved now, rather than postponing partial change until the historical moment for radical change might be seized.

One of his activities illustrates his frustrations in an overpoliticized society. When he helped form the Groupe de liaison internationale in 1948, he had socialist and syndicalist support in helping political refugees. Camus was extremely effective in getting visas and work-permits, and was impatient with members who wanted to spend time defining their creed and calling for self-criticism and rehabilitation (McCarthy, pp. 241–42). The group finally broke up because of ideological infighting, which seemed far less important to Camus than providing refugees with the opportunity for a new life.

In 1945, when Camus published his *Notes on Revolt*, he had

asserted that the answer might be found in art (*E*, p. 1696). *The Rebel* reveals that Camus still questioned political action based on a utopian ideology, and believed that art might prove a better guide than philosophy. Camus may serve as his own case in point. Certainly *The Plague* is a more successful text than *The Rebel*, because Camus controlled the elements he could use. He could "correct" creation in a fictional text because the writer has unlimited power to impose order. In political terms those means amount to unacceptable tyranny.

The *Rebel* had a mixed reception. The fact that many favorable and even laudatory reviews came from critics other than Catholics and conservatives has been obscured by the notoriety of the public quarrel between Sartre and Camus. In May 1952 Francis Jeanson wrote a damning review of the book in *Les Temps modernes*. Camus, believing that Sartre, as editor-in-chief, was indirectly responsible, wrote a reply addressed to "Monsieur le Directeur." This letter, followed by lengthy rebuttals from both Jeanson and Sartre, was published in *Les Temps modernes* in August 1952.

The attack on Camus was almost inevitable in view of the political climate in 1952. Polarization was extreme: the Communists were under heavy attack and Jeanson's review coincided with the famous incident of the "carrier pigeons" and Jacques Duclos's arrest.[2] The comic aspects of the affair did not detract from the alarm aroused by arbitrary and illegal police methods. Camus's book could not be interpreted as a personal statement in such a heavily polarized atmosphere; *Les Temps modernes* had to denounce it as a political statement related to the current situation.

The major thrust of Jeanson's criticism lay in his accusation that Camus, by denouncing Marxism as the revolutionary ideal, betrayed the working class and objectively served the interests of the bourgeoisie. In a television program commemorating the twentieth anniversary of Camus's death, Jeanson reiterated this viewpoint with undiminished anger. The position of Sartre and

Jeanson was that although Russian Communism had many defects, the Communist movement was the only one that had any chance of effectively engendering a social and economic revolution, and should therefore be supported. Sartre commented that if Camus denounced both Fascism and Communism, he should retire to the Galapagos Islands. Camus's unpublished response to this sally reiterated the need to search for an alternative. "I do not believe that this liberation [of the working-class] will have advanced a single step if we have merely replaced bankers with policemen" (*E*, p. 1708).

The *ad hominem* barbs were perhaps more painful than objective criticism of a philosophical and political viewpoint, and Camus himself was not blameless in the exchange of personal comments. An unfortunate tone was set by Jeanson in the title of his first article, "Albert Camus, ou l'âme révoltée" ("Albert Camus, or the soul in revolt"); it indicated a satirical comment on the man rather than on the ideas expressed in the book under review. Camus was equally unjust in accusing his critics of never having "placed more than their armchair in the direction of history" (*Les Temps modernes*, August 1952, p. 332). Sartre's perceptive comment on the climate of the times noted that "friendship too tends to become totalitarian" (ibid., p. 334).

But Sartre's letter voices a feeling of personal betrayal. "You were for us—tomorrow you may be again—the admirable union of a person, an action, and a work. It was in '45: we discovered Camus the resistant, as we had discovered Camus the author of *The Stranger*. . . . You were close to being exemplary. For you summed up the conflicts of the time, and you transcended them by your ardent living of them. You were a *person* of the most rich and complex kind" (ibid., pp. 345–46). Sartre had helped place Camus on his "portable pedestal," and now blames the idol for having feet of clay. He criticizes Camus for refusing to change as the real world was altered by historical events, yet voices disappointment that he is no longer the same heroic figure "discovered" in 1945.

The quarrel and its attendant publicity obfuscated other problems associated with the text of *The Rebel*. Apart from the basic disagreement on the role of the Communist party, and on the dividing line between rebellion and revolution, another subject was raised that would continue to haunt Camus's thought and work. Jeanson, who had been actively engaged in the liberation movement in Algeria, emphasized the fact that in his survey of oppression, Camus had not mentioned colonialism. Richard Crossman, in an article expressing all the irritation of the active politician reading "a book about politics written by a distinguished man of letters," also points out that "M. Camus's account of Marxism . . . contains no reference to the colonial problem, an omission all the more extraordinary on the part of a Frenchman writing in 1952." Sartre felt that Camus's inability to discuss the issue of colonialism in Indo-China was due to his confusion over the identity of the masters and the slaves. "If we apply your principles, the Vietminh are the colonized and therefore slaves, but they are Communists and therefore tyrants" (*Les Temps modernes*, p. 343). This explanation does not account for Camus's omission of any analysis of the Algerian situation, however, for the Communist party was never a factor in the struggle, and the situation was quite different from that in Indo-China.

His failure to deal with colonialism specifically in a work about oppression obviously needs some explanation. There is in fact one reference to colonialism in the text, in a footnote. Camus describes the total destruction by the Nazis of Lidice, a village in Czechoslovakia, as a kind of mystical vengeance that went as far as emptying the graveyard of its dead. "It is striking to note that atrocities reminiscent of these excesses were committed in the colonies (India, 1857; Algeria, 1945, etc.) by European nations that were in fact acting in accordance with the same irrational belief in racial superiority" (*E*, p. 590).

There are several possible explanations for Camus's failure to deal specifically with the phenomenon of colonialism, apart from this footnote that drew analogies with Nazism. Events in Indo-China as well as in Algeria at the time of writing made the process of decolonization a contemporary issue in European politics. Camus had always maintained that colonialism was a particular facet of Fascism; in prior and subsequent articles, he repeatedly brought out the similarities between the colonialist venture and other forms of totalitarian rule. The common denominator was servitude, justified by a mystique. In *The Rebel* Camus explained his view of the difference between Fascism and the Russian example of Communism: "It is inaccurate to consider the aims of Fascism and of Russian Communism as identical. The former represents the exaltation of the executioner by the executioner himself. The latter, which is more dramatic, the exaltation of the executioner by the victims. The former never dreamed of liberating all mankind, but only of liberating a few by subjugating the rest. The latter, in its fundamental principles, aims to liberate all men by enslaving them all, provisionally" (*E*, p. 648).

Colonialism obviously fits into the Fascist world of selective liberation and servitude. But by 1950 Camus felt that the Marxist view of history was founded on a "mystification" similar to that which had been used to justify colonial conquest. "The end of history, within the limits of our condition, can have no definable meaning. It can only be the object of a faith or of a new mystification. A mystification that today is just as powerful as that which once based colonialist oppression on the need to save the souls of the infidel" (*E*, p. 801). Although he attacks both Fascism and Stalinism, he finds the latter worse, "more dramatic," a more insidious danger than the almost universally abhorrent Fascism that most Europeans have now experienced at close hand. Stalinism is his main target in *The Rebel*, rather than rightist oppression. The latter he had always opposed, but his resolutely anti-Communist stance was of more recent origin, and had become obsessive.

A hypothesis based on the character of the writer himself rather than on his text is also viable. While Camus, as an Algerian, could be more objective about the French political scene than those raised in the hothouse of the Parisian intelligentsia, he was physically involved in the Algerian tragedy. He not only knew that the situation could have been avoided, but he also realized that his own action had been useless, "the story of a failure" (*E*, p. 899). *The Rebel* was an attempt to intellectually rationalize his political beliefs, which were based, more often than not, on visceral reactions to situations. If these beliefs were impossible to justify rationally, then it would be less painful to suppress them than to evaluate them openly.

The Rebel is uncharacteristic of Camus in its polarized presentation of differences. But his view of the situation in Algeria could not allow him to see it simply in terms of master and slave. As Alastair Horne has shown, the struggle for Algerian independence involved seven separate wars; some of the factions involved may have been more just than others, but Camus never gave unmitigated support to any of them, for he could never ignore the rights of the losers in any single solution.

Whether Camus omitted discussion of the problem of colonialism in *The Rebel* unconsciously, or objectively deemed it irrelevant to his argument, he was certainly stung by allegations that he no longer cared. "It has been rashly stated that I am not interested in the victims of colonialism, despite hundreds of pages that prove that for the last twenty years, even when M. Hervé and his friends abandoned the struggle for tactical reasons, I have never really engaged in any other struggle but that one" (*E*, p. 747). The reference to Pierre Hervé and his article in *La Nouvelle Critique* reveals Camus's bitterness at criticism from the Communists, who had turned away from the PPA in 1937, and who had supported the brutal repression of disturbances in Sétif in May 1945. "Repression is not the answer to the questions raised by colonized peoples, by the politics of the slums or social injustice" (*E*, p 779).

Within the text of *The Rebel*, Camus offered no philosophical or political answer to the conflict in Algeria. His situation was such that "he was bound to harvest the suspicion of the colonized people and the anger of his own family" (Memmi, "Camus," p. 95). And if his aim was to meet the Parisian intelligentsia on its own ground, then he certainly would not wish to include Algeria in his discussion, for he felt that the view from Paris was a simplistic one, and the solution naïve and short-sighted.

The extent to which Camus was involved in the problems of his time is revealed in the fictional worlds he created during the early and mid-1950s. *The Fall* and *Exile and the Kingdom* bear witness to the conflicts that continued to obsess him and which he tried to resolve through the medium of creative work. They reflect too the increasing complexity and ambiguity of the world that *The Rebel* had failed to capture. *The Rebel* and its aftermath marked a distinct break with the Parisian intellectual scene; Camus's confession of ignorance was hardly a compelling argument except to conservatives. But Camus's view of the world and its reality was wider, and in the long term, his humanistic stance led him to a more accurate premonition of future trends and of the failure of Communism as a political means of achieving social justice and freedom in Europe.

It did not, however, help him to come to terms with Algerian independence. He had no illusions as to the effects of such a move; a permanent exile. Nadine Gordimer, writing more than twenty years later of her comparable situation in South Africa, voices an awareness of lost identity: "However hated and shameful the collective life of apartheid and its structures has been to us, there is, now, the unadmitted fear of being without structures. The interregnum is not only between two social orders, but between two identities, one known and discarded, the other unknown and undetermined" (p. 22).

The last published fiction of Camus reveals his search for an identity. *The Fall* is centered on Camus the Frenchman, *Exile and the Kingdom* on the Algerian within him: the texts attempt a synthesis of French and Algerian, as well as of artist and political man.

8

True Believers or False Prophets

Je vous refuse le droit de
vous croire vous-même les
mains nettes. Nous sommes
dans un noeud de l'histoire
où la complicité est totale.
—Réponse à Emmanuel d'Astier

Oui, croyez-moi, pour vivre
dans la vérité, jouez la
comédie.
—"Pourquoi je fais du théâtre"

"You are not on the right, Camus, you are up in the air."
Thus Jeanson defined Camus's political stance in 1952, a year
after the publication of *The Rebel*, during the bitter exchange
between its author and the staff of *Les Temps modernes*. Jeanson's comment was designed to reduce Camus to irrelevancy in
the current political arena. Camus subsequently withdrew from
public participation in most political activities, with the notable exception of his 1956 appeal for a civilian truce in Algiers,
and appearances in aid of refugees from Franco's Spain.

As he was nearing the end of the manuscript of *The Rebel*, a
work which had demanded laborious preparation and rewriting
during a period of declining health, he twice mentioned in the
Notebooks his need to compose something entirely different.
"In the spring when everything is completed, write *everything I*

155]

feel. Little things at random. . . . When everything is completed, write a jumble. Anything that comes to mind" (*CII*, p. 299). This need for spontaneous self-expression, combined with Camus's period of stocktaking in the aftermath of the furor over *The Rebel*, resulted in a transformation of his experience into fiction. *The Fall*, originally planned as the opening story of the collection *Exile and the Kingdom*, eventually grew into an independent work.

It is the most brilliant and complex of Camus's texts, and is quite different in its form and tone from any of the earlier narrative works. It contains many themes with which the reader is already familiar, but what is clearly new is the heavily ironic mode, a mode also found, but in a lighter vein, in "Jonas." The sharpness of the irony might lead us to suppose that the narrative closely resembles the author's personal experiences, the pain of which can be alleviated by mockery: Camus invites us to consider this possibility by including details of his own life in Clamence's biography.

In an intricate monologue directed at a fellow Frenchman whom he meets in a bar in the port area of Amsterdam, Jean-Baptiste Clamence relates the story of his life and the philosophy that has influenced his decisions. After a highly successful career as a defense attorney in Paris, Clamence's perception of himself and the world is changed, first by his failure to dive into the Seine to save a drowning woman, then by the mocking laughter he hears one night on the Pont des Arts. Subsequent attempts to escape the memory of the event—in sexual excess or travel—prove ineffective, and he decides on a radical change of life and milieu. He moves to Amsterdam and takes up the role of "judge-penitent," accosting strangers in the bar and inducing them to indulge in a similar confession.

In an article published in *L'Express* on 8 October 1955 Camus described the experience of an intellectual in a

> country torn apart by the shopkeepers who own it and the po-
> licemen who covet it. . . . The intellectual may speak, in a hesi-

tant voice, but in vain. It is not a response that will greet him, but curses and idiotic polemics. According to what he says, his topic and his mood, he will indirectly help the shopkeepers, or unwittingly encourage the policemen. He will thus have rendered a disservice to those he loves, and as sole recompense will have to endure the fact of having enemies, even though it goes against his nature. In preference to such sorrow, should he not opt for silence, and that irony that helps him live his life? Thus the man with scabies tosses in his bed, scratching his sores. (*E*, pp. 1747–48)

The Fall represents the scratching and bleeding of those wounds, even though in the text it is not the hero Clamence who suffers from mange, but his camel coat.

Certainly Camus shares with Clamence the expression of self-awareness, of a radical reevaluation of past stands (cf. Girard, "Camus's Stranger Retried"). The last published Notebooks speak of the pain: "Henceforth I knew the truth about myself and others. But I could not accept it. I squirmed under it, cut to the quick" (*brûlé au rouge*, which recalls Clamence tossing in his bed, alternating between heat and cold; *CII*, p. 337). Clamence learned the same truth: "First I needed this perpetual laughter, and those laughing, to teach me to see clearly inside myself, to discover that I was not simple." Only then does he recognize "the profound duplicity of the [human] creature" (*TRN*, p. 1518). This duplicity is echoed by the text itself; truth and falsehood are hard to distinguish. Indeed, the distinction becomes irrelevant.

It is not surprising that those who knew Camus stressed the autobiographical aspects of the work. As Lottman remarks, the refusal of a man to save a drowning woman had obvious symbolic significance during the Algerian war, and the literal quotations from Sartre's letter in *Les Temps modernes* revealed barely disguised keys to Camus's responses. But *The Fall* is certainly more than Camus's autobiography. It provides a caricatural portrait of the Camus whom Sartre depicted in his "Reply to Albert Camus," as well as aspects of Sartre's own brand of existentialism. "*The Fall*, while it constitutes a parody of existentialist man, which was meant as a counter to Sartre's attacks, is nevertheless, on the level of the psychology of its hero at least, a profoundly existentialist work" (Fitch, "Une Voix," p. 65). It gives an ironic picture of the postwar French intellectual, and it debunks the idealized view of Camus that his admirers had created. Camus once said in an interview that the creative writer expresses in his work not so much his personal experience as his desires and temptations. Clamence's portrait is an accurate study of the Don Juan neurosis as well as of the Icarus complex (see Lazere and Sperber); perhaps the writing of it exorcised at least some of the temptations that beset the author.

According to the psychoanalyst Barchilon, "It is highly probable . . . that in order for Camus to write this masterpiece, he had to achieve some distance from what he described, that to a degree it was *located in his conflict-free sphere*" (p. 237). It did not, however, solve the gnawing problem of sterility; the award of the Nobel Prize for literature in 1957 coincided with a crisis that would suggest that an objective appraisal of the past had not successfully cleared away all inner conflict. Indeed, his exclamation of *Je suis châtré* ("I'm castrated") in reaction to the award is in itself an instance of unresolved feelings.

Conor Cruise O'Brien has suggested that Clamence poised on the bridge reflects Camus's position on the Algerian situation; he was unable to take the plunge into what would certainly prove uncomfortable waters. This would compare Clamence's choice between a dangerously cold dip and a guilty conscience with Camus's choice between what he regarded as two evils: the reactionary colonial administration in Algeria and the increasingly violent FLN. But just as he sought a middle way between Communism and capitalism, so Camus sought a moderate alternative in Algeria. Clamence could have looked for an alternative too—that of summoning help for the drowning woman. But he deliberately failed to do this and carefully neglected to discover any further details of the event. He refused to compromise between two absolutes. O'Brien's comparison thus suggests that Camus chose to withdraw from the mêlée and let

Algeria die, and there may well have been times when he wished
the whole problem would go away. But Clamence refused to take
the plunge because there was no one present to witness his
cowardice, whereas Camus was in a situation where every action, or lack of it, took place in the spotlight of publicity. The
action he did choose sought to avoid the public eye. In the circumstances, supporting the FLN would have been the easier
way out of the impasse: the failure to make that decision did not
necessarily denote cowardice, nor a refusal to take a political
stand.

In *The Rebel*, Camus had rejected two forms of escape from
the state of permanent rebellion: religion and history. The political movements that lie on the same axes as these philosophical
tenets are Fascism and Marxism—a vertical, hierarchical movement and a horizontal, egalitarian one. Camus had always denounced Fascism, first in its paternalistic, colonialist form in
Algeria, and then during its Nazi period. And he found the notion of history as an inevitable progression on a horizontal plane
untenable too. In *The Fall* the background reflects a world
where history reigns supreme.

Clamence's Amsterdam is a special kind of hell. Nominally
the epitome of a merchant-class city, it is here endowed with a
dreamlike quality quite untypical of the Dutch mentality. In
contrast to Dante's descending circles of Hell, Clamence's con-
centric rings formed by canals are on a horizontal plane. Everything is flat, and the horizon is not visible. It is a foggy
landscape, hemmed in by sterile waters, a cycle of endless repetition. History repeats itself as irony: Descartes's house now
shelters the insane. There is no sun, no warmth from the sky to
make the waters a welcoming environment, a source of inspiration. Even the doves circle but never descend. "It has been said
that great ideas come into the world on the feet of a dove"
(*E*, p. 1096). Clamence, among other things, portrays the writer
robbed of his creative environment, his inspiration. The murky
gray surroundings suppress the creative spirit.

The bourgeois Clamence had been used to looking at the

world in terms of vertical hierarchies. Images of "high" and "low" pervade the text. He had seen himself as a liberal humanist, the advocate of the widow and the orphan, generous and altruistic. Successful and self-assured, he looked down on the judges to whom he presented his cases, and was looked up to by the needy who sought his aid. Actor, Don Juan, conqueror—he fitted all these roles. But his whole personality is undermined by the strange laughter he hears one night on the Pont des Arts; his success as the "artist" of his life is called into question. Then his outlook undergoes a revolution: "I made a sudden about-face" (*faire une volte-face* can also mean "to change sides"; *TRN*, p. 1495). He enters the "universe of the trial" and comes face to face with "the affirmation of general guilt. All men are criminal without being aware of it. The objective criminal is precisely the one who believed he was innocent" (*E*, p. 645). The word *objective* can be understood also in the Marxist sense—all men are criminal by force of circumstance. Nothing is what it once seemed when subjected to this new optic; commonplace values are revealed as sham, virtue is pride, and kindness an assertion of superiority. Clamence had assumed the father's role in relation to widows and orphans, even while despising the paternalism of judges. Being a man of absolutes, he seeks a total escape from the scorn he now suspects on all sides, and plunges into a life of debauchery and excess. "Thus I lived from one day to the next with no other continuity but of me-me-me" (*TRN*, p. 1501). Finally, in failing health and bereft of friends, he leaves Paris and his past behind him, and settles in a bare room in Amsterdam, with no books, in threadbare clothes and the garb of a new identity.

This is the stage of the *malconfort* or little-ease, the medieval prison cell designed to prevent the prisoner from standing upright or lying down. Clamence lives on the horizontal plane of history, but his instincts still lead him to think in terms of vertical planes: "I had to live in the *malconfort* . . . live on the diagonal" (*TRN*, p. 1531), a transversal position somewhere between the two axes.

The *malconfort* is the alternative in the modern age to a choice between absolutes. It symbolizes the state of constant discomfort and wakefulness that makes rebellion so difficult to maintain. In that cell, "sleep was a fall [*une chute*], wakefulness a cramped crouching position" (p. 1531). Clamence reflects the taste for absolutes in his assumption that while lack of self-awareness implied total innocence, so self-knowledge must imply total guilt. His monologue is self-criticism and at the same time a parody of its practice. The text of *The Fall* constitutes Clamence's attempt to talk his way out of the *malconfort*, and into the ease of an absolute stance. Having renounced one personality, that of the comfortable bourgeois liberal, he must now forge another. "When one has no personality, one must get hold of a method" (*TRN*, p. 1481). Clamence's method is simple: by becoming a penitent and denouncing his past, he may invite others to confess similar sins, so that he may in turn judge them and recapture his dominant position. In the past, Clamence had been able to live "with impunity; free of any duty, shielded from judgment as from sanctions, I reigned freely in an Edenic light" (p. 1489). His liberty was without responsibility, since others pronounced judgment: when judgment came in the form of mockery, he found it unbearable.

He discovers, as had Camus, that "these days judges, defendants and witnesses exchange places with exemplary speed" (*E*, p. 800). So he finds himself in Amsterdam, free of his past life and its stigma, but in a world with no points of reference. Thus the hero of our time, to escape the ambiguous demands of this limbo, looks for another system, "an impeccable organization" (*TRN*, p. 1535). His *volte-face* sets him in search of a new totalitarian order, in which he can leave the indecisive parameters of the *malconfort* for the clear-cut, roomy dimensions of a cell. "Prison . . . prison or the islands, the peace of the cell"[1] is what Clamence dreamed of in an earlier draft of the text (*TRN*, p. 2036). In *The Rebel* Camus asserted that "they run . . . to party headquarters[2] as they used to fling themselves down at the foot of the altar. That's why the period that boldly claims to be the most rebellious offers only a choice between two orthodoxies. The real passion of the twentieth century is servitude" (*E*, p. 637). Clamence, by looking down on French values and institutions, thought himself a rebel, whereas in fact he was only a conformist.

The theme of Clamence as a failed artist and political turncoat is also supported by a comment in Camus's Notebooks: "Most failed men of letters turn to Communism. It's the only position that allows them to judge artists from above. From this point of view, it's the party of thwarted vocations" (*CII*, p. 272). And like the Parisian philosophers he mocks, Clamence turns to the cruellest party: "I discovered within myself sweet dreams of oppression" (*TRN*, p. 1504); the ambiguity is pointed up by the fact that he desires to be both oppressor and oppressed.

Clamence thinks only in terms of absolutes; he exchanges a world of fast-flowing rivers like the Seine for a world of still, stagnant waters, the canals of Amsterdam. He is a prisoner of history, whereas d'Arrast, in "The Growing Stone," who can control the course of the river and use it for the benefit of others, remains free to act according to his values. Clamence, who considered himself a rebel, exemplifies the ease with which the unwary rebel can become an ideologue: he reveals the cycle of modern revolution, betrayed by the desire for power. Hence his "fall," a constant slippage into a new form of oppression.

For Clamence is searching for a father. Germaine Brée believes that he represents a whole generation of men during the mid-twentieth century who had been deprived of fathers as a result of two world wars (Barchilon, p. 222). The absence of father-figures in any sphere of interpretation is remarkable, and helps to explain the desire for a structure of authority. Not only does Clamence not have a father, but neither did his namesake, John the Baptist. The man who threatens to put Clamence in his place at the traffic light might have been a father-figure, but he turns out to be "a lean little man with a pincenez and knickers" (*TRN*, p. 1501), over whom Clamence towers by a head. The sun, the masculine principle in nature, exists only in Clamence's memory, for it never shines on the soggy hell of Amsterdam. God the Father is dead, no longer in fashion among twentieth-century intellectuals: "For the person who is alone, without a god and without a master, the days weigh terribly. So one must choose a master" (p. 1544). Once the defender of liberty, Clamence is now "an enlightened partisan of servitude" (p. 1543). Even the just judges have disappeared.[3] The public is taken in by a clever imitation, but the judges are fakes. So without fathers, man must make his own rules, his own judgments, create his own values. In the whirling mists, "we walk on with no landmarks [repère], we cannot estimate our speed. We move forward and nothing changes. It is not sailing, but dreaming." Clamence longs for the clarity exemplified by classical Greece: "No confusion: in that clear light, everything was a landmark" (p. 1525).[4]

The story of Clamence in the prison camp in North Africa illustrates the same theme. The pope, spiritual father to millions of believers, has lost touch with his people, so the prisoners need a new, personal pope who will take care of their needs. Clamence puts forward his candidacy half in jest, and once elected, exercises absolute power, since he controls the distribution of water. What Quilliot calls the "theme of the degeneration of power" (TRN, p. 2014) is exemplified by Clamence's change of attitude from "we" to "I," the exact reverse of the rebel's path; his own survival becomes his paramount concern, even though he tries to veil this truth behind the assertion of altruistic motives. Thus Clamence fails too as a father.

Having rejected one paternalistic system, Clamence now seeks another. Since he deems himself to have been a fake philanthropist, there is no reason for him not to become a fake Marxist. "Do not lies eventually put you on the path of truth?" (TRN, p. 1537). The only way to establish truth is through power. "Every man needs slaves as he needs fresh air. . . . 'You don't talk back to your father,' you know the expression?" Discussion can only lead to ambiguity, while "power, on the contrary, decides everything." Clamence joins his contemporary philosophers in their current mode. "We no longer say, as we did in more naïve times, 'I think this. What are your objections?' We've become lucid. We have replaced dialogue with communiqué. 'This is the truth,' we say. 'Argue if you like, we are not interested. But in a few years you'll have the police to show you that I'm right'" (pp. 1498–99).

The whole *récit* illustrates the terrorism of the monologue, a topic already noted by Camus in the second volume of his Notebooks. "Progress and true greatness lie in dialogue between equals and not in the gospel, soliloquized and dictated from the top of an isolated mountain" (*CII*, p. 162). Though Clamence has now stripped himself of wealth, position, and possessions, he still sees himself as a "burning bush" with a special mission. By adopting the patrons of the sleazy Mexico-City bar as his new clients, he has not changed his attitudes. The grunting barman and the petty thieves in the establishment are viewed with the same scorn as Clamence sensed in the gaze of others upon himself. The important thing is still hierarchy; Clamence is a more daring thief than the professionals in the port area of Amsterdam.

Clamence is an untrustworthy narrator, and language can no longer be considered a trustworthy tool of communication. It purports to speak the truth but remains ambiguous. It has a dreamlike quality, like Amsterdam itself. The whole situation might well seem like a bad dream to Clamence's guest, and yet the voice haunts the reader, rather like a subtle Big Brother intruding on his sleep. Clamence's newly adopted role of judge-penitent is a falsehood: he is neither truly penitent, since he has retained the basic structure of his past life, nor is he a true judge, because justice has been locked away in his cupboard, and separated from mercy. In 1949 Camus had written in his Notebooks: "Marxism is a philosophy of litigation, but without jurisprudence" (*CII*, p. 286). Clamence typifies this interpretation of

Marxist philosophy at the same time as he reveals the insidious links with the bourgeois mentality. Camus commented in 1954, in relation to *The Stranger*, that "the universe of the trial . . . is just as bourgeois as it is Nazi or Communist" (*E*, p. 1611). For all his radical change in the way he lives, Clamence's nature is fundamentally unaltered.

Clamence begins by denouncing others—"them"—and then moves slyly to include himself and his interlocutor. But this "deliberate and paternalistic recourse to the 'we' " is not a fraternal gesture; rather, it is a means of dominating the other, another example of the untrustworthy nature of language (Abbou, "Structures," p. 123). *The Fall* echoes Camus's remarks on Brice Parain in 1944. "This world, in which words are prostituted" has scarcely changed, and Clamence himself personifies the notion that language expresses "the definitive solitude of man in a silent world" (*E*, p. 1673).

Clamence interprets the world for his interlocutor, in the same way as Meursault's lawyer speaks on his behalf, using the "I" form, in *The Stranger* (Lévi-Valensi, "*La Chute*," p. 51). Clamence's victim has no chance to offer any argument or defense, since Clamence picks up the beginning of his responses and then interprets the unspoken end of the sentence. Like Meursault's lawyer, he seems to be on the side of his current "client," but in fact he is not interested in spontaneous reactions to his presentation, only the reactions he has orchestrated in advance. His monologue represents the dictatorship of the police state, dialogue replaced by communiqué. Not only is the victim unable to defend himself, he is also unable to pass judgment, since his words are suppressed (cf. Maillard, p. 11). Allowing the other to speak can be dangerous, as Meursault discovered. In the second part of his story, Meursault allows others to judge, and even to assume his identity, and is condemned to death.

The text also represents the demise of language. "All things considered, is not Clamence an allegory of speech [*la parole*]:

not only a man who speaks, but language itself, indulging in a desperate attempt to take over a world which it knows, however, to be bereft of its splendor and its innocence?" (Lévi-Valensi, "*La Chute*," p. 51). Language as a form of power has been abused to such an extent, particularly by politicians and lawyers, that it has lost its ability to discriminate, to play with nuances. Good style is out of fashion; the terse forms of command are more popular. Yet Clamence's discourse is as elusive as the setting of the narrative. Time sequences are deliberately misordered, and at times the rational thread of meaning is lost in a feverish logorrhea. "I'm losing the beat," says Clamence (*TRN*, p. 1544), as he weaves an ever more elaborate web.

Clamence is not only a hero of our time, but he is also an artist of our time, struggling to create in a hostile and ambiguous environment. The dual role of judge-penitent is analogous to that of activist-artist, and the essential duplicity of that role lies in the fact that the rules are different for life and art. Political activism involves judgment. In 1940 Camus had declared it immoral to judge a historical situation from the outside; one had to be involved in order to know the truth. Camus denounces Marxism as an accusatory system, yet he recognizes that judgment is an inevitable factor in any political action. The artist, on the other hand, needs to withdraw from history in order to create. "For me, working conditions have always been those of monastic life: solitude and frugality. Apart from frugality, they are contrary to my nature, so that work is a violence I inflict upon myself" (*Corr.*, p. 231). Another letter to Grenier refers to work as "these long days of penitence" (p. 173). And in his Notebooks, Camus refers directly to the duplicity of the artist: "Dishonesty of the artist when he pretends to believe in the democracy of principles. For he then denies the most profound aspects of his experience and that which is the great lesson of art: hierarchy and organization. That this dishonesty is sentimental does not diminish it. It leads to the slavery of the factories and the camps" (*CII*, p. 338). And the final entry in the published Notebooks declares that "every accomplishment is a servitude. It obliges you to seek a higher accomplishment" (CII, p. 345).

Withdrawal, violence, penitence, hierarchy, servitude: these are all aspects of political life that Camus decries, yet they are fundamental to his function as an artist. How can he denounce a concept in one realm and submit to it in another? Ambiguity is no longer an attribute only of language, but also of what words denote. If the artist-penitent submits to the tyranny of his art, can he also be a rebel? Or, to rephrase the dilemma in Gordimer's words: "The morality of life and the morality of art have broken out of their categories in social flux. If you cannot reconcile them, they cannot be kept from one another's throats, within you" (p. 26).

For Camus, life and art could not be totally separate. But their conflicting demands created more and more anguish, and exacerbated the ever-present fear of sterility. In 1957 he wrote to Grenier: "[I am] so discouraged that I no longer dare sit down in front of a white page. Wouldn't it be better to drop everything, to give up this fruitless effort that for years has prevented me from being completely happy and relaxed anywhere, which takes me away from other people in a rather reprehensible way, and from a large part of myself? I could work in the theater, I'd be free, happy perhaps. . . . I find it hard to write even a letter" (Corr., p. 213).

It is significant that Camus's preoccupation with his art and its conflicts with political activism reaches an obsessive pitch in both The Fall and Exile and the Kingdom; that is, during a period in which he withdrew from public participation in politics. The Stranger and The Plague, written during periods of active commitment to an unambiguous political cause, reveal a positive integration of the dual claims. But the war in Algeria left him with no clearcut parameters; his ideas were proving inadequate in the face of political choices that contradicted human values.

The *malconfort*, which reflects the necessary tensions involved in maintaining rebellion, is also a metaphor for the situation in which Camus found himself in relation to Algeria, as
well as that of the artist unable to write. When Clamence
dreams of a roomy prison cell, it is of a place where the limits are
such that creative activity can take place. But the *malconfort*
makes it impossible to forget one's body: like illness, it can
make one sterile. The universe of the prison can be a creative
one, provided the links with the outside world remain intact:
the universe of the trial is sterile.

The dual nature of the *malconfort* with its two-way torture is
reinforced by the duplicity of the landscape, of human nature,
and finally of moral philosophy itself. Thus judgment becomes
invalid too. That is why Clamence is not wholly at ease in the
police state he envisages. Even as he tries to escape the ambiguity of his environment to find clarity, he realizes that it merely
constitutes another kind of hell. Judging, labeling, classifying:
these are the occupations of an orderly world. "But that would
be hell! Yes, hell must be like that: streets with signs and no way
of explaining yourself. You're classified once and for all" (*TRN*,
p. 1499). Here Camus is crying out from his own experience,
having long borne the classification of "moralist." According to
Charles Rolo, "He once said wryly that if he were to rape his
grandmother in a public garden, someone would argue that it
was a moral act." Clamence is uncomfortable at being unable to
classify his interlocutor—"So you are just more or less"
(p. 1480)—yet the only title he will allow on his own visiting
card is *comédien* ("actor"), a thoroughly ambiguous label that
can imply any role and no basic reality.

Clamence conducts his own trial and judgment in order to
forestall the judgment of others. But his self-criticism is designed to implicate others: "The trial of others was taking place
incessantly in my heart" (*TRN*, p. 1514). "The real question is
no longer 'who is innocent, who is guilty?' but 'why do we, all of
us, have to keep judging and being judged?'" (Girard, p. 532).

This is the universe created by Marxism: "Just because Christian governments have a natural bent for complicity, we should not forget that Marxism is a doctrine of accusation, whose dialectic can only succeed in the universe of the trial" (*E*, p. 386). Clamence, in his role of judge-penitent, embodies the concepts of accusation and complicity, and the form of the text—the monologue—reflects the characteristic shared by Christianity and Marxism. The ironic mode is perfectly apt for the theme of complicity, for it forges a complex link of allusion and collusion between reader and narrator as it does between Clamence and his interlocutor.

Camus's preoccupation with judgment was exacerbated by the criticism to which *The Rebel* and he personally had been subjected. His own passionate reaction surprised many people, for he was normally too private a man to air his hurt feelings in a public and hostile forum. But it should be remembered that he felt he had been judged unjustly, and that this was not the first time it had happened. In Algiers in 1937, when the PCA investigated instances of defiance of party strategy in certain cells, Camus was invited to defend his dissident position, but policy had already been dictated by the Central Committee, and there was no possibility of a just and pragmatic judgment. Other members of Camus's cell had similar personal feelings, but were disciplined militants who fell into line. When Camus was expelled from the party, his only visible reaction, according to friends, was "a gentle smile" (Lottman, p. 158). After the second judgment in Paris, it took Camus four years to develop a text that would convey all the emotions behind that smile. "One true fact, in any case, in this careful play of mirrors: pain, and what it augurs" (*TRN*, p. 2015).

Clamence is not Camus, but in portraying a hero of our time, Camus included characteristics that he shared with his contemporaries. He recognized errors in his own thinking as well as in others; "my speech is less sure" (*TRN*, p. 1497). "Weak too, a noisy accomplice, have I not cried out in the wilderness?" he asks in "Return to Tipasa" (in *E*, p. 876). The author, however, resisted the temptation to accept the dictatorship of a new paternalistic order of left-wing intellectuals, and elected to stay in the *malconfort*, even at the risk of losing his ability to write. With reference to the intellectuals who eagerly condemned French Algerians rather than the French government for the injustices perpetrated in Algeria, Camus asserted, "I find it disgusting to confess one's sins like our judge-penitents, by beating their *mea culpa* on other people's breasts" (p. 897).

For him, the fact that justice was an imperfect approximation meant that mercy was all the more necessary. Philip Thody suggests that the name Clamence is close to *clémence*, and is an ironic contradiction of Clamence's philosophy. Camus had supported judgment without mercy for a short period after the Liberation, but had later recognized that Mauriac's position on this matter was right: "After the Liberation, I went to watch one of the purge trials. The accused was guilty in my opinon. But I left the trial before the end because *I was on his side* and I never went back to this kind of trial. In every guilty man there is a share of innocence. That's what makes any absolute condemnation revolting. People don't think enough of the pain" (*Corr.*, p. 141). In 1950 he noted: "If the times were merely tragic! But they are vile. That is why they should be impeached—and pardoned" (*CII*, p. 328).

Although Camus's stand may have seemed irrelevant to those committed to one side or the other, it was not necessarily so from a wider, long-term perspective. On the issue of Algerian independence, his position was a conservative one. When he had formulated this position, it had been profoundly radical for the times, and had cost him his livelihood in Algeria. He held those beliefs then without any internal division, because the struggle was between an absolute fact, colonialism, and a flexible human factor, the emancipation of the oppressed Moslem community. When the latter factor changed, Camus was emotionally, though not necessarily intellectually, unable to move from his position in the middle, and the signs of this internal conflict are evident not only in *The Fall* and throughout the stories of *Exile and the Kingdom,* but more significantly in his growing obsession with death and sterility during the latter half of the 1950s.

9

Exile from the Kingdom

Si loin que je vive main-
tenant de la terre où [je
suis né], elle est restée
ma vraie patrie et sa
lumière me nourrit jusque
dans la ville d'ombres, où
le sort me retient.
—"L'Enigme"

In the aftermath of the famous quarrel, Camus withdrew
from Parisian social and intellectual circles: nor could he return
to his roots, as Algeria resembled less and less the possible
kingdom. All the stories in *Exile and the Kingdom*, published in
1957, deal with people who do not belong in the world in which
they find themselves. In 1947 Camus had declared Algeria "my
true homeland" (*E*, p. 850). But by 1950 he would write in his
notebook: "Yes, I have a native land: the French language" (*CII*,
p. 337).[1] There was no longer a land to which he belonged, but
merely a form of expression; he became increasingly aware of
his francophone core, an "Algerian Frenchman," while his sympathy for France and its values declined. And his recurrent episodes of artistic sterility were exacerbated by the fact that the
French language was his medium; his inability to use it fruit-
fully underlined his feelings of exile.

Algeria was a paramount factor in political debate in France
during the 1950s. The tug-of-war between East and West in Europe seemed to have ended in a stalemate, at least for the time

being, and events in France's colonies were giving cause for alarm. The conflict in Indo-China was decided in 1954 with the fall of Dien Bien Phu to the Vietminh. Once Mendès-France had negotiated a settlement in 1955, he had to turn his attention to North Africa. Tunisia and Morocco were already suffering terrorist attacks by rebels and European right-wing extremists; the situation in Algeria had not yet deteriorated to the same degree, but the likelihood of violence was imminent, particularly since the problems of poverty and overpopulation were even more acute there than in the two neighboring countries. Decolonization dominated French political life in the fifties and sharply divided the country.

Camus returned briefly to journalism in 1955; he contributed articles to *L'Express* to support Mendès-France's candidacy for the premiership and to express his views on the Algerian situation. After an unsuccessful appeal for a civilian truce in Algiers in 1956, he withdrew from regular journalism, and limited his activities to behind-the-scenes interventions on behalf of imprisoned activists. The publication in 1958 of *Actuelles III: Chroniques algériennes,* elicited scant reaction at a moment when violence was at its height, and de Gaulle had once more been called in to save France. Camus's call for a confederation seemed irrelevant, when the ultimate choice now lay between massive repression and the granting of independence.

The short stories of *Exile and the Kingdom* return to Camus's early themes of estrangement and misunderstanding. Many of the characters are misfits in their environment, even when they feel they belong there. Colonialism constitutes a major motif in the collection. Only one story, that of the artist at work, takes place in Paris, and the artist's name, significantly, is Jonas, the Douay name for the man who refused to prophesy against the city. Three of the stories—"The Adulterous Woman," "The Guest," and "The Silent Men"—are set in Algeria. "The Silent Men" presents an ironic portrayal of the myth of colonial conquest, a reversal of the prevailing view in France of the wealthy, oppressive *pied-noir*. In this story, the conflict is not racial but social: the workers, both European and Algerian, are united in defiance of the owner of the small cooper's shop where they are employed. The other two stories reveal an awareness of the changes in the political situation in Algeria that had occurred since Camus lived there, but they seem to deliberately evade an understanding of the polarization which both sides in the conflict underwent during the 1950s. Camus's characters fail to comprehend or even recognize their misunderstanding of the world.

In his preface to the first edition of "The Adulterous Woman," published by Schumann in Algeria in November 1954, Camus acknowledged the autobiographical element in the story: "In Laghouat I met the characters of this story. I am not certain, of course, that their day ended as I have told it. Doubtless they did not go forth to the desert. But *I* went, some hours after that, and during all that time their image pursued me and challenged what I saw."[2] This impression of opposition, of conflict, is apparent in the portrayal of Janine and her husband Marcel as they travel in unknown territory in the Algerian interior. On the most obvious level, Janine finds the desert the opposite of what she had expected: instead of warm sand and palm trees, there is a bitterly cold wind blowing over a landscape of stone. Physical discomfort is a dominant feature of the couple's experience.

Marcel is a stereotype of the petty-bourgeois *pied-noir* whom Camus ridiculed in his notebooks, who believes that Arabs are uncivilized and whose aim is a house full of furniture from the Galeries Barbès (cf. *CI*, p. 225). Marcel's attitude is that of the fault-finding tourist, who complains of anything that is different. Even in the final version of the story, Marcel's comments are full of racial slurs; it is significant that in earlier versions his comments are even stronger. The typical racist epithets—lazy, dishonest, incompetent—are applied to various Arabs. Marcel expresses a commonly held attitude towards emancipation:

"They're supposed to be making progress, said Marcel. To make progress, you have to work. And for them, work is like pork, forbidden" (*TRN*, p. 2042).

Camus may, in Quilliot's view, have diluted Marcel's racism because of the worsening situation in Algeria between 1952, when the story was first drafted, and 1954, when it was published in Algiers (*TRN*, p. 2042). It seems more likely, however, that Camus wanted to make his character more sympathetic by emphasizing his limitations and the narrowness of his outlook in general, rather than presenting him as a hardened racist. Marcel is just another frightened human being, who works hard and takes no risks in order to assure both economic and emotional security. It is the exposure to a strange land with undefined parameters that elicits his hostile criticism. On a realistic level, his racist attitude arises from fear of two well-documented threats: economic and sexual competition. The economic crisis that followed World War II had forced Marcel to dispense with intermediaries, and to try and sell his fabrics directly to the Arabs. For the first time, he must deal with Arabs in the small towns of the interior, and to be successful he must deal with them as equals. Also for the first time, perhaps, he must speak Arabic. In the city, where French is the language of the dominant class, he can assert that dominance with his perfect mastery of that language. Now he finds the roles reversed, and the Arab has the upper hand because of his linguistic fluency. Marcel resents the Arabs' haughtiness, and his own position of suppliant: "He became irritable, raised his voice, laughed awkwardly, he seemed like a woman who is trying to be attractive and is unsure of herself" (p. 1567). His manhood is put in doubt, and his response is to make scornful comments to Janine about Arab conceit. The final insult is administered by the magnificent Arab who crosses the town square and almost walks over Marcel's case of samples. "They think they can get away with anything nowadays," remarks Marcel (p. 1568). Even Arab cooking is inferior: "*We* know how to cook" (p. 1565); the French rendering of the emphatic "we" (*nous autres*) underlines the otherness Marcel feels in a predominantly Arab town.

Marcel does not actually voice his fears for Janine's security, yet her reaction to the strange environment is physical. "Adulterous" may seem an extreme epithet in view of the reality of Janine's experience, but she is disloyal to the structure of the little world she lives in with her husband, to their marriage. She feels drawn toward the autonomy of these people of the interior, who seem not to depend on material comforts or possessions for their well-being. Janine is encumbered by overweight, luggage, a complaining husband, a heavy meal, the years of conjugality: in the oasis town, people display a freedom and independence such as she enjoyed in her youth. The Arabs do not even seem to notice her existence: "She found that even when they were dressed in rags, they had a proud demeanor, which was not the case with the Arabs in their home town" (*TRN*, p. 1566). The Arabs in the coastal towns depend on the Europeans for a living, and therefore adopt a more servile attitude, but here in the interior the French presence is minimal—pork served in the hotel restaurant, and a military decoration on the chest of the old Arab waiter. Out in the desert, the nomads are sovereign.

Hostility or serene indifference greet the French couple, both inside and outside the town. The local people and their landscape are at one in their autonomy vis-à-vis the strangers. All is cold and hard; even Janine's experience of physical union with the world is like a cold flood rather than a warm glow, as she leans against the stone parapet of the fortress. But Janine's fear is stronger than her yearning for freedom, and she returns to the warmth of her husband "as her safest haven" (*TRN*, p. 1571).

The impression of physical weight that Camus evokes in his portrayal of these characters makes them real and tangible people, what E. M. Forster would call "round" characters rather than the somewhat abstract characters of *The Plague*. Marcel and Janine are among Camus's most successful fictional creations: they are creations of flesh and blood rather than the stereotypical image of the *pied-noir*. Marcel may represent the reactionary racist European in Algeria, yet at the same time he is just a man, beset by the fear of death, loneliness and poverty like any other. Camus's old Algiers friend, Charles Poncet, suggested that, living in Paris as he did, "Camus may have felt more of a duty to defend the interests of the *pied-noir* against the unanimous hostility of the French left" (Lottman, p. 624). Camus certainly wanted to dissipate the "image d'Epinal" disseminated by some of the French press, which portrayed Algeria as a colony "inhabited by a million *colons* with whips and cigars, riding around in Cadillacs" (*E*, p. 973).

"The Adulterous Woman" does not defend the interests of the *pied-noir*, but rather reveals the extent to which fear inspires scorn and hostility. Marcel and Janine are quite literally out of their element in central Algeria: they need the definition of a coastline to feel secure, for the desert is as limitless as the ocean; the prevailing imagery of the descriptive passages is drawn from the open sea. Even in their home town, the couple no longer goes to the beach, but exists in an ever more restricted area: "The years had passed in the shadowy light they maintained with the shutters half-closed" (*TRN*, p. 1562). It is only a half-life, and what characterizes both the conjugal relationship and Janine's experience in the desert is sterility. The story suggests that the couple has no future, only a precarious present. Janine's encounter with the desert makes her newly aware of the vastness of space and time, into which the Arabs seem to fit while she remains excluded, unable to read "the obscure signs of a strange writing whose meaning had to be deciphered" (p. 1569).

Camus's attitude to the Algerian situation at this point is revealed as more humanistic than political. Marcel's opinions are obviously distasteful, yet Camus mitigated them in order to make the character more universal. The two sides are not black and white, and a solution does not lie in the eviction or enslavement of one party in the dispute. And yet in this story as in "The Guest," the characters are not really at home in the country they regard as their own.

In "The Adulterous Woman" a hostile natural environment is handled with equanimity by the Arabs, while the Europeans are acutely uncomfortable. A sandstorm is blowing, a "mineral mist" surrounds the bus on which Janine and her husband are traveling. A few palm trees seem to be "cut out of metal," and Janine's dream of a desert of soft sand is disappointed: "The desert was not like that, but was only stone, stone everywhere, in the sky that was still overcast with the dust of the stone, cold and rasping" (*TRN*, p. 1559). In the jolting bus, the Arabs "looked as though they were asleep, wrapped up in their burnoose. Some had tucked up their feet on the seat and swayed more than the others with the movement of the vehicle. . . . The passengers . . . had sailed in silence through a kind of pale night" (p. 1560). Janine notices that "despite their voluminous garments, they seemed to have plenty of room on the seats which were only just wide enough for her and her husband" (p. 1561). She and Marcel are impeded by their clothes and their baggage, but "all these people from the South apparently traveled empty-handed" (p. 1563).

Only when Janine stops all movement can she begin to understand the desert and its people. "For a long time, a few men had been traveling without respite over the dry earth, scraped to the bone, of this unbounded land, men who had no possessions but were no man's slave, wretched but free lords of a strange kingdom" (*TRN*, p. 1570). The scene recalls the end of *Crime and Punishment*, where Raskolnikov sees the nomads across the river from his prison. For a moment Janine shares this accord, but she is brought back to reality by her husband. "She felt too tall, too solid, and too white for this world she had just entered" (p. 1571). She is a misfit in the landscape.

So too is Daru, the protagonist of "The Guest." The ambiguity of the title word, *l'hôte*, meaning both "guest" and "host," and of which meaning should be applied to which character, is resolved by the landscape. Paul Fortier has shown how the landscape and its changing aspects offer an interpretation of historical events and of moral values ("Décor," pp. 535–42). Daru believes himself in harmony with the natural world around him. But it is an illusion. The sun is dominant during the drought, "the plateaus charred month after month, the earth gradually shrivelling, literally scorched" (*TRN*, p. 1612). The snowfall represents a brief reprieve, a temporary truce before hostility is renewed. When the sun shines again, Daru feels a kind of exaltation, but it is as if the sun were in league with the rocks against him, quickly drying out the puddles of melting snow and returning the landscape to its former rockiness. Now the sun becomes destructive, and "began to devour his brow ... sweat trickled down it" (p. 1623).

The physical attack portends the human violence with which the teacher is threatened on his return to the school. The wind "lurking" around the school building parallels the activities of the rebels who are following his movements. And the precise location of Daru's school, on an isolated plateau, an intermediate stage between the coastal plain and the mountains, reflects the moral stance of neutrality and isolation maintained by the schoolteacher (Fortier, *Une Lecture*, p. 29). The Arab prisoner, as Fortier points out, resembles the desert, "his skin sunburnt but slightly discolored by the cold" (*TRN*, p. 1613). He fears what the Frenchmen may do to him, but he does not fear the desert. Of course in reality the natural world is hostile to the Arabs too: Daru is well aware that "in the desert, all men, both he and his guest, were nothing" (p. 1617). But Camus's landscapes are never innocent. A welcoming environment can become inimical and can inflict pain and even death on the unwary individual.

In all Camus's works, it is the mineral element of the world that proves hostile to mankind. The Algerian sun, which has such a positive and beneficent influence on the bronzed young bodies on the Mediterranean beach, can at times be deadly. It is

portrayed as metallic in its destructive role in the short stories
(Weis, p. 54).

This is also the case in other texts. In *A Happy Death*, for
example, Mersault falls asleep in the afternoon sun: "Now the
sun struck with ever swifter blows on every stone on the
path. . . . The slopes were rocky and full of flint. . . . The entire
mountain vibrated beneath the light and the crickets, the heat
increased and besieged them beneath their oak tree. Patrice . . .
could feel in his stomach the dull blows of the mountain, like a
woman in labor" (*MH*, p. 179). When Mersault wakes and begins
his descent, he faints; the French *syncope* denotes a break in
rhythm, a break that is repeated during Mersault's last swim
before the onset of his fatal relapse, when the harmonious
movements of his body in the warm water are abruptly thrown
out of gear by a sudden cold current: "He had to stop, his teeth
chattering and his movements uncoordinated [*désaccordés*]"
(p. 193). In contrast to this disharmony, Camus portrays the
Arabs who appear riding donkeys, against a background of lux-
uriant and fruitful vegetation: "The paths were still embroi-
dered with prickly pear, olive and jujube trees" (p. 178). The
series of long vowel sounds in the French text contributes to the
feeling of relaxed, smooth, and rhythmic movement.

A similar juxtaposition occurs in *The Stranger*. When Meursault is walking on the beach at noon, both sun and sea become
metallic: "each rapier of light," "an ocean of boiling metal," "the
light splashed on the steel and it was like a long sparkling
blade," "the cymbals of the sun," "the dazzling blade," "this
burning sword." The reality of the knife is indistinguishable
from the sun's rays and the light reflected off the sea. And in
Meursault's hand is the gun, modern man's contribution to
deadly metallic objects. In direct contrast to this portrait of
physical disarray, of jangling nerves and assaulted senses,
Camus depicts the Arabs, who experience none of this hostility.
They are lying in the shade beside a little spring: "They seemed
quite calm and almost contented. Our coming changed

nothing" (*TRN*, p. 1165). One of the Arabs plays a flute, and the impression of harmony is accentuated by the movement of the Arabs' bodies, which "slipped [*coulés*] behind the rock" (p. 1166): it is as if they were absorbed into the landscape. Even in the unnatural surroundings of the prison, the Arab prisoners communicate with their visitors in a gentle murmur, while the Europeans have to shout to make themselves heard.

The opinions Camus expressed in a political context are apparently contradicted by the fictional worlds of these short stories.[3] Camus opposed independence because it would lead to the expulsion of his own people. Yet the European characters he places in an Algerian setting are uncomfortable strangers in a country they regard as theirs. In "The Guest," for example, despite the sympathetic portrayal of characters, it is clear that Daru's position is untenable. Warm human bonds between individuals are not enough to assure a peaceful settlement of struggle in the political arena.

Daru fits in with Albert Memmi's portrait of the left-wing colonizer. He "refuses to become a part of his group of fellow citizens. At the same time it is impossible for him to identify his future with that of the colonized. Politically, who is he? Is he not an expression of himself, of a negligible force in the varied conflicts within colonialism?" (*The Colonizer*, p. 41). Daru has isolated himself from his fellow Europeans, and lives alone on a barren plateau in the foothills. As a schoolteacher he is obviously committed to the welfare and education of his pupils, and sympathetic towards their impoverished and illnourished condition. He feels at home: "Daru had been born there. Anywhere else he felt an exile" (*TRN*, p. 1613). In earlier versions of the manuscript, Daru was a disenchanted businessman from the coast, who had given up his old life and become a teacher. In the final version, Camus stresses Daru's roots in this harsh landscape; yet his origins continue to separate him from the indigenous population: "Faced with this wretchedness [Daru], who lived almost like a monk in this isolated school, yet was happy with the little he had and with this simple life, had felt like a lord" (p. 1612). Colonialist rule is symbolized by the drawing on the school blackboard of the four rivers of France: the local schoolchildren follow the same curriculum as children in metropolitan France, even though it may be irrelevant to their culture and their needs. The colonial administration uses the schools as distribution centers for emergency supplies of food during the drought, so that children have to come to school to receive their allocation. Daru is thus placed in the position of an overlord, separate from "that army of ragged ghosts" (p. 1612). The word *army* evokes a sense of hostility and violence which runs through the whole narrative and explodes across the map of France at the end of the story.

The advent of Balducci and his Arab prisoner brings the reality of the current situation into Daru's monastic retreat, brings movement into a static world, and forces him to take a position. "Commitment comes like a guest who does not want to leave" (Cryle, *Bilan critique*, p. 142). It is his failure to choose in a positive way that leaves him helpless to affect the course of events. His attitude toward Balducci and the Arab is entirely laudable: Balducci is a tough but sympathetic Corsican who dislikes mistreating an Arab, but who believes in discipline, while the Arab, despite his act of violence, is nevertheless a man who deserves to be treated with human dignity. By refusing to take the Arab to prison, Daru offends Balducci personally; by allowing the Arab a choice he does not understand, he alienates himself from the local people. His actions are misunderstood by the groups represented by the two individuals, just as Daru fails to recognize the political reality behind those two people.

On a personal level, ambiguity and humanitarian instincts are possible; but on a political level, actions cannot bear any nuance without being misconstrued. Thus the colonial administration will view Daru's refusal as a treacherous act, while the Arabs interpret the result of his inaction as a betrayal too: "You have handed over our brother. You will pay" (*TRN*, p. 1623). The words "hand over" recall mockingly Daru's thrice-repeated "I will not hand him over" (p. 1616); Camus obviously had some biblical references in mind, for in an earlier version of the story, the teacher's name is Pierre (Peter), and at one time he considered "Cain" as a title (p. 2048). Daru's future in Algeria is precarious, and the use of the pluperfect in the final sentence bears out this sense of finality. "Daru looked at the sky, the plateau, and beyond it the invisible landscape that stretched out to the sea. In this vast country he had loved so much, he was alone" (p. 1623). The reference to the sea indicates the direction in which Daru will now have to travel, into his exile.

The individual's viewpoint cannot be reduced to a single vision, and yet circumstances often demand it. By refusing to commit himself to one side or the other, Daru loses all. He deplores the Arab's resigned decision to accept his fate, and yet his own indecisiveness allows him also to be swept away by events; he is no better than the Arab at choosing his own future. The text clearly shows that Daru's behavior is understandable but sterile. In a polarized situation, one must choose between black and white and put aside all the shades of gray that intervene, if one is to have any impact on the situation.

The criticisms leveled at Camus during the late 1950s dealt mainly with his unwillingness to ignore the gray nuances: in a situation where two hostile *groups* were involved, *individuals* would surge into view and temper the objective evaluation with a visceral sympathy. Like his character Daru, Camus became "suspect to the nationalists of both sides. I am blamed by one side for not being sufficiently . . . patriotic. For the other side, I'm too much so" (Mallet, quoted in Lottman, p. 639).

There is no doubt that Camus suffered intense anguish over his role in the Algerian tragedy. When an old Algerian friend asked him why he had accepted the necessity of violence during the Resistance but rejected it with respect to the Moslem independence movement, his response reveals what Daru ignored— an awareness of his fundamental identity: "It's true that I wasn't shocked by resistance to the Nazis, because I was French and my country was occupied. I should [*devrais*] accept the Algerian resistance, but I'm French" (ibid., p. 624).

Camus's reaction to the political struggle was never objective, but was colored by fear for the safety of his family in Algiers as well as by the pressure of more reactionary views within his family in France. After the failure of his mission in 1956, his participation in events was limited to private action to help individuals. He knew that he was going against the tide of his time; decisions were being made on a national rather than a local level. "All the power of science today is aimed at strengthening the state. Not one scholar has thought of directing his research towards the defense of the individual. But that is where a freemasonry would have some meaning" (*CII*, p. 328).

"The Silent Men" depicts another aspect of the ambiguity of political action, and of the way in which it can divide men rather than unite them. The artisans in this story are the people Camus knew in his youth, and remind us of the men in *The Wrong Side and the Right Side*, old before their time, remembering with nostalgia the sunlit beaches and freedom of their youth. This is no romantic portrayal of the worker: physical fatigue and a sense of hopelessness in a dying trade are the predominant sentiments of Yvars and his co-workers.

In the conflict between boss and workers, there are no winners. The shopowner, who is depicted as honest and sympathetic, cannot afford to raise wages because the cooperage business is in crisis. The workers, humiliated by the failure of their strike and the lack of union support for their cause, decide to remain silent in the presence of their boss. Benevolent though he may be, he cannot understand what life is like for the poor, and they are unable to communicate it to him. Their own solidarity cuts across racial lines; the conflict is centered on the relationship between employer and employees. No one seems to have conceived of it in terms of "class" conflict: like Daru, they relate to each other as people rather than as representatives of a social or political reality.

Their action, however limited, is an assertion of human dignity rather than political revolt. Hence their evident confusion when faced with the illness of the boss's daughter; they suppress their feelings of common humanity in the face of the scandal of the death of a child, but they are not happy about it. They cannot formulate ideas on the complex issues involved, and so they cling stubbornly to the one decision they have made, to remain silent, even at the expense of a vital part of their humanity.[4]

In this story Camus shows through the complexities and ambiguities of a particular situation how irrelevant political theory can be. Politics itself must be ambiguous if it is to take account of reality. "The Silent Men" portrays people struggling for economic survival, ignorant of the wider theoretical application of their dilemma.

"The Guest" also demonstrates an individual situation, but one in which the hero chooses not to be part of a group. It reveals the failure of a stand that refuses total commitment to either side. "The Renegade," on the other hand, affirms the dangers inherent in such a commitment.

Paradoxically, this story's subtitle, "A Confused Mind," contradicts the world in which the renegade functions, although the form of the story, a frenzied monologue, does bear witness to a crazed mind. The renegade's progression in life, however, follows a straight and determined line: from a sickly and depressed childhood, he plans a course of action that will lead directly to the exercise of power. "Powerful, yes, that was the word that I constantly rolled on my tongue, I dreamed of absolute power, the kind that brings people to their knees" (TRN, p. 1581). Thus the seminary is merely a means to an end, the theft from the bursary in Algiers a necessary step in the direction of the attainment of his dream. But on arrival in Taghâsa, the city of salt in the desert (again the hostile mineral element), he discovers that instead of wielding power, he must become a slave. The distinct line of his own progression is halted, for the world of Taghâsa is overwhelming in its geometric patterns, and its stark setting of black and white. The renegade's dream of power comes to an abrupt end in a cell of salt. He no longer has any control over the situation, because his potential power lay in the propagation of the word, and he is now speechless, for his captors have cut out his tongue. Physical force reigns in Taghâsa, and the renegade embraces his new servitude with delirious passion. "The maddest passion of the twentieth century: slavery" (*CII*, p. 334). The renegade's conversion fits in with Camus's definition of the aim of Russian Communism—"the exaltation of the executioner by his victims" (*E*, p. 648).

Taghâsa is the perfect example of the totalitarian state: symmetry and efficient organization imposed by violence rather than by reasonable persuasion, absolute values suggested by the stark contrast of black on white, and the sterility of the world of salt. Only when the renegade leaves the city to lie in wait for the French missionary do any colors reappear in the landscape, or the lines lose their rigid angles.

The renegade can be seen as an example of the modern intellectual in search of ideological absolutes; when one fails, another takes its place (Brombert, p. 230). Certainly he is willing to accept any tyranny in order to attain the "kingdom" he envisages. But the major thrust of the narrative is to show how violence, when used as a means to what may be a laudable end, becomes a way of life. The violence implicit in the renegade's dream of power is camouflaged by the explicit mission of the conversion of a ferocious people to Christianity. But when violence is used to convert the potential conqueror to slave, it is received with a pathological pleasure, and the renegade can conceive of no other means of action when threatened by the arrival of a new missionary. Thus violence is not limited to the attainment of a certain goal, but pervades the whole landscape, the human mind, and the verbal expression of the confused workings of that mind.

It is significant that the renegade was regarded as a young man of limited intelligence, unsure of himself or his capabilities. "Order, an order . . . yes, I have always wanted order" (*TRN*,

p. 1579).[5] The order of the Church is replaced by the more powerful order of violence: "the city of order, in fact, right angles, square rooms, inflexible men" (p. 1589). Camus's comment on Rebatet and Morgan is relevant here too: "Universal definition of Fascism: having no character, they found themselves a doctrine" (CII, p. 193). And that doctrine requires total submission and loss of liberty. "Truth is square, heavy, dense, it will not tolerate nuance" (p. 1589).

The title of the story obviously refers to the narrator's treachery to his Church when he adopts the pagan religion of his captors. But he had already betrayed the ideals of that Church before leaving France. He is a colonialist who has swallowed the myth that conquest is justified by the need to "save the souls of the infidel" (E, p. 801), a myth that disguises a lust for power. This disguise proves no match for the rulers of Taghâsa: the renegade betrays the myth too, and "goes native." He is a renegade in both the religious and political senses of the word. His mind is confused because he has no moral values on which to base his decisions. It is the attraction of power that provides his only motivation.

There are obvious links between "The Renegade" and The Fall, both in form and content. The renegade realizes Clamence's dream of tyranny, and his text is also monologue, but this time there is no interlocutor, for the words are never formed. Speech is totally suppressed in favor of violent gesture. The inhabitants of Taghâsa are also silent men, but this is the silence of certainty rather than that of doubt. The only sound uttered by the renegade is the repeated "râ râ" of his tongueless mouth. A striking image in Camus's 1956 "Appeal for a Civilian Truce" in Algiers suggests that the renegade represents the course of history when men accept cruelty and inhumanity with a passive fatalism. Then history "repeats itself, like a bleeding mouth that spews out only a furious stuttering" (E, p. 999).

The theme of violence, which relates to the political level of interpretation, also reiterates the problems of writing.[6] The last sentence of the story, which is the only one outside quotation marks, refers to the "garrulous slave,"[7] an extraordinarily harsh portrait of the writer, particularly since his "words" communicate nothing. The mouthful of salt is the final assertion of the sterility of his endeavor.

"The Renegade" marks the low point in Camus's view of his art, and probably coincides with the period around 1954 when, in a letter to René Char, he confessed that he was "literally vitriolized by doubt" (E, p. 1629). The last two stories in the collection, however, are more optimistic. "Jonas, or the Artist at Work" deals with the conflicting demands of the world and the artist's need for solitude. The ironic tone is reminiscent of *The Fall*, but the pain it hides is less intense and distanced by the benevolent attitude of the narrator.

A considerable number of details relate to Camus's own experience, from the description of the apartment to the problem of organizing his work and family life. "The fight to the finish between me and my children is over, with the children the winners," Camus wrote to Grenier in 1949. "I no longer work at home, but try to do so in my office at the NRF, with the door locked and the telephone off the hook. The victors now occupy all the conquered territory and behave like all conquerors, cynically" (*Corr.*, p. 151). In "Jonas," the bantering tone of the satire of Parisian life gradually gives way to a more somber note as Jonas's vocation is threatened, first by his own lack of responsibility, then by the invasion of friends, critics, and hangers-on. The opening line of "Jonas" states simply that he "believed in his star"[8] but he allows other aspects of his life to take precedence. He tries escape from the apartment, but wine and women provide no inspiration. He must find the solution within the confines of the apartment, and each new attempt involves a rearrangement of the space available (Cryle, "Written Painting," pp. 124–26). Like that other artist, Grand, he must continually start again without altering the basic structure of the givens, reorganize within limits. The words *recommencer* and *organisation* recur constantly in the text.

Just as Jonah chose to neglect the dictates of God, so Jonas allows the exigencies of his "star" to be swamped by the demands of outside influences. He enjoys the adulation of disciples, even though he realizes that he is merely a fashion; these admirers showed an interest "in painting when they could just as easily have been mad about the English royal family or gourmet restaurants" (*TRN*, p. 1643). The ironic juxtaposition suggests Camus's modesty with regard to his estimate of the importance of the artist.

Jonas's ultimate solution is to build a loft, making use of the excess height of the apartment, where he can be alone while still retaining at least aural contact with his family. The only evidence we have of Jonas's activity is his subsequent physical collapse and the canvas with one word, *solitaire* or *solidaire*, perhaps both. The loft, a compromise comparable to Clamence's *malconfort*, is not an ideal situation but a possible balance between two absolutes. The reader can only imagine Jonas's anguish before the blank white canvas: his retreat and self-discipline do not lead to the creation of a work of art, but at least he has succeeded in conceptualizing the problem, and will recover his health.

The ironic tone and the relatively optimistic ending—Jonas can begin again—reveal an upswing in Camus's vision of his work. His conclusions about the role of the artist are not new: he needs the inspiration of the world of men as well as the solitary cell to be creative; his duty is a double one, and the balance must be constantly reassessed and reasserted.

Jonah defied God's orders because they seemed arbitrary. Jonas ignores the demands of his star, which also requires obedience to certain laws and structures, like the celestial body it resembles. The tyranny of art is compared to that of the Old Testament God: it must be recognized as such before the artist can evolve his admittedly ambiguous response to its dictates, and avoid the sterility that total submission or irresponsibility produces.

The idea of organization over anarchy is evident in the last story in the collection, "The Growing Stone." In the earlier stories, sterility is linked with the desert, parched earth, dust. In "The Growing Stone" the ambiance is suffused with water, an element that encourages fertility, but left unmanaged it leads to decay, rotting overcrowded vegetation, and muddy roads. The hero d'Arrast is an engineer, and it is in this story that the rules of a person's profession are most closely integrated with the human and social demands to which that person responds.

Although the setting of the story is quite specific, and is based on Camus's personal experiences during his visit to South America in 1949, the main character, d'Arrast, is not developed in depth. Indeed, during the initial scenes of the story, he is referred to simply as "the man" (*l'homme*), and the reader's only impression is that of a gentle giant. Even when some details are filled in, the engineer's past remains mysterious. In contrast to Marcel and Janine, and to Daru, who cling to their past, d'Arrast has closed it off, leaving the future open and uncertain.

His current role is to build a dam that will prevent seasonal flooding in the small town of Iguape. The notables who gather at the club to welcome the French engineer typify the petty colonial elite, benevolent and paternalistic toward the local populace, obsequious and gushing toward the foreign visitor. The judicial system is a parody: the judge is an effusive dandy, the chief of police a drunken lout who bullies d'Arrast until put in his place by the judge, at which point he assumes the air of "a child who has been caught out," and "sidles out like a dunce in trouble" (*TRN*, p. 1664). To d'Arrast's dismay, the judge insists that he select a suitable punishment for the transgressor: he eventually succeeds in persuading the judge to forget the matter, but in the meantime the chief of police remains in the ridiculous situation of being in his own jail.[9]

D'Arrast is welcomed by the local people, and he feels a greater affinity with them than with the notables. But a barrier remains: he cannot share the simple faith of the ship's cook, and during the celebrations for Saint George he is rejected as a

stranger: "They don't want you to stay now" (*TRN*, p. 1677).
D'Arrast accepts his dismissal: "I don't know how to dance," he
tells Socrate, his driver (p. 1679).

D'Arrast's position is like that of Daru. He has rejected his
roots in the European aristocracy as well as the new regime of
policemen and shopkeepers, but he has not found a new place
for himself. "Over there, in Europe, it was shame and anger.
Here, exile or solitude" (*TRN*, p. 1678). He is a man without an
identity. The notables look on him as one of themselves, and so
the native people view him with suspicion or indifference. In
this he is like Meursault, who had to be considered an enemy by
the Arab on the beach. It will need a striking gesture to overturn
the assumptions of the people of Iguape.

During the religious procession d'Arrast is invited to join the
town notables on a balcony of the judge's house facing the
church: the significance of the position of the ruling class is
evident. But d'Arrast goes down among the people to look for
the cook, who is staggering under the rock he has sworn to carry
to the church.[10] D'Arrast has to go against the tide to reach the
cook: "He had to struggle against the joyful crowd, the candle
bearers, the offended penitents. Slowly but surely, bearing all his
weight against the human tide, he opened up a path" (*TRN*,
p. 1682). When he finds the cook, he sees that the man's com-
panions keep replacing the rock every time he stumbles. Again
d'Arrast defies the will of the people: ignoring the cries of "to
the church, to the church" (p. 1685), he turns to the left and
carries the stone down to the slums instead. His gesture is not
understood immediately; he has defied the oppressive rule of
the Church just as he defied an unjust system of power that
states that "punishment is necessary" (p. 1667).

There is certainly a link between d'Arrast and the figure of
Christ, but it would be an exaggeration to view him as a personification of Christ. Camus uses the word *resurrection* rather
than *reappearance* or *resurgence* to describe the figure of d'Arrast in the car's blinking headlights. Like the statue of Christ

that floated upstream to the town of Iguape, d'Arrast goes against the tide. But Christ is appropriated by the notables, and incorporated into the system of oppression and submission: d'Arrast refuses to be annexed by the ruling elite, and so perhaps he, rather than Meursault, can be considered the only Christ we deserve. A similar opposition exists between the two stones. "The real growing stone is not the one in the grotto, an object of selfish superstitions and false hopes . . . [but] the one that symbolizes a friendship . . . between two people. On the stone is founded not the Church of God, but the community of men" (Crochet, p. 205).

Of all the characters in *Exile and the Kingdom*, d'Arrast is the only one of heroic stature. But he resists the role: he has left a position of social prominence in Europe, he rejects the power offered him by the judge, and the stone he carries to the slums puts out the fire in the middle of the hut, an anti-Promethean gesture. Once more we are back with the stone of Sisyphus, "but this time two men have carried it together" (Barnes, p. 241). Sisyphus accepted his daily task because he so loved life, and it is "life beginning anew" (*TRN*, p. 1686) that reveals to d'Arrast the possibility of creating a kingdom in the midst of exile.

D'Arrast is a man who can change the order of this small world: not only can he tame the natural world by controlling the river, but he can also change a system of power in human society. The poor people of the town are treated as children by the Church and State that rule them. D'Arrast shows them the way to independence, symbolically by carrying the rock to the poorest hovel, realistically by providing work on the dam project. He acts not according to the dictates of an abstract ideology, but in response to an instinctive human compassion. It is his *body* that shows him the way. The final words, "Sit down with us," justify d'Arrast's joy; the stranger is invited to join the group. The underlying inference is that a process of emancipation can be achieved by peaceful means, for the dominant imagery of the story has none of the violence of "The Guest" or "The

Renegade"; the flowing of water, which permeates the text, water that d'Arrast will direct to make it serve these people rather than dominate them, denotes a peaceful transition over time.

This was Camus's dream for Algeria: "I love [Algeria] as a Frenchman who loves Arabs, and wants them to be at home[11] in Algeria without himself having to feel a stranger there because of that" (Mallet, quoted in Lottman, p. 639). But it harked back to a period when federation of some kind was still a viable policy. The situation depicted in "The Growing Stone" is still relatively simple because it takes place prior to the awakening of political consciousness among the masses, and d'Arrast is the first man to rebel against the status quo. He illustrates Camus's conception of true freemasonry: by aiding an individual he can influence a community. Once violent means are introduced, however, human beings lose their liberty, both of speech and action. "The Renegade" offers an explanation of Camus's public silence on Algeria after 1958. In a situation where violence is the order of the day, the word has no power for good. The cutting out of the renegade's tongue removes all hope of achieving his mission through reasonable dialogue. It is left to the French army to impose control by force, making a mockery of the Christian message.

The stories of *Exile and the Kingdom* reveal the impasse in which Camus found himself with regard to the Algerian situation. His existence as a writer depended on his identity as a Frenchman, yet his experience as an Algerian made liberty his foremost social ideal. There was no political solution to his personal dilemma. Had he lived, he would doubtless have accepted the inevitable tide of events, just as Daru did. But his vision of the trends in society, of the triumph of violence over dialogue, of the state over the individual, is now generally recognized as a relevant indictment of the modern world.

10

Conclusion

> The distinction between theories
> and values is not sufficiently
> recognized, but it is fundamen-
> tal. On a group of theories,
> one can found a school; but on
> a group of values one can found
> a culture, a civilization, a
> new way of living together among
> men.
> —Ignazio Silone

The aim of this study has been to approach Camus's fiction from a new perspective, to interpret that fiction in the light
of nonfictional texts and thus elucidate the author's political
vision. Left-wing intellectuals among Camus's contemporaries
looked to him for answers and were disappointed. This disappointment is evident in Sartre's response to Camus in *Les
Temps modernes*, in which he describes Camus as the active
embodiment of all the conflicts of his time, a heroic figure who
then failed to live up to the expectations of his friends. His
failure to support Algerian independence provoked further disillusionment and convinced his critics that he was too fastidious
to dirty his hands in the real stuff of politics.

What led Camus into this impasse in the late 1950s? His work
reveals an ever-widening gap between his theoretical positions
and his values—that is, between the intellectual and political
side that grew up as a result of his education and was closely
linked with the French language, and the view of the world that

was formed by his origins in a *pied-noir* milieu in Algiers. The question that Camus had posed in 1947 remained unanswered: "Is it possible, legitimate, to be in history while using as points of reference values that go beyond history?" (*CII*, p. 202).

In the early years of Camus's political commitment, the gap between his political ideals and his values was minimal, and as Sartre commented, he lived positively the conflicts of his time. But the times changed, and Camus was not alone in feeling a yawning gulf between those poles during the period of disillusionment that followed World War II. But the extreme case of Algeria became an anguish that no Frenchman could share. The image of the changing nature of the gap between the two sides in the conflict is summed up in an article written for *L'Express*, 10 January 1956: "Tomorrow, [the two populations] will not face each other across a ditch, but over a communal grave" (*E*, p. 984). The gap that once offered a tension that sparked creative energy and the possibility of "a new way of living together among men" had become a grave that signaled the death of that energy. When Camus returned to writing toward the end of the decade, he started work on an autobiography, going back to a period of unity, the period when he bridged the gap and when history and the values that transcended it were in accord.

Camus's position on Algerian independence has been a source of embarrassment and puzzlement for his admirers, and a proof of his reactionary political views for his detractors. There is no doubt that he opposed independence, although not in the interest of continuing French rule. "The era of colonialisms is over," he wrote in 1958 (*E*, p. 898). But he feared the rising tide of nationalism, and the pan-Arab dreams of a Moscow-oriented Nasser. His ideal solution was a federation along the lines of the Swiss Confederation, with proportional representation in a parliament made up of Moslem and European members. Camus defended the rights of those whose racism and bigotry he decried, and whose shouts of "Down with Camus! Camus to the stake!" had greeted his call for a civilian truce in 1956. It is significant that members of the FLN who knew Camus were more sympathetic to his dilemma than were the French supporters of the liberation movement within France.

The tenuous bridge on which Camus had stood became a seesaw; justice he had claimed for twenty years on behalf of the Algerians could now be achieved only by imposing injustice on the European population. Camus's language develops an almost tribal accent; he withdrew, unable to separate himself from his own, *les miens*. The silence cloaked an identity crisis, a coming to terms with a kind of ethnic solidarity within himself. Racism is not the appropriate term because it implies a hatred of the other, which was never true of Camus. And this solidarity was not with France, but with that heterogeneous group of Mediterranean people he had known in his old neighborhood of Belcourt. "Must these hardworking Frenchmen . . . be offered up for slaughter to atone for the enormous sins of colonialist France?" (*E*, p. 974).

Camus's anguish in the face of the violence of decolonization can be attributed to several factors. The conflict between *pied-noir* and Arab was not being fought out on an ideological plane, but in the city streets and cafés and in remote villages. Camus felt sympathy for the motive common to both sides—the desire for a homeland. During World War II, Camus's loyalties had been undivided, and if in *The Plague* the enemy is transformed into microbes, it is because they represent the abstraction of the ideological cause. Camus's target was not other people, but the ideas in whose name they were mobilized. In Algeria, violence on a personal basis had become the order of the day, and the words on which Camus the artist relied were powerless. The suppression of speech leads to violence, as Camus had foreseen when he left the Communist party in 1937. He must have recognized the danger of being contaminated by that violence and of being unable to contain it within himself.[1] Public silence and private efforts to combat injustice through letters, money, personal influence, provided a way of surviving without contributing to the bloodshed. "Speech always implies betrayal" (*CII*, p. 107).

This refusal to allow violence to impose itself on him is reflected in the stresses evident in his life as an artist. The years after 1956 saw no original literary endeavors. Camus's publications included his Nobel Prize speeches, an essay on capital punishment, a collection of his journalistic articles on Algeria, and the preface to a new edition of *The Wrong Side and the Right Side*. Most of his energies were directed toward the theater, and he adapted and produced a number of successful plays during the period. In this sphere he found freedom from the tyranny of art, and respite from the tyranny of history. It was a pragmatic solution to the problem of integrating conflicting demands.

These latter publications were greeted with little critical comment. Camus had gone out of style. The closed world of the Parisian intelligentsia, with its tightly knit *chapelles* and sectarian allegiances, provided the major criteria for evaluating literary production in France. Camus was classified as a has-been, suitable reading only for secondary-school pupils. His journalism was not read once the moment that had inspired it had passed, even though his positions have frequently been vindicated by subsequent events. Many articles have a rhetorical quality that now seems dated and needlessly moralistic. Camus's plays are rarely performed, with the exception of *Caligula*, and his literary works have often been interpreted through the filter of his political position in the 1950s, without reference to his earlier militant writings.

The continuing fidelity of readers of Camus's fiction, both in France and abroad, thus demands some explanation. One reason for his appeal is that although the problems and themes presented in his work anchor him firmly in his moment in history, he was at the same time ahead of that moment, not only in his political perspicacity, but in his art too. It is generally agreed that *The Stranger* is a precursor of the "new novel" in France: Robbe-Grillet talks of the empty consciousness of the narrator and the "implosion" of the world; Barilli considers Meursault's point of view a forerunner of the narrator's eye in the new novel.[2] *The Plague* debunks the carefully nurtured myth that most of the French were heroic resistants to the Nazi occupation. While former resistants published memoirs and French filmmakers portrayed the few as many, Camus, without diminishing the stature or the self-sacrifice of the resistants, depicted a society in which self-interest and passive collaboration were the most common reactions to the crisis. *The Fall* is a tour de force as a monologue, and constitutes a new departure in that it breaks out of the written genre and enters the sphere of oral expression. The stories in *Exile and the Kingdom* exhibit Camus's skill and range in experimenting with narrative techniques. His work has proven a rich and open source for contemporary critics; rereading Camus is not a repetition but a new beginning.

Thus Camus has found favor again among "professional" readers, but they constitute a small percentage of the total. Why does Camus appeal to such a wide audience? Why can so many readers of different cultures and education feel a personal identification with his work?

First Camus, as an outsider, was not bound by the limits of contemporary intellectual circles, and could bring a new vision to his work. Even though it shares many of the same themes and basic concerns that are typical of much of European literature since World War I, its originality of both form and content has withstood the test of time.

Secondly, Camus's independence and his refusal to lie appealed to the majority of readers who are neither as politicized nor as conventionally radical as many French intellectuals. The consistent level of readership suggests that Camus was successful in attaining the ideal he had proposed for himself as an artist.

Camus described his notion of the artist's role in his Nobel

Prize speech in Stockholm in 1957: "In my view, Art is not a solitary delight. It is a means of touching the emotions of the greatest number of people by offering them an exceptional representation of shared sufferings and joys" (*E*, p. 1071). The experience of sharing has to be combined with trust in the writer in spite of an age of suspicion. "Whatever our individual frailties may be, the nobility of our craft will always be rooted in two difficult commitments: the refusal to lie about what we know and resistance to oppression." "By definition, [the writer] cannot serve those who make history: he serves those who have to live it" (p. 1072).

Early in his career, Camus had found in a myth-figure the embodiment of the principles of both artist and rebel. Sisyphus forms the basis for such fictional characters as Grand and d'Arrast. But Camus's creatures have an added dimension, a "correction": integration with the world of men. It is by sharing the suffering of others that these two characters find personal fulfilment and creative freedom. Grand has already experienced the pain of his wife's departure, but he cannot translate it into art, for he cannot find the right words. It is the shared suffering of the plague that brings him into contact with the world of history, and which at the same time teaches him the limits of art. In this little portrait of an unsung hero of resistance lies Camus's view of what a writer can hope to achieve, and by what rules he can attain his goal. In the character of d'Arrast we find an inverted portrait, in the sense that a heroic figure becomes humble, but his task is the same, to put his talents to the service of mankind, and to share the burden of suffering.

Camus presents his readers with unpretentious men rather than heroic models, poetry rather than ideology, anguished questions rather than placid answers. The tension and ambiguities he lived himself are communicated to the reader through the text; rather than passively receiving it, he finds himself drawn into active participation. Camus, through his "exceptional representation," invites us to experience the world in a new light. He made no claims to being the guide of his generation:

> That kind of opinion strikes me as funny. I speak for no one; I have enough trouble finding my own language. I guide no one: I do not know, or I scarcely know, where I am going myself. I do not live on a pedestal: I walk through the streets of time at the same pace as everyone else.
>
> I ask myself the same questions as other men of my generation, that is all, so it is natural that they should find them in my books if they read them. But a mirror informs, it does not teach. (*E*, p. 1925)

The enduring value of a body of work does not lie merely in satisfactory answers to specific questions. Camus's creative work reflects and throws light on the history of his times, but also remains relevant today, not because he had the "right" answers, but because he persistently asked the right questions.

Notes

Introduction

1. Abbou reported the following sales in 1980 ("Deuxième vie," p. 277):

> *The Stranger:* 4,300,000 copies
> *The Plague:* 3,700,000
> *The Fall:* 1,300,000
> *Exile and the Kingdom:* 930,000

2. For details of Camus's life, see the biographies of Herbert Lottman (1978) and Patrick McCarthy (1982).

3. Jean Grenier referred to "La Pasionara" (i.e., Camus's Spanish heritage via his mother's family) and "North African blood" as sources of such violence (*Corr.*, pp. 185–86).

4. McCarthy (p. 101) claims that while Camus *talked* of teamwork, he in fact ran the show in Algiers, but this may have been the result of his feverish activity between bouts of tuberculosis rather than of a conscious desire to dominate.

Chapter 1

1. Camus mentions in the letter a forthcoming visit to the Balearic Islands, which took place in the summer of 1935. See also *Fragments*, p. 20.

2. Amar Ouzegane was a member of the political bureau of the PCA in the late thirties, spent the war years undergound or in prison, and in 1946 was elected deputy from Algiers in the Constituent Assembly in Paris. He was expelled from the Communist party in 1948, and joined the Algerian Front de libération nationale (FLN) in 1955.

3. Camus's sense of religion is not associated with any particular faith. "I recognize the greatness of the Gospels. . . . I am well aware, believe me, that there are mysteries. But I am more sensitive to those of nature. . . . I have never felt any religious soul except in the presence of the sea or the night" (*Corr.*, p. 181).

4. *The First Man* is the title of an unfinished manuscript that remains unpublished at the express wish of Camus's executors.

5. Camus frequently mentions the need for sexual abstinence as part of the askesis necessary for artistic activity.

6. Cf. *Nuptials at Tipasa*, where Camus states that the body's retreat into and merging with nature can last only one day (*E*, p. 59).

7. On Camus and the class struggle, see Lottman, p. 158. His understanding of racism developed early: "Even though I learned . . . in high school, for example, that wealth was unequally distributed . . . social classes are not as distinct as [in France] (things would have been different, of course, if I had been Arab) . . . (*Corr.*, p. 180).

Chapter 2

1. This translation of the title is not strictly accurate: the original French title implies "happy death" in general, rather than a particular occurrence of such a death.

2. This leads to some confusing juxtapositions when Mersault is talking specifically about women: "Man diminishes man's strength" (*l'homme diminue la force de l'homme*), p. 132, and "taking refuge in humanity" (*réfugié dans l'homme*), p. 161.

3. The original French text reads: *le jeu plié à la technique*. When rendering the phrase as "play linked with technique," the translator obviously read *lié* for *plié* (in *Notebooks I*, p. 92).

4. The French text reads: "un paradis qui n'est donné qu'aux animaux les plus privés ou les plus doués d'intelligence." Richard Howard's translation is incorrect; he renders it "a paradise given only to the most private or the most intelligent animals" (*Happy Death*, p. 122). The phrase "d'intelligence" is dependent on both "privés" and "doués."

5. Paradoxically, from a grammatical point of view, he achieved distanciation in *The Stranger* in part by using a first-person narrator and the *passé composé*.

Chapter 3

1. The quotations are from Abbou and Lévi-Valensi, eds., *Fragments*, pp. 31, 40. Until 1978 only one segment of Camus's journalistic work in Algeria was readily available, the report entitled "Poverty in Kabylia." This was republished in 1958 as part of *Actuelles III, Chroniques algériennes*, and reprinted in the Pléiade edition of *Essais* (1965); but the major portion of his contributions remained in obscurity, stored on poor microfilm copy in the Bibliothèque Nationale in Paris. Abbou

and Lévi-Valensi have now edited a two-volume collection of all the articles signed by, or attributed to, Camus.

2. The details of the Hodent affair have been fully documented by Emmett Parker, Abbou and Lévi-Valensi, and Lottman, as have those of the El Okbi and incendiaries of Auribeau trials. In all cases, the political motivation behind the judicial decisions is exposed.

3. The series of articles on Kabylia was not included in a selection of Camus's journalistic work published in English under the title of *Resistance, Rebellion and Death*, although those articles stand today as a lasting indictment of colonialism and racist oppression.

4. These aspects of the colonial regime appear in "The Guest" and in "The Adulterous Woman," two stories in the collection *Exile and the Kingdom*.

5. The *caïd* was a local notable appointed by the French colonial administration, who was in charge of affairs concerning the indigenous population. Those in the south were particularly influential because of the limited numbers of French officials in such remote areas.

6. It is interesting to note that in a literary context, Janine, the main character in "The Adulterous Woman," fails to observe such a ban. Her response to a similar moment is to experience the scene in an almost epic mode. But this vision is part of the colonial myth, the tourist brochure, and Camus deliberately suppresses a poetic response in his journalistic work in order to concentrate on the reality of wretchedness.

7. Jacques Léenhardt, in his political reading of Robbe-Grillet's *La Jalousie*, also stresses the dominance of language in a colonial situation.

Chapter 4

1. In an introduction to the American edition of *L'Etranger*, Camus called Meursault "the only christ we deserve" (*TRN*, p. 1929).

2. The French text reads: "L'idée qu'on se fait de lui lui est préférée." Philip Thody's translation, "other people prefer their idea of him" (*Notebooks I*, p. 32), is incorrect. By missing one word in the original, the second "lui," Thody changed the meaning of the sentence.

3. Balibar (*Français fictifs*, p. 289) mentions the word *asile* ("old-age home") as one of the puns on the French educational system that appear in the text:

```
        asile       - école maternelle
   instruction   (judiciaire) - instruction   (scolaire)
   interrogatoire      (")     - interrogation     (")
```

4. See Jules Brody for a perceptive analysis of the way in which Meursault maintains the balance of natural elements in their effect upon his body.

5. Stuart Gilbert translates the French *le fond de mon coeur* as "all the thoughts that had been simmering in my brain" (*The Stranger*, p. 151), which makes Meursault a far more cerebral character than Camus intended.

6. According to his wife, Camus had nightmares about the guillotine all his life. The theme recurs in his writings: Clamence dreams of being beheaded like his namesake, John the Baptist; the renegade has his tongue cut out. Apart from being a barbarous injustice (*Reflections on the Guillotine*), such punishment constituted a separation of a vital link between mind and body—the power of speech. For a psychoanalytical study of this obsession, see Jean Gassin, "De Tarrou à Camus."

Chapter 5

1. The tow fire refers to the old custom of burning tow at the installation of a new pope, to remind him of the temporal nature of his power and glory.

2. The first in *Revue libre*, no. 2, 1943; the second in *Cahiers de la Libération*, no. 3, 1944. The last two were written for the *Revue libre*, but remained unpublished until all appeared in *Lettres à un ami allemand* in 1945.

3. Camus's hard-line colleagues of the Comité National des Ecrivains (CNE) objected to the tone of the article, and insisted on the inclusion of a disclaimer stressing their view that a lack of imagination was not an unfortunate natural characteristic, but a voluntary choice (Lottman, p. 311).

4. Camus used the same image in his polemical exchange with *Les Temps modernes* in 1952. In response to the assertion that he had betrayed the course of history, Camus accused Sartre of having turned only his armchair in the direction of history.

5. On 21 October 1937 Camus mused in his notebooks about the discomfort of travel when one is poor, and limited by the conditions imposed on those taking advantage of reduced fares. "But after all, it protects you against dilettantism: of course I would not go so far as to say that what is lacking in Gide and Montherlant is that they never traveled at a reduced fare that forced them to spend six days in the same city. But I do know that basically I cannot see things in the same way as

Gide and Montherlant—because of the reduced fares on trains" (*CI*, p. 93).

Chapter 6

1. These physical and metaphysical experiences were Camus's own, and their application to the plague may have been suggested by Antonin Artaud: "... the only two organs actually affected and damaged by the plague: the brain and the lungs both happen to be under the direct control of consciousness and will" (4:26). Artaud's theory of the plague as a purgative experience is not, however, reflected in Camus's concept of the sickness.

2. It is noteworthy that Rambert, the only "professional" writer, does not contribute directly to the text. McCarthy asserts that it is because Camus knows that journalism is "a particularly inadequate form of language" (p. 226), but it is more likely that his testimony is unacceptable because he is not free to write the truth (*TRN*, p. 1126).

3. I am indebted to Edwin Moses for his illuminating article "Functional Complexity," which forms the basis of this and the following paragraphs.

Chapter 7

1. For a detailed study of the complexities and ambiguities of *The Rebel*, see Werner.

2. When Duclos was arrested, "a loaded pistol, a truncheon, a wireless transmitter, and two carrier pigeons" were allegedly found in his car. The pistol and the truncheon belonged to Duclos's driver-bodyguard; the transmitter was an ordinary car radio; and the pigeons, already dead, were, as Duclos explained, intended for his Sunday lunch (see Werth, pp. 578–79).

Chapter 8

1. The French *cellule* could mean a prison cell, a party cell, or a monk's cell. Meursault also came to love the peace of the prison cell where he could "write."

2. The French *la permanence du parti* also contains a double meaning: "party headquarters" or "the permanence of the party" as an anchor.

3. In the Van Eyck altarpiece as it has come down to us, Hell is also missing (Denis, p. 55). The depiction cited by sixteenth-century commentators was probably part of a hanging above the altarpiece that has not survived. In any case, Clamence does not need to wait for the Last Judgment: Hell is created daily by living people. For a convincing interpretation of the altarpiece as a *mise en abyme* of the essential themes of Camus's work, see Gassin, "La Chute."

4. The repetition of the French *repère* suggests a pun on the word *père*.

Chapter 9

1. The Russian poet Inna Lisnyanskaya, on quitting the Soviet Writers' Union, expressed a similar feeling: "My homeland is the Russian language. Only on its soil can I conceive of my existence" (*New York Times Book Review*, 2 March 1980, p. 3).

2. Quoted in English in Lottman, p. 523. "Challenged" is not an apt translation of *s'opposait* in this context, as it gives too active an impression of defiance. "Contrasted with" would be closer to the meaning.

3. See the articles on the Algerian situation published in *L'Express*, 1955–56, reprinted in *Chroniques algériennes* in 1958 and in *E*, 1965. That his politics are not reflected in his fiction has since been supported by Camus himself in a recently published letter to Grenier dated 4 August 1958: "Like you, I believe it is probably too late for Algeria. I did not say so in my book because lo peor no es siempre seguro— because one must allow historical fate its chances, and because one does not write to say that it's all over. In that case, one remains silent. I'm getting ready for that" (*Corr.*, p. 222).

4. For a detailed analysis of solidarity and fraternity as unifying themes of the collection, see Cryle, *Bilan critique*.

5. The word *ordre* is played on just as clearly in the French text: (1) order in contrast to disorder, a system; (2) order as a command; (3) the order of religious missions.

6. On the stories as allegories of the writer at work, see Linda Hutcheon on "Le Renégat" and Fitch on "Camus's Desert Hieroglyphics."

7. In the preface to the 1958 edition of *The Right Side and the Wrong Side*, Camus refers to himself as the "admiring slave of a strict artistic tradition" (*E*, p. 12).

8. In the French text there is frequently a play on the words *l'étoile* and *les toiles*, canvases.

9. Camus found himself in exactly the same situation as d'Arrast during his visit to Brazil. See his *Journaux de voyage*.

10. David H. Walker interprets this scene as a symbolic representation of the wretchedness of blacks struggling under the burden of colonialist exploitation.

11. "At home" translates *chez eux*, which has the added sense of possession, of being master in one's own house.

Conclusion

1. McCarthy documents incidents where Camus violently attacked an adversary (pp. 90, 236).

2. Alain Robbe-Grillet, "Monde plein, conscience vide"; Renato Barilli, "Camus et le nouveau roman." Papers delivered at the Camus colloquium at Cerisy-la-Salle, June 1982, forthcoming in the series *Cahiers Albert Camus* (Paris: Gallimard).

Bibliography

Primary Sources: Works by Albert Camus

Carnets I (1935–1942). Paris: Gallimard, 1962.

Carnets II (1942–1951). Paris: Gallimard, 1964.

Correspondance, 1932–1960. Albert Camus and Jean Grenier. Edited by Marguerite Dobrenn. Paris: Gallimard, 1981.

Ecrits de jeunesse. Edited, with introduction and notes, by Paul Viallaneix. Paris: Gallimard, 1973.

Essais. Edited by Roger Quilliot. Paris: Gallimard, 1965.

Fragments d'un combat: Alger-Républicain, 1938–1940. 2 vols. Cahiers Albert Camus 3. Paris: Gallimard, 1978.

Journaux de voyage. Paris: Gallimard, 1978.

La Mort heureuse. Edited, with introduction and notes, by Jean Sarocchi. Paris: Gallimard, 1971.

Théâtre, récits, nouvelles. Edited by Roger Quilliot. Paris: Gallimard, 1962.

Secondary Sources

Abbou, André. "Un Débutant nommé Camus." In *Nouvelles littéraires*, 15 April 1971, p. 3.

———. "La Deuxième Vie d'Albert Camus: Les Paradoxes d'une singulière aventure de notre culture." In *Albert Camus 1980.* Gainesville: University Presses of Florida, 1980.

———. "Les Structures superficielles du discours dans *La Chute.*" In *Revue des lettres modernes* (Cahiers Albert Camus 4), 1970.

———, and Jacqueline Lévi-Valensi, eds. *Fragments d'un combat.* Paris: Gallimard, 1978.

Aho, James. "Suffering, Redemption and Violence: Albert Camus and the Sociology of Violence." *Rendezvous* 9, nos. 1–2 (1974): 51–62.

Artaud, Antonin. *Le Théâtre et son double.* In *Oeuvres complètes*, vol. 4. Paris: Gallimard, 1964.

D'Astorg, Bertrand. "L'Homme engagé—de *La Peste* ou d'un nouvel humanitarianisme." *Esprit* 10 (October 1947): 615–27.

Balibar, Renée. "L'Affaire Meursault-Camus." In *Les Français fictifs.* Paris: Hachette, 1974.

———. "Le Passé composé fictif dans *L'Etranger* d'Albert Camus." *Littérature* 7 (October 1972): 102–19.

Barchilon, José. "A Study of Camus's Mythopoeic Tale, *The Fall*, with Some Comments about the Origin of Esthetic Feelings." *Journal of the American Psychoanalytic Association* 19, no. 2 (April 1971): 193–240.

Barnes, Hazel. *The Literature of Possibility: A Study in Humanistic Existentialism.* New York: Tavistock, 1959.

Barthes, Roland. "*La Peste*, annales d'une épidémie ou roman de la solitude." *Club*, February 1955, p. 6.

Bertocci, Angelo. "Camus's *La Peste* and the Absurd." *Romanic Review* 49, no. 1 (February 1958): 33–41.

Bieber, Konrad. *L'Allemagne vue par les écrivains de la Résistance française*, with a preface by Albert Camus. Geneva: Droz, 1954. Preface reprinted in *Essais*, pp. 1487–91.

Bourdet, Claude. "Camus ou les mains propres." *France-Observateur*, 7 January 1960, p. 18.

Brée, Germaine. *Camus.* New Brunswick, N.J.: Rutgers University Press, 1959.

———. *Camus and Sartre: Crisis and Commitment.* New York: Delta, 1972.

———, ed. *Camus: A Collection of Critical Essays.* Englewood Cliffs, N.J.: Prentice-Hall, 1962.

Brody, Jules. "Camus et la pensée tragique: *L'Etranger.*" *Saggi e ricerche della letteratura francese* 15 (1976): 513–54.

Brombert, Victor. *The Intellectual Hero.* Chicago: University of Chicago Press, Phoenix Books, 1964.

Champigny, Robert. *Sur un héros païen.* Paris: Gallimard, 1959.

Chiaramonte, Nicola. "Sartre versus Camus: A Political Quarrel." In *Camus: A Collection of Critical Essays.* Edited by Germaine Brée. Englewood Cliffs, N.J.: Prentice-Hall, 1962. Originally published in *Partisan Review* 19, no. 6 (Nov. to Dec. 1952): 680–87.

Crochet, Monique. *Les Mythes dans l'oeuvre de Camus.* Paris: Editions Universitaires, 1973.

Crossman, Richard. "A Frustrated Intellectual." *New Statesman and Nation*, 16 January 1954, pp. 72–74.

Cruickshank, John. *Albert Camus and the Literature of Revolt.* New York: Oxford University Press, 1960.

———. "The Art of Allegory in *La Peste.*" *Symposium* 9, no. 1 (Spring 1957): 61–74.

Cryle, Peter. *Bilan critique: L'Exil et le royaume. Essai d'analyse.* Paris: Minard, 1973.

––––––. "The Written Painting and the Painted Word in 'Jonas.'" In *Albert Camus 1980.* Gainesville: University Presses of Florida, 1980.

Daniel, Jean. "Cet Etrange Recours à Camus." *Le Nouvel Observateur,* no. 73 (27 November 1978).

Denis, Valentin. *All the Paintings of Jan van Eyck.* New York: Hawthorne Books, 1961.

Doubrovsky, Serge. "The Ethics of Albert Camus." In *Camus: A Collection.* First published in *Preuves,* no. 116 (October 1960), pp. 39–49.

Dunwoodie, P. "*La Mort heureuse* et *Crime et châtiment:* Une Etude comparée." *Revue de la littérature comparée,* no. 4 (Oct. to Dec. 1972).

Fitch, Brian. "Camus' Desert Hieroglyphics." *Proceedings of the Comparative Literature Symposium* 8 (1975): 117–31.

––––––. *L'Etranger d'Albert Camus: Un Texte, ses lecteurs, leurs lectures.* Paris: Larousse, 1972.

––––––. *The Narcissistic Text.* Toronto: University of Toronto Press, 1982.

––––––. "*La Peste* comme texte qui se désigne. Analyse des procédés d'autoreprésentation." *Revue des lettres modernes* (Cahiers Albert Camus 8), 1975.

––––––. "Une Voix qui se parle, qui nous parle, que nous parlons, ou l'espace théâtral de *La Chute.*" In *Revue des lettres modernes* (Cahiers Albert Camus 4), 1970.

Forster, E. M. *Aspects of the Novel.* 1927; New York: Harcourt, Brace and World, 1955.

Fortier, Paul. "Le Décor symbolique de 'L'Hôte' d'Albert Camus." *French Review* 46, no. 3 (February 1973): 535–42.

––––––. *Une Lecture de Camus: La Valeur des éléments descriptifs dans l'oeuvre romanesque.* Paris: Klincksieck, 1977.

Fouchet, Max-Pol. Untitled article in *Dossiers Albert Camus: Magazine littéraire,* no. 67–68 (September 1972), p. 32.

Gadourek, Carina. *Les Innocents et les coupables.* The Hague: Mouton, 1965.

Gassin, Jean. "De Tarrou à Camus: Le Symbolisme de la guillotine." *Revue des lettres modernes* (Cahiers Albert Camus 8), 1975.

––––––. "*La Chute* et le retable de 'L'Agneau mystique': Etude de structure." In *Albert Camus 1980.* Gainesville: University Presses of Florida, 1980.

_____. *L'Univers symbolique d'Albert Camus: Essai d'interprétation psychanalytique.* Paris: Minard, 1981.

Gay-Crosier, Raymond. *Les Envers d'un échec: Le Théâtre d'Albert Camus.* Paris: Minard, 1967.

_____, ed. *Albert Camus 1980.* Gainesville: University Presses of Florida, 1980.

Girard, René. "Camus's Stranger Retried." *PMLA* 79, (December 1964): 519–33.

Goldmann, Lucien. *Le Dieu caché.* Paris: Gallimard, 1955.

_____. *Pour une sociologie du roman.* Paris: Gallimard, 1964.

Gordimer, Nadine. "Living in the Interregnum." *New York Review of Books* 20 (January 1983): 21–29.

Grenier, Jean. *Albert Camus: Souvenirs.* Paris: Gallimard, 1968.

Hartman, Geoffrey. "Camus and Malraux: The Common Ground." In *Beyond Formalism.* New Haven: Yale University Press, 1970.

Hirdt, Willi. "*La Mort heureuse* von Albert Camus." *Archiv für Studium der neueren Sprachen,* no. 211 (December 1974), pp. 334–39.

Horne, Alastair. *A Savage War of Peace.* New York: Viking Press, 1978.

Hutcheon, Linda. " 'Le Renégat ou un esprit confus' comme nouveau récit." *Revue des lettres modernes* (Cahiers Albert Camus 6), 1973, pp. 69–87.

Jeanson, Francis. "Albert Camus, ou l'âme révoltée." *Les Temps modernes,* no. 79 (May 1952), pp. 2070–90.

_____. "Pour tout vous dire." *Les Temps modernes,* no. 82 (August 1952), pp. 354–83.

Kréa, Henri. "Le Malentendu algérien." *France-Observateur,* 5 January 1961, p. 16.

Kriegel, Annie. *Les Communistes français.* Paris: Seuil, 1968.

Lazere, Donald. *The Unique Creation of Albert Camus.* New Haven: Yale University Press, 1973.

Léenhardt, Jacques. *Lecture politique du roman: "La Jalousie" d'Alain Robbe-Grillet.* Paris: Editions de Minuit, 1973.

Lévi-Valensi, Jacqueline. "*La Chute,* ou la parole en procès." In *Revue des lettres modernes* (Cahiers Albert Camus 4), 1970.

_____. "Le Temps et l'espace dans l'oeuvre romanesque." In *Albert Camus 1980.* Gainesville: University Presses of Florida, 1980.

Lottman, Herbert. *Albert Camus: A Biography.* New York: Doubleday, 1979. Also published in French, Paris: Le Seuil, 1978.

McCarthy, Patrick. *Camus.* New York: Random House, 1982.

Maillard, Claudine, and Michel Maillard. *La Parole en procès.* Grenoble: Presses universitaires de Grenoble, 1977.

Mallet, Robert. "Présent à la vie, étranger à la mort." In *Hommage à Albert Camus*. Paris: Gallimard, 1967.

De Man, Paul. "The Mask of Albert Camus." *New York Review of Books*, 23 December 1965, pp. 10–13.

Marx, Karl. *Economic and Philosophical Manuscripts*. Translated by T. B. Bottomore in Erich Fromm, *Marx's Concept of Man*. New York: Ungar, 1961.

Memmi, Albert. "Camus ou le colonisateur de bonne volonté." *La Nef*, 12 December 1957, pp. 95–96.

_____. *The Colonizer and the Colonized*. Boston: Beacon Press, 1967.

Morot-Sir, Edouard. "Logique de la limite, esthétique de la pauvreté." In *Albert Camus 1980*. Gainesville: University Presses of Florida, 1980.

Moses, Edwin. "Functional Complexity: The Narrative Techniques of *The Plague*." *Modern Fiction Studies* 20 (1974): pp. 419–29.

Neilson, Frank. "The Plague: Camus's Pro-Fascist Allegory." *Literature and Ideology*, no. 15, pp. 17–26.

Nora, Pierre. "Pour une autre explication de *L'Etranger*." *France-Observateur*, 7 January 1960, pp. 16–17.

O'Brien, Conor Cruise. *Albert Camus of Europe and Africa*. New York: Viking Press, 1970.

Ouzegane, Amar. *Le Meilleur Combat*. Paris: Julliard, 1962.

Pariente, Jean-Claude. "L'Etranger et son double." *Revue des lettres modernes* (Cahiers Albert Camus 1), nos. 170–74 (1968), pp. 53–80.

Parker, Emmett. *The Artist in the Arena*. Madison: University of Wisconsin Press, 1965.

Picon, Gaëtan. "Notes on *The Plague*." In Germaine Brée, ed., *Camus*. Originally published in *L'Usage de la lecture*. Paris: Mercure de France, 1960.

Pierce, Roy. *Contemporary French Political Thought*. New York: Oxford University Press, 1966.

Poirot-Delpech, Bertrand. "Justice pour Camus." *Le Monde*, 5 August 1977.

Popkin, Samuel. *The Irrational Intellectual*. Ithaca: Ingrate Press, 1981.

Quilliot, Roger. "L'Algérie d'Albert Camus." *La Revue socialiste*, no. 120 (October 1958), pp. 121–31.

_____. *La Mer et les prisons*. Paris: Gallimard, 1956.

Reich, Wilhelm. *The Mass Psychology of Fascism*. New York: Farrar, Straus and Giroux, 1970.

Rolo, Charles. "Albert Camus—a Good Man." *Atlantic Monthly*, May 1958, pp. 27–33.

Sarocchi, Jean. "Albert Camus et la recherche du père." Thesis, University of Paris, 1975.

Sartre, Jean-Paul. "Albert Camus." *France-Observateur,* 7 January 1960.

———. "Une Explication de *L'Etranger.*" In *Situations I.* Paris: Gallimard, 1947.

———. "Réponse à Albert Camus." *Les Temps modernes,* no. 82, August 1952.

Seghers, Pierre. *La Résistance et ses poètes.* Paris: Seghers, 1974.

Silone, Ignazio. Untitled essay on his membership in the PCI, in *The God That Failed.* Edited by R. H. Crossman. New York: Harper and Brothers, 1949.

Sivan, Emmanuel. *Communisme et nationalisme en Algérie, 1920– 1962.* Paris: Presses de la Fondation Nationale des Sciences Politiques, 1976.

Sperber, Michael. "Camus' *The Fall:* The Icarus Complex." *American Imago* 26, no. 3 (Fall 1969): 269–80.

Tall, Emily. "Camus in the Soviet Union: Some Recent Emigrés Speak." *Comparative Literature Studies* 16, no. 3 (Sept. 1979): 237–49.

———. "Correspondence between Albert Camus and Boris Pasternak." *Canadian Slavonic Papers* 22, no. 2 (June 1980): 276–78.

Thody, Philip. *Albert Camus: A Study of His Work.* New York: Macmillan, 1957; Grove Press, 1959.

———. "Camus et la politique." *Revue des lettres modernes,* nos. 212–16 (Cahiers Albert Camus 5), 1969, pp. 137–47.

Treil, Claude. *L'Indifférence dans l'oeuvre d'Albert Camus.* Montreal: Editions Cosmos, 1971.

Van-Huy, Pierre N. "Camus et le conflit traditionnel des valeurs paternelles et maternelles." *USF Language Quarterly,* no. 13 (1974), pp. 10–14.

Viallaneix, Paul. *Le premier Camus.* With introduction and notes to Camus's *Ecrits de jeunesse.* Paris: Gallimard, 1973.

Walker, David H. "Image, symbole et signification dans 'La Pierre qui pousse.'" *Revue des lettres modernes* (Cahiers Albert Camus 11), 1982, pp. 77–104.

Weis, Marcia. *The Lyrical Essays of Albert Camus.* Ottawa: Editions Naaman de Sherbrooke, 1976.

Werner, Eric. *De la violence au totalitarisme: Essai sur la pensée de Camus et Sartre.* Paris: Calmann-Levy, 1972.

Werth, Alexander. *France, 1940–1955.* New York: Holt and Co., 1956.

Willhoite, Fred H., Jr. "Albert Camus's Politics of Rebellion." *Western*

Political Quarterly 14, no. 2 (June 1961): 400–414.

————. *Beyond Nihilism: Albert Camus's Contribution to Political Thought*. Baton Rouge: Louisiana State University Press, 1968.

Works by Albert Camus in English

Knopf editions:

The Stranger. Translated by Stuart Gilbert. New York: Knopf, 1946.
The Plague. Translated by Stuart Gilbert. New York: Knopf, 1948.
The Rebel. Translated by Anthony Bower. New York: Knopf, 1956.
The Fall. Translated by Justin O'Brien. New York: Knopf, 1957.
Exile and the Kingdom. Translated by Justin O'Brien. New York: Knopf, 1958.
Resistance, Rebellion and Death. Translated by Justin O'Brien. New York: Knopf, 1961.
Notebooks I. Translated by Philip Thody. New York: Knopf, 1963.
Notebooks II. Translated by Justin O'Brien. New York: Knopf, 1965.
Lyrical and Critical Essays. Edited by Philip Thody, translated by Ellen Conroy Kennedy. New York: Knopf, 1969.
A Happy Death. Translated by Richard Howard. New York: Knopf, 1972.
The First Camus and *Youthful Writings*. Translated by Ellen Conroy Kennedy. New York: Knopf, 1976.

Hamish Hamilton editions:

The Rebel. Translated by Anthony Bower. London: Hamish Hamilton, 1953.
Collected Fiction. The Outsider and *The Plague*, translated by Stuart Gilbert; *The Fall* and *Exile and the Kingdom*, translated by Justin O'Brien. London: Hamish Hamilton, 1960.
Carnets I. Translated by Philip Thody. London: Hamish Hamilton, 1963.
Carnets II. Translated by Philip Thody. London: Hamish Hamilton, 1966.
Lyrical and Critical. Translated by Philip Thody. London: Hamish Hamilton, 1967.

Index

Abbou, André, 15, 25, 127; analysis of Camus's journalism, 52, 53, 63, 64
Absurd: Cycle of the, 93; Nazism associated with, 99–100; notion of, 2–3, 5, 6, 34, 35, 42, 88, 120; plague as symbol, 127–29, 134; revolt against, 39; as ultimate problem, 6–7. *See also* Camus, works, *Myth of Sisyphus, The*
Algeria: Communist party, 17–24, 32; early years in, 9, 10, 15–33 passim, 201 (n. 4); as fictional setting, 70–74, 173–74, 178, 179, 181–82; French rule in, 18, 31, 32, 58, 89, 203 (n. 3); French society in, 70–74; involvement in, 153–54, 158–59, 173, 183–84, 195; political situation in, 9–10, 17–18, 22–26, 173–74; vision for, 27, 29, 32, 56–58, 65, 170–71, 193, 195. *See also* Arabs; Kabylia; Oran
Algerian independence: views on, 10–11, 151–52, 153, 194–96, 206 (n. 3)
Alger-Républicain, 47, 48; aims, 50–51; articles for, 11, 15, 51–62 passim, 66; censorship of, 62, 63, 65; demise of, 62–64; review in, 16
Arabs: Camus as bridge to and for, 25, 59, 196; and Communist party, 18, 21, 31, 32; defense of, 9, 24, 26; education for, 56–57; in fiction, 67–68, 69, 73–81, 175–76, 182; and nature, 76–78, 79, 180–81; solutions for, 56–58
Artaud, Antonin: theory of the plague, 205 (n. 1)
Askesis: notion of, 17, 19, 38, 42, 202 (n. 5); and luxury, 46; and Meursault, 88, 89

Balibar, Renée, 67
Barthel, Jean (Jean Chaintron), 21, 22
Barthes, Roland: letter to, 126–27
Bidault, Georges, 101, 102
Blum-Viollette project, 22, 23, 57
Body: and nature, 202 (n. 6); role of, 4–5, 136; and the theater, 31; vulnerability of, 134
Bonnel, Pierre: letter to, 93–94
Bourdet, Claude, 108, 112
Bourgeoisie: and Camus, 4, 40, 47; attacks on, 109–10; scorn for, 111, 123
Brasillach, Robert, 109
Brée, Germaine, 162
Brisville, Jean-Claude, 19
Bruel, François, 110

Camus, Albert
—assessments of, 1–2, 64, 109, 197
—criticism of, 108–9, 112, 141, 149–50; by both sides, 118–19, 120; by Communists, 116–18, 153; by leftists, 194; by Paris intelligentsia, 197; response to, 149, 153, 207 (n. 1). *See also* Jeanson, Francis; Sartre, Jean-Paul
—fiction: autobiographical elements in, 7–8, 157–58, 168, 188–89; evaluation of, 197–200; and journalism, 10, 11–12, 121; and political commitment, 2–3. *See also* Characters, literary; Style; Themes, literary
—journalism, 2, 3, 173; aims, 102; Camus on, 50, 60, 102; editions of, 15, 103, 202–3 (n. 1); and fiction, 10, 11–12, 121; importance, 10–11, 51, 64; later assessment of, 197; as political commitment,

ABOUT THE AUTHOR

Susan Tarrow teaches French in the Department of Romance Studies, Cornell University. She received her bachelor of arts and master's degrees from Oxford University, England, and her doctorate from Cornell University. She has published several translations, but this is her first book.